ANCIENT SECRETS OF MYSTERIOUS AMERICA

Revealing Our True Cosmic Destiny

By W. R. Drake

Added Material by Timothy Green Beckley, and Sean Casteel

With Joshua Shapiro, Brent Raynes, Angela Sangster

Global Communications

Ancient Secrets of Mysterious America

New Edition © 2011

by W. R. Drake

A PRIVATELY PUBLISHED MANUSCRIPT

Added material by Timothy Green Beckley and Sean Casteel
with Joshua Shapiro, Brent Raynes, Angela Sangster

Copyright © 2011
DBA Global Communications, All Rights Reserved

EAN: 978-1-60611-102-4
ISBN: 1-60611-102-7

Nonfiction

Timothy Green Beckley: Editorial Director
Carol Rodriguez: Publishers Assistant
Sean Casteel: Associate Editor
Cover Art: Tim R. Swartz

Printed in the United States of America

For free catalog write:
Global Communications
P.O. Box 753
New Brunswick, NJ 08903

Free Subscription to Conspiracy Journal E-Mail Newsletter
www.conspiracyjournal.com

Contents

Unsolved Mysteries of America: What Is To Come?

By Timothy Green Beckley

✴ Erich von Daniken is the most popular researcher/author of the Ancient Astronaut concept, but did you realize that others have postulated similar ideas and theories? Learn how the work of W.R. Drake can be said to have preceded von Daniken's, but to little fanfare.

✴ Did an angel of God appear to a weary and embattled George Washington in order to enlighten him about the future of America and thus restore his sagging will to fight? Did the American nation truly depend on the blessings sent through extraterrestrials/ angels to survive in an increasingly hostile world?

✴ The presence of guiding aliens/angels in the past has a crucial importance for us today. Will they reveal themselves to the entire world sometime soon? Will they inevitably return to guide us to safety and sanity once again?

*   *   *   *   *

There is a buzzing, a stirring in the air.

It's all around us and people are feeling it in every part of the world.

You can tell something is going to happen. But when? Where? And who will be involved?

Some people see significance and a link to the last month of 2012 and the closing of the Mayan calendar. They point to the return of the mysterious Planet X hurtling toward Earth from the far reaches of the cosmos. Or they turn the pages of the Holy Bible, quoting chapter and verse out of the Book Of Revelation, as well as awaiting the appearance of the antichrist and the Great Tribulation, before which the true believer will be lifted up into heavenly realms facilitated by the return of Jesus of Nazareth.

Many of today's visionaries speak of the homecoming of the Star Gods, a theory involving "Divine Kings" who descended from the heavens to Earth in ages past, long ago establishing contact and openly communicating and passing on their sophisticated technological skills and arts to a humankind that was still attempting to work its way up the ladder of civilization from a primitive intelligence.

Swiss author Erich von Daniken is generally credited with having popularized the notion that extraterrestrials sent their craft here eons ago and left behind numerous clues to their existence while on Earth. TV shows such as *Ancient Aliens* on the History Channel currently probe this concept. Numerous other researchers have expanded on von Daniken's ideas and thoughts, creating an entire intellectual cottage industry.

Two authors from the United Kingdom, Brinsley Le Poer Trench and W. R. Drake, actually beat von Daniken to the punch, hammering out the astronauts of antiquity concept several years prior to Erich's then very controversial pronouncements in what was to become the number one best seller *Chariots of the Gods*? Trench, who later in life became a member of the House of Lords due to his lineage as the 8th Earl of Clancarty, pioneered the trend with the publication of *The Sky People* in 1960, a book that postulated that space visitors from Atlantean and Biblical times remain with us today.

But most impressive is the massive investigative work of the late British historian W. Raymond Drake. Drake spent many years digging through huge archives of material, looking in his case for supposed anomalies that could support his scenarios of space aliens impacting human history. As Drake himself said, "I aspired to collect as many facts as possible from ancient literature to chronicle for the past what Charles Fort has so brilliantly done for the present century."

In the 1970s, several American paperback publishers issued works by Drake with such scintillating titles as "Gods and Spacemen In The Ancient Past," "Gods and Spacemen Throughout History," and his most notable book, "Gods or Spacemen?" Not to toot my own horn, but it's more than likely that I was the one to publish Drake's material earlier than anyone else in my mimographed zine "The Interplanetary News Service Report" sometime during the mid to late 1960s. In short, I have always felt that "Sir" Drake is doubtlessly the most credible reseacher of the "ancient astronaut" theory who has utilized dozens of writers of antiquity to fortify his findings, scrutinizing their most important works through a high powered literary "lens."

Somewhere buried deep within over 40 file cabinets are rough carbon copies of several full length manuscripts Drake gave me first dibs on publishing. Unfortunately, in those "early days" our printing methods were crude and we engaged no professional staff who could properly edit and retype the material that had been submitted for publication. Nor did we possess a distribution network that would allow for disseminating these works widely. Thus, we suggested W. Raymond Drake contact our comrade-in-UFOlogical-arms, Raymond A. Palmer, who was both a printer (Tomorrow River Press) and publisher (Amherst Press) for authors, including Brinsley Le Poer Trench and the highly controversial George Hunt Williamson (a/k/a Brother Philips) whose works "Other Tongues – Other Flesh" and "Secrets of the Andes" were getting a fair share of attention due to RAP's having garnered their exclusive North American Rights.

Among the literary works Drake passed on to Palmer was the "lost manuscript" you are now about to dig into. I won't reveal how it was recently returned to my hands, nor how only a few copies of the work were ever printed and then with the incorrect title unfortunatley "switched" with another manuscript that Drake had mailed to Palmer at around the same time. It's one of those "coincidences" I like to write about but its meaning is clouded and anyway what's important is that this material has finally managed to reach its rightful audience even if it's a couple of decades later than the deceased researcher might have desired.

But better late than never seems to apply amply at this juncture.

Other researchers, whose credentials may be mostly unvetted at this point, have conjectured just like Drake that these off-world visitors have taken a personal liking to the Americas (both North and South), but in particular to that portion which has become the United States. It is strongly accepted by ancient astronaut theorists that space beings have helped in the formation our government, if only from behind the scenes.

As the chaos of economic default and natural disasters seems to swirl around us on a daily basis, Drake realized even "back then" when he originally summarized his findings for a handful of truth seekers, that "America's fate may ultimately depend once again on the spacemen who left all around us physical proof of their regular visits if we would only open our eyes and properly evaluate the evidence that they are about to show up once more."

Washington's Strange Visitation

General Washington is said to have gone into a thicket to pray
only to have an angel appear and show him the
destiny of America and its three conflicts. Was the angel an alien?

Shadowy figures whose identities and origins have been clouded by design have appeared throughout the history of America. It is if we were being "watched" from upon high for a grand purpose.

It was the winter of 1777 and General George Washington's troops had suffered severe setbacks. At Valley Forge the weather had turned so cold the troops stood a good chance of freezing to death. It was at times like this that the father of our country could be seen deep in contemplation with tears rolling from his eyes.

Washington's vision was reprinted in December of 1880 by "The National Tribune," the U.S. war veterans' paper, and on December 21, 1950 by "The Stars and Stripes." It had been taken down verbatim by Anthony Sherman and has become perhaps the most important vision centering on the birth of America and its connection to unseen forces.

Anthony Sherman was in Valley Forge and received the report of the vision firsthand from George Washington. Sherman recalled: *"You doubtless heard the story of Washington's going to the thicket to pray in secret for aid and comfort from God, the interposition of whose Divine Providence brought us safely through the darkest days of tribulation.*

"One day, I remember it well, when the chilly winds whistled through the leafless trees, though the sky was cloudless and the sun shown brightly, he remained in his quarters nearly all the afternoon alone. When he came out, I noticed that his face was a shade paler than usual. There seemed to be something on his mind of more than ordinary importance. Returning just after dusk, he dispatched an orderly to the quarters who was presently in attendance. After a preliminary conversation of about an hour, Washington, gazing upon his companion with that strange look of dignity which he alone commanded, related the event that occurred that day."

Washington stated: "This afternoon, as I was sitting at this table engaged in preparing a dispatch, something seemed to disturb me. Looking up, I beheld standing opposite me a singularly beautiful female. So astonished was I, for I had given strict orders not to be disturbed, that it was some moments before I found language to inquire the cause of her presence. A second, a third and even a fourth time did I repeat my question, but received no answer from my mysterious visitor except a slight raising of her eyes.

"By this time I felt strange sensations spreading through me. I would have risen but the riveted gaze of the being before me rendered volition impossible. I assayed once more to address her, but my tongue had become useless, as though it had become paralyzed.

"A new influence, mysterious, potent, irresistible, took possession of me. All I could do was to gaze steadily, vacantly at my unknown visitor. Gradually the surrounding atmosphere seemed as if it had become filled with sensations, and luminous. Everything about me seemed to rarify, the mysterious visitor herself becoming more airy and yet more distinct to my sight than before. I now began to feel as one dying, or rather to experience the sensations which I have sometimes imagined accompany dissolution. I did not think, I did not reason, I did not move; all were alike impossible. I was only conscious of gazing fixedly, vacantly at my companion.

The First Peril – The Revolution

"Presently I heard a voice saying, *'Son of the Republic, look and learn,'* while at the same time my visitor extended her arm eastwardly. I now beheld a heavy white vapor at some distance rising fold upon fold. This gradually dissipated, and I looked upon a stranger scene. Before me lay spread out in one vast plain all the countries of the world - Europe, Asia, Africa and America. I saw rolling and tossing between Europe and America the billows of the Atlantic, and between Asia and America lay the Pacific.

"*'Son of the Republic,'* said the same mysterious voice as before, *'look and learn.'* At that moment I beheld a dark, shadowy being, like an angel, standing or rather floating in mid-air, between Europe and America. Dipping water out of the ocean in the hollow of each hand, he sprinkled some upon America with his right hand, while with his left hand he cast some on Europe. Immediately a cloud raised from these countries, and joined in mid-ocean. For a while it remained stationary, and then moved slowly westward, until it enveloped America in its murky folds. Sharp flashes of lightning gleamed through it at intervals, and I heard the smothered groans and cries of the American people.

The Second Peril – The Civil War

"A second time the angel dipped water from the ocean, and sprinkled it out as before. The dark cloud was then drawn back to the ocean, in whose heaving billows it sank from view. A third time I heard the mysterious voice saying, *'Son of the Republic, look and learn.'* I cast my eyes upon America and beheld villages and towns and cities springing up one after another until the whole land from the Atlantic to the Pacific was dotted with them.

"Again, I heard the mysterious voice say, *'Son of the Republic, the end of the century cometh, look and learn.'* At this the dark shadowy angel turned his face southward, and from Africa I saw an ill-omened specter approach our land. It flitted slowly over every town and city of the latter. The inhabitants presently set themselves in battle array against each other. As I continued looking I saw a bright angel, on whose brow rested a crown of light, on which was traced the word 'Union,' bearing the American flag which he placed between the divided nation, and said, *'Remember ye are brethren.'* Instantly, the inhabitants, casting from them their weapons became friends once more, and united around the National Standard.

The Third Peril – America's Judgment?

"And again I heard the mysterious voice saying *'Son of the Republic, look and learn.'* At this the dark, shadowy angel placed a trumpet to his mouth, and blew three distinct blasts; and taking water from the ocean, he sprinkled it upon Europe, Asia and Africa. Then my eyes beheld a fearful scene: From each of these countries arose thick, black clouds that were soon joined into one. Throughout this mass there gleamed a dark red light by which I saw hordes of armed men, who, moving with the cloud, marched by land and sailed by sea to America. Our country was enveloped in this volume of cloud, and I saw these vast armies devastate the whole country and burn the villages, towns and cities that I beheld springing up. As my ears listened to the thundering of the cannon, clashing of sword, and the shouts and cries of millions in mortal combat, I heard again the mysterious voice saying, *'Son of the Republic, look and learn.'* When the voice had ceased, the dark shadowy angel placed his trumpet once more to his mouth, and blew a long and fearful blast.

"Instantly a light as of a thousand suns shone down from above me, and pierced and broke into fragments the dark cloud which enveloped America. At the same moment the angel upon whose head still shone the word Union, and who bore our national flag in one hand and a sword in the other, descended from the heavens attended by legions of white spirits. These immediately joined the inhabitants of America, who I perceived were well nigh overcome, but who immediately taking courage again, closed up their broken ranks and renewed the battle.

"Again, amid the fearful noise of the conflict, I heard the mysterious voice saying, *'Son of the Republic, look and learn.'* As the voice ceased, the shadowy angel for the last time dipped water from the ocean and sprinkled it upon America. Instantly the dark cloud rolled back, together with the armies it had brought, leaving the inhabitants of the land victorious!

"Then once more I beheld the villages, towns and cities springing up where I had seen them before, while the bright angel, planting the azure standard he had brought in the midst of them, cried with a loud voice: *'While the stars remain, and the heavens send down dew upon the earth, so long shall the Union last.'* And taking from his brow the crown on which blazoned the word *'Union,'* he placed it upon the Standard while the people, kneeling down, said, *'Amen.'*

"The scene instantly began to fade and dissolve, and I at last saw nothing but the rising, curling vapor I at first beheld. This also disappearing, I found myself once more gazing upon the mysterious visitor, who, in the same voice I had heard before, said, *'Son of the Republic, what you have seen is thus interpreted: Three great perils will come upon the Republic. The most fearful is the third, but in this greatest conflict the whole world united shall not prevail against her. Let every child of the Republic learn to live for his God, his land and the Union'.* With these words the vision vanished, and I started from my seat and felt that I had seen a vision wherein had been shown to me the birth, progress, and destiny of the United States.

This ended General George Washington's vision and prophecy for the United States of America as told in his words.

Many have asked – In the third peril, is Washington talking about invaders coming from Europe (Russia), Asia (China and Iran), and Africa (Libya)?

Regardless of the interpretations placed on Washington's three visions of peril, it is difficult to relate this experience in other terms than a meeting with a spiritual or celestial being. Perhaps an angel? Well, angel only means "messenger," and this messenger can easily be interpreted in the context of an encounter with an extraterrestrial intelligence. As history reveals, Washington says the air in the room where the vision took place appeared to glow. He later stated that he felt as though he might be dying, that the sensation thus could have been akin to a near death experience, which is the same feeling that UFO contactees seem to undergo during their moments of illumination. Did an attractive, humanlike alien speak with our first president? The answer may be a definite Yes!

Previously, in my work "Prophecies of the Presidents – The Spiritual Destiny of America Revealed," along with co-author Arthur Crockett, I pointed out how I felt

that we have long had a bond with powers and principalities watching over us from what might be interpreted as a "safe distance." W. Raymond Drake says the ancient Gods are about to return – it could be they have never left!

The Great Seal and Alien Intervention

On the one dollar bill you will see the Great Seal of the United States. Have you ever wondered about it? Did you know that one of the most puzzling mysteries connected with the growth of our country is associated with the Great Seal?

History tells us that the Continental Congress asked Thomas Jefferson, Benjamin Franklin and John Adams to put their heads together and arrange a seal for the colonies. But despite their combined efforts, nothing they did would produce the desired results.

It was late at night and Thomas Jefferson told the others that he needed some fresh air. He excused himself and took a walk in his garden.

Suddenly, from out of the darkness, Jefferson saw a strange man approach dressed in a long black cloak. Jefferson was unable to see the face of the unfamiliar person as his appearance seemed foggy and his eyes were blacked out. The visitor told Jefferson that he knew what the three great statesmen were trying to accomplish and that he had a design which would be appropriate and meaningful.

Jefferson listened while the man described what he had in mind. The plans were perfect! They were exactly what were needed. Jefferson hurried back into the room to tell the others what he had experienced. He rushed away from the stranger so quickly that he forgot the thank him and ask for his name.

A mysterious stranger appeared before Thomas Jefferson and gave him the mysterious symbol to appear on the reverse side of the Great Seal of the U.S. which include an eye in the middle of the capstone of the Great Pyramid.

Moments later, when the excitement was over and the situation fully assessed, the three men went into the garden to see if they could find the strange man in the cloak. But he was nowhere to be found.

So it is that the three Founding Fathers and all of the other patriots of the day never knew who really designed the Great Seal of the United States. The mystery is one which will probably never be

solved, though some theorize that this man may have been a space voyager or an alchemist with a secret society.

Unseen Forces And Our Presidents

President Eisenhower is said to have had at least one meeting with extraterrestrials at Edwards Air Force Base, still known as Murdoc at that point.

Interest in the subject of UFOs and ancient astronauts seems to be contagious even among successful candidates voted into the Oval Office. Unfortunately, the presidents do not appear to be approved for Disclosure despite their being the highest elected official in the land. Our presidents have been left in the dark regarding these fascinating subjects just like the man in the street.

But this is not to say that they haven't had their own experiences or managed to go around the forces that try to keep them in check. If our cosmic voyagers want to say something, they have the ability to do so, though it would seem for the most part they are planning to play dumb until the right time to openly show themselves, maybe through a mass landing or a takeover of our broadcasting systems.

For example, it's been reported all-too-many times that President Dwight D. Eisenhower met with aliens – maybe related to the ones who came in the more distant past – at Edwards Air Force base in the California desert. It is said he entered a landed spacecraft and spoke for hours with the craft's crew. Supposedly, Ike was offered a deal – the exchange of "their" advanced technology for earthlings who could be prodded and probed for medical and psychological reasons.

There was also Jimmy Carter, who had a UFO sighting in the presence of other eyewitnesses, and Ronald Reagan, who warned of a war between worlds and was apparently chased or followed in his private plane by a bogie up and down the California coastline. To say nothing of John F. Kennedy, who might have been ready to scrub the deck and reveal tattletale files on UFO crashes and the existence of a super secret quasi-military/government agency known as Majestic, whose sole purpose was to keep all UFO information out of the public's hands. JFK was assassinated before he could accomplish the task before him. His brother Robert Kennedy was to continue the legacy of UFO release, but was warned to back off and gunned down sometime after this warning by a demented assassin who may have been under the influence of some sort of New World Order mind control program.

What Are The Signs To Look For That The Gods of Antiquity Are About To Return?

As publisher of this work, I am convinced that its prime contributor, W. Raymond Drake, remains overall one of the most thorough researchers of the ancient astronaut concept and that his extensive body of investigative material proves that something extremely important is about to transpire in the next few years that will rock the very fabric of civilization.

Beyond Drake's research, there are others who have begun to add to the evidence through their research into other aspects of antiquity, including revelations regarding the crystal skulls, the Star Child phenomenon, the appearance of crop circles as well as various Native American myths and legends that are obviously based on real episodic encounters with these great inter-dimensional and intergalactic beings who are coming for us from out of the past.

Indeed, we live in interesting times.

And things are about to get more interesting than we ever even imagined possible!

Timothy Green Beckley
UFO & Paranormal Pioneer

Tim Beckley has had so many careers that even his own girlfriend doesn't know what he does for a living. He has been described as the Hunter Thompson of UFOlogy. Since an early age his life has more or less revolved around the paranormal. His life was saved by invisible beings around the age of three. The house he was raised in was thought to be haunted. Tim saw his first of three UFOs when he was but ten, and has had two more sightings since – including an attempt to communicate with one of these objects.

Tim started his career as a writer early on. At age 14 he purchased a mimeograph machine and started putting out the Interplanetary News Service Report. Over the years, he has written over 25 books on everything from rock music to the secret MJ-12 papers

He is one of the few Americans ever to be invited to speak before closed door meetings on UFOs presided over by the late Earl of Clancarty at the House of Lords in England. He visited Loch Ness in Scotland while in the UK and went home with a belief that Nessie was somehow connected with the dragons of mythology as well as strange discs engraved on cathedrals and ghostly phenomena.

The Inner Light Publications and Global Communications' catalog of books and video titles now number over 200, including the works of Tim Swartz, Sean Casteel, T. Lobsang Rampa, Commander X, Brad Steiger, John Keel, Tracy Twyman, Wendelle Stevens and a host of many other authors

Tim has written over 30 books himself including:

TIMOTHY BECKLEY'S BIG BOOK OF WEREWOLVES
OUR ALIEN PLANET-THIS EERIE EARTH
STRANGE SAGA
JOHN LENNON – WE KNEW YOU
SECRET PROPHECY OF FATIMA REVEALED
SUBTERRANEAN WORLDS INSIDE EARTH
MJ 12 AND THE RIDDLE OF HANGAR 18

Tim is known among horror movie fans as Mr. Creepo. When asked his major cinema influences, he mentions Nancy Reagan as having gotten him involved as a horror host. During the heyday of double features and Time Square grind houses he worked as a movie review critic as well as a publicist for several small film companies. His recent efforts include "Skin Eating Jungle Vampires" and "Blood Sucking Vampire Freaks."

MRUFO8@hotmail.com
www.ConspiracyJournal.com

Ancient Secrets
of
Mysterious America

By
W. R. Drake

\

Forward

Mysterious America haunts Man more than ever in our space age. Behind the modern glamor today we sense that muted wonder of the ancients and feel those silent, shrouded lands of the sunset slumbered under some secret spell cast by the gods. From the Arctic to the Amazon colossal mounds with buried treasures, strange sculptures crowning mountain-tops, unknown writings carved on cliffs, challenge us with some civilization lost in dim prehistory. Legends of white gods from the stars confirm those classic tales of the Titans, that stellar race of supermen who once ruled Earth in a golden age shattered by wars and cataclysms drowning continents and smashing to desolation the culture of the west. Lemuria and Atlantis still trouble our dreams, fitful memories bedazzle our minds with marvels beyond belief.

The red Indians worshipped a great spirit in the sky who descended to Earth in human form to teach warriors and heal the sick. In Mexico Montezuma surrendered himself and all his people to Cortes and the conquistadores believing them to be the white gods returning like Quetzalcoatl long ago. The amazing ruins of the Mayas hint at some wondrous civilization once ruled by the gods. The brilliant realm of the Incas still basks in the sun destroyed by Pizarro; the vast green forests of the Amazon shroud fabulous cities luring explorers to their death; cyclopean ruins perched forlorn from a far-forgotten past crown dizzy crags touching the sky; mountain-tracks mark airfields inviting the stars; down deep canyons cryptic petroglyphs tell mysteries of lost peoples from Lemuria even Babylon. Golden El Dorado, white gods, giants, dwarfs, warrior-women, humanoids, fearsome creatures of the night; surely the secret of the spacemen lurks in those fascinating ancient lands of South America so haunted today.

ACKNOWLEDGEMENTS

The warmest gratitude is due to Brinsley le Poer Trench, that illumined
Leader in Cosmic Understanding for his inspired encouragement.

To my Wife
MARJORIE

Chapter One
Extraterrestrials

From those forgotten multitudes in far Antiquity who like ourselves paused for a brief moment in their cosmic pilgrimage on our green planet, few records remain, yet down the ages tantalizing echoes tell us of that Golden Age when the Sky Gods winged to Earth and taught their wisdom to men. After many millennia the glorious civilization dissolved in wars; then cataclysms devastated countries, changing climates. The celestials returned to the stars leaving the survivors to rebuild their shattered world. On treasured occasions extraterrestrials would descend to direct through chosen initiates the destinies of nations advancing evolution; the gods would mate with virgins to father heroes whose wondrous deeds inspired their people to new glories. Their task accomplished these prophets were translated to the skies in chariots of fire; later some might return to prove men's souls survived death.

Traditions tell of shadowy figures, not born of woman, flitting down the dusty corridors of time to preach some new philosophy or invent some novel machine revolutionizing contemporary culture. The Bible abounds in tales of angels, devils, divine interventions, paralleled in world-wide folk-tales and in ominous significance by extraterrestrials appearing today.

Who were the ancient gods? Who was the Lord of the Old Testament? Who were the great culture heroes civilizing primitive societies all over the world?

The universe, seen and unseen, thrills with life. Extraterrestrials have visited Earth for thousands of years; they appear now. Whence do they come?

Recent research into micro-particles leads physicists to suspect an infinite number of parallel universes with properties fundamentally different from our own. Atoms appearing in empty space postulated by the Hoyle-Bondi Theory of Continuous Creation may intrude from another universe; new stars and notably supernovae manifesting with immense bursts of energy may conceivably have broken through the universal barrier. It may seem idle fancy to wonder whether those mirages of strange cities seen in the sky somehow reflect a real metropolis in some other universe, inexplicable lightnings and fireballs, especially the baffling disappearances of people, ships and aircraft do suggest some random contact with other realms. The ancient gods might have materialized from a parallel universe to which they returned—fortunately not one composed of anti-matter, otherwise on landing they would have destroyed our Earth and themselves too.

In olden times few people ever left their own village; to them the world seemed so vast beyond comprehension. Four centuries ago when Sir Francis Drake circumnavigated the globe in three years men marvelled at this daring adventure and for the first time since lost Antiquity could think of Earth as one immense sphere; today satellites circle in only ninety minutes and astronomers reduce it to a grain of dust. Surely limitation is only an attitude of mind conditioned by contemporary thought; even Plato who discoursed on Atlantis dared hardly imagine men sailing around the world—a fantasy undreamed of millennia ago, though men now circumnavigate in

4

yachts alone. Mystics view all creation as divine manifestation; each atom vibrates in harmony with all the others; astrologers echo a most ancient science teaching that the stars exert a subtle influence on men's destinies, now suspected by psychiatrists probing people's minds and confirmed from exquisite experiments by Dr. Georgio Piccardi, Professor of Geophysics at Florence University, who proves that chemical reactions vary significantly according to our fluctuating forcefield. Since the universe constitutes one whole harmonious cosmos expressing the divine plan, surely its creator intends the most highly evolved men to marvel at its myriad wonders and view it as one single living world. Can extraterrestrials infinitely more wise than us with transcendent techniques beyond our science circumnavigate the universe as we now fly around our own Earth?

Aristotle whose alleged omniscience mesmerized science for centuries could not conceive a technology producing the aeroplane and nuclear-submarine which circumnavigate our Earth; so we with our present knowledge cannot imagine the cosmic craft of extraterrestrials millions of years more advanced than ourselves mastering techniques and forces beyond our dreams. Super-intelligences may take short-cuts across the universe through hyper-space, a fourth-dimension, or teleport themselves here instantaneously by thought, though such esoteric travel baffles us. Scientists speculate on spaceships speeding at more than 290,000 kilometers a second requiring about twenty-five years "ship-time" to cross our Milky Way for cosmonauts benefitting from Einstein's Time-Dilation paradox, while a hundred thousand years rolled by on Earth.

Suppose a flying saucer lands manned not by Martians or Venusians but by Earthmen from a trip to Sagittarius returning to Atlantis long submerged beneath the sea? Would we welcome our ancestors home or treat them as aliens here on their own Earth?

Physicists hope that some day matter may be converted into energy transmitted like those photographs from Mars then rematerialized at destination. In theory a cosmonaut could be transformed into photons modulated to his key-frequency beamed toward a distant star, then on arrival reconstituted to his normal body, a science-fiction conception which if ever achieved would still limit motion to the speed of light leaving the problem of galactic travel yet unsolved.

Can Man never reach another galaxy, or is "never" a word which should never be used?

A generation ago it seemed that aeroplanes could never exceed the speed of sound, roughly 360 meters a second. After breaking the sound-barrier they were threatened by the heat-barrier. Now that these are conquered there looms the light-barrier, for Einstein's Special Theory insists that nothing can travel at more than 300,000 kilometers a second, the speed of light, when time stops and mass becomes infinite. Skeptics feel obliged to accept Einstein's limitation as valid for observational phenomena but suspect from experience that barriers exist only in the minds of men. God has destined Man like some colossus to bestride the whole glittering universe.

In January, 1966 Maarten Schmidt, the American astronomer of Dutch extraction, announced the discovery of a quasar receding at 83% of the speed of light. Quasars have a hundred times more energy than an ordinary galaxy comprising a hundred thousand million stars yet are not much bigger than a common star; their existence known only since 1963 still baffles astronomers. Some now speculate whether some quasars may actually exceed the speed of light despite Einstein's Theory. In 1968 Gerald Feinberg, Professor of Physics at Columbia University, tilting his lance to demolish Einstein, checked his calculations carefully and was obliged to agree with them; hardly surprising since conditioned to a similar thought-pattern his mind followed the same logic. However an extraterrestrial evaluating light from concepts transcending our knowledge and viewing the whole universe from a totally different perspective might have corrected Einstein as he qualified Newton. For many centuries men thought Earth was flat; reaching the edge they might fall off; only when adventurers ignored such limitation did exploration really begin. Perhaps we must forget the finite speed of light before we can see the universe in all its wonder. With a sudden flash of genius Gerald Feinberg realized that if the speed of light was actually a barrier, some phenomena must exist on the other side. He then theorized beyond the wall a whole universe with particles called "tachyons" capable of motion faster than light. Tachyons, if they do exist, will have the strange property that as their energy diminishes their velocity accelerates to millions of light-years per second until at infinite velocity the particles have neither mass nor energy. A suitably designed spaceship would break the light-barrier with a light-boom analogous to the sound-boom on breaking the sound-barrier, visible to astronomers as a light-flash; the ship, fantastic as

5

it seems, transformed into a beam of tachyons losing energy would accelerate to incredible speeds, reaching the nearest star in five seconds to cross our Milky Way in one minute. Isaac Asimov suggests that a spaceship modulated to a tachyon-beam would attain the most distant galaxies in a week, giving ready access to the entire universe since the cosmonauts would experience the same time-element as their ship. Tachyons have not yet been detected, but physicists are searching for them. Extraterrestrials with most advanced science may view the whole universe as one world and devise techniques for spanning it as we now speed around our own Earth.

Astronomers agree that our sun is similar to countless stars whose slow rotation suggests attendant planets. Exobiologists assert that primeval nitrogenous atmospheres at high temperatures charged by electrical storms must inevitably vivify inorganic matter into organic molecules, the basic cells of life throughout the entire universe, apparently confirmed by organic substances often discovered in meteorites from outer space. Many people believe in pan-spermia, the propagation of seeds of life swept by spatial currents or solar-wind from planet to planet, others insist that the destiny of Cosmic Man is to people the universe; long ago extraterrestrials colonized our Earth; soon we too shall land on other worlds. Some civilizations more advanced than our own may be linked in galactic federations whose duty is to survey and inspire backward planets like Earth.

Supermen may cross the universe to visit the dazzling social centers of the Milky Way; it is difficult to conceive them straying toward the edge to slum on lowly Earth, althought Al Bender, an American UFO investigator, complained of menaces from three mysterious Men in Black allegedly originating from a distant galaxy dominated by an immense burning mass beyond human conception, suggesting a quasar, if life within its proximity be possible. Dr. G.H. Williamson in 1952 claimed radio and telepathic contact with Hatonn, a planet in our nearest galaxy, Andromeda.

In our own Milky Way Dr. S.S. Huang of Dearborn Observatory, suggests as many as eight thousand million inhabited star-systems; statistical assessments differ widely, the lowest estimates at least a million planets with advanced civilization. Dr. Harrison Brown of the California Institute of Technology computes more than a thousand inhabited planets comparatively near—only forty-four light-years from Earth. It seems certain that the peoples on other worlds would advertise their presence by light-signals, radio-beams or other means to attract attention and possible response. Josef Schlovsky theorizes that super-intelligences could impregnate a star with millions of tons of the artificial element technetium, a short-lived radio-isotope, which is already in the spectra of certain stars. Super-novae flares may be deliberate explosions by cosmic engineers. Freeman Dyson of Princeton University calculates that extraplanetary civilizations could live in immense spheres, very powerful sources of infra-red radiation, artificial stars detectable from Earth by optical or radio-telescopes. Dr. Philip Morrison of Cornell University suggest that advanced scientists might launch a comet made from millions of tons of dust which glowing through space would reveal obvious signs of its artificial origin. Quasars, each emitting more energy than an entire galaxy, may be superdense stars composed solely of protons or in a state of gravitational collapse, however they could be some fabrication of stellar engineers with techniques beyond our dreams.

On the night of 12/13th April, 1965 the Tass News Agency announced that Soviet scientists had discovered a most distant civilization on an unknown planet situated in a zone of the sky designated CTA 102. Josef Shklovsky and Nicholas Kardaschev of Moscow's Sternberg Observatory believe these signals with regular variations throughout a hundred days were emitted by extraterrestrials; photographs revealed two stars probably with planets. Our own civilization is said to use about four thousand million kilowatts of electrical energy increasing by 3 or 4 per cent per year, eventually this might be measured by people of another planet, thus revealing the presence of intelligent life on our Earth. The electrical power needed for transmissions from CTA 102 and a similar source CTA 21 is quite incredible by terrestrial standards but to a most highly advanced civilization may not be relatively more difficult than the building of the pyramids or our landing a man on the moon. Astronomers still most reluctant to specify extraterrestrial intelligences cannot agree on a satisfactory explanation for these cosmic miracles.

While scientists were debating CTA 102 they received another shock. During the summer of 1967 the Mullard radio-telescope at Cambridge detected strange rhythmic pulsations from some source in space; this "Pulsar" as it became called, beats at intervals of 1.33730109 seconds varying at less than one second per year, regular enough to

6

correct astronomical clocks. Several more have been discovered; some detected optically like NP 0532 in the Crab Nebula believed to be the residual core of the star seen to explode by the Chinese astronomer, Wei-Tei in AD 1054; all pulsate with fantastic precision making natural phenomena seemingly impossible. Dr. Thomas Gold of Cornell University explains a pulsar as a stellar core collapsed to form an extremely small neutron-star spinning at fantastic rotation in a super-colossal powerful magnetic-field slowing down and losing energy at a steady pulse-rate. Sir Martin Ryle of Cambridge christened the first pulsar by the initials L.G.M., "Little Green Men", signifying extraterrestrial intelligence. Giancarlo Barbadoro, the Vice-Director of the Ceres Observatory near Turin, suggests that pulsars may be artificial objects with regular beams like lighthouses—celestial beacons, as points of reference for spacemen travelling in the galaxy; a space direction-system like those beacons guiding our civil aircraft. Who knows?

The Americans and Russians are experimenting with telepathy as a means of communication with cosmonauts and crews of nuclear-submarines. Soviet scientists, ignoring the occult, believe thoughts are transmitted on extremely short electromagnetic wavelengths generated by mental electricity. It seems likely therefore that the spatial intelligences may detect our Earth by the morbid thought-miasma befogging the planet's aura; perhaps, as often claimed, they can project thoughts to certain sensitives, which Earthlings consider inspirations or prophetic dreams.

No optical telescope could view a planet around even the nearest star, Alpha Centauri, only four light-years distant. Astronomers believe invisible planets are denoted by the periodic perturbations in any star's rotation. In 1964 Peter Van de Kamp after twenty-five years observation discovered a dark companion around Barnard's Star, six light years away with a mass only fifty per cent greater than Jupiter. Epsilon Eridani and Tau Ceti within eleven light years were the first stars investigated under Project Ozma by Dr. Frank Drake's 27 meter-antenna at the National Radio Astronomy in Green Bank, Virginia, devised to detect interstellar radio-signals of intelligent origin at 21 cm wavelength, the radio-frequency line of neutral hydrogen. Dr. Zend Kopal of Manchester University announces that a red star in Epsilon Aurigae appears to be the center of a solar-system of its own. He adds: "If they were highly advanced beings we could not learn from them. We could not

bridge the communication-gap." Professor Clyde Tombaugh, discoverer of the planet, Pluto, states: "It would be disaster to contact another planet."

Scientists on other planets may monitor our Earth with radio-sondes which may have fed back the signals heard by Marconi and Tesla, also later by Van Stormer. From September 14th-17th 1953 some viewers in Britain were astonished to see on their screens the T.V. identification-card of the Station KLEE in Houston, Texas, which had closed down there years before, presumably beamed from space, surely an uninspiring telecast not quite so dramatic as the hand which Belshazzar saw write on his palace wall in 538 BC heralding Babylon's sack by the Persians. Two Russian astronomers, Genrikh Altov and Valentina Zhurvelvo believe that extraterrestrials on a planet in 61 Cygnus sent powerful signals to Earth received in 1894 answering the flash from the volcano Krakatoa which exploded in 1883.

Astronomers by statistical analysis of stellar civilizations suppose that spacemen from outside our solar-system would visit Earth only once every thousand years. Orthon, Adamski's Venusian friend, who should probably know better, stated that "people are coming Earthward from planets in our system and from planets of other systems beyond ours." Eugenio Siracusa of Catania, Sicily, leader of "Centro Studi Fratellanza Cosmica" claims to be inspired by beings from the Pleiades and Alpha Centauri whom he met on the slopes of Mt. Etna. Arthur Shuttlewood, in Warminster received phone-calls from aliens from an unknown planet, Aenstria; Bob Renaud in Massachusetts claimed regular short-wave contact with a planet, Korendor, four hundred light-years distant. Dr. G.H. Williamson with masterly erudition tells of a planet called Tyrantor which five hundred thousand years ago was capital of the old decadent Empire of the Stars in the Milky Way; its subject planets rebelled and after devastating space war this confederation won victory; hopes of galactic pacts are still frustrated by evil entities on Orion who have agents here on Earth. Many people now claim contacts with beings from the stars. Such revelations strain our credulity, yet a dispassionate critic must reluctantly admit that the evidence, doubtful though it be, does seem as valid as those encounters with angels revered in our Bible.

We are living today in the golden age of astronomy; with radio-telescopes, infra-red photography and space-probes more fundamental discoveries have been made in the last decade than in all the centuries since Galileo. Quasars, pulsars,

7

microwave background radiation, x-ray stars, invisible planets. What new wonders await us? Our astronomers number men of genius, whose triumphs do rare honor to Man's intellect. When such brilliant scientists insist that though countless inhabited worlds circle distant stars, Earth lives alone around our sun, not one of the other eight planets can support life, what can we say but dismally admire their judgment? Gradually we become aware from meteorological experts studying the cloud-patterns that every single one of the thousands of photographs being constantly telemetered from satellites only a few hundred miles away and their stream of scientific data show, indeed prove, beyond all doubt that life cannot possibly exist here on our own Earth. Lost in wonder, love and praise for the great astronomers, as we really are, yet sadly conscious of all the troubles threatening our over-populated planet, we must suspect that even the cleverest men can make mistakes. If all the wonderful techniques of astronomy so strikingly fail when analyzing our Earth from such close range, surely across many millions of miles through spatial radiation and obscuring atmospheres they may be equally wrong about Venus and Mars, perhaps even more wrong about those other solar planets much further away?

In his controversial work "GODS OR SPACEMEN?" the present writer stated: "Space intelligences are reported as stating that our sun does not actually emit light itself but a primal positive force producing light on interaction with the secondary negative force of a planet. Much chemical light is produced by atomic interaction of atmospheric gases or from certain vegetation; heat emanates from the body of the living planet increased by high frequency radiation from the sun and by atmospheric phenomena; gravity is said to be a combination of a universal pressure modified by a planet's etheric and magnetic fields, density and temperature; oxygenated surface air exist beyond the range of our atmosphere-obscured instruments. The reported landings from flying saucers show the planets are inhabited not by monsters made of silicon but by passionate, wise and sensitive humans like ourselves."

There may be two intramercurial planets invisible to us because of the sun's luminescence; observed during the solar eclipse of 1876, they have not been seen since.

A century ago Leverrier, Director of the Paris Observatory, from six observations of a tiny planet which he named Vulcan, calculated it would transit the sun on 22 March, 1877. Astronomers still wait in vain.

Mercury is believed to be too close to the sun to support life, its distance varying between 28 million and 43 million miles. It is not known whether Mercury does rotate or whether it always turns the same face to the sun. Extraterrestrials are said to reveal that the planet is protected by a vast etheric covering which increases gravity for the retention of a breathable atmosphere and filters the sun's rays to permit graceful inhabitants with fine intelligence. The ancients identified Mercury with Hermes, Thrice Greatest, Inventor of Magic, worshipped as Nebo, God of Wisdom, by initiates in Palestine. Swedenborg, the Swedish mystic, claimed to have spoken with spirits from Mercury "whose sole study is to acquire knowledges, finding in them their only delight." Dr. George King, the metaphysician, states Mercury operates the communications of the solar system. Is that why the ancients knew Mercury as the messenger of the gods?

Venus, Earth's nearest neighbor, 67 million miles from the sun, is veiled in a mystery which still confounds astronomers, who argue that its atmosphere consists of carbon-dioxide or of sodium-and-magnesium-chloride or of formaldehyde or of water-vapor; it has oxygen or no oxygen with a temperature of minus 50 degrees C., or 3 degrees higher than Earth or 270 degrees C. or 400 degrees C. With such wild conflict that would paralyze any other profession astronomers declare that the surface of Venus may be covered with gigantic tropical vegetation or be a dustbowl racked with volcanic eruptions or have storm-swept islands in boiling seas or be completely drowned in oceans of soda-water. These descriptions may amuse Venusians even more than the satellites' pronouncement of no life on Earth amuses us. Alleged contacts report a wondrous heliocentric civilization where men live out a wisdom-religion of non-violence, love and beauty. Most ancient traditions agree that wonderous teachers winged down from Venus to become the first priests-kings of Atlantis. Some early Christians and modern metaphysicians believe that Jesus was a great soul from Venus. Agents from Venus and Mars are believed to survey Earth and neutralize excessive atomic-radiation in our atmosphere. The well-known ashen-light seen on the planet, once regarded as a natural auroral glow is now thought by some astronomers to be an electrical illumination suggesting the reflection from populous cities. About 12:30, noon, on Thursday,

8

20th November, 1952 there occurred in California in the desert the most famous—or most notorious—contact of modern times. George Adamski and six friends saw a flying saucer land from which alighted Orthon, a Venusian, who later took Adamski for a trip in a spaceship.

In 1686 Cassini observed a satellite of Venus seen several times during the eighteenth century; recent researchers could not find it. A large body has been seen near Venus called "Neith" by the astronomer, Houzen. Could it have been an immense spaceship?

Mars at a solar distance varying from 129 million to 154 million miles approaches about every two years as close as 35 million miles to Earth. During these oppositions waves of UFO sightings considerably increase, suggesting some correlation with the red planet. Astronomers who once agreed that the very thin atmosphere of Mars contained 98% nitrogen are now somewhat confounded by contradictory data telemetered from the space-probes. Mariner IV, 15 July, 1965 revealed the absence of a magnetic-field and consequently no Van Allen radiation-belts, and analyzed the atmosphere only 2% as dense as Earth's as 72% nitrogen, 16% carbon-dioxide, 0.8% water, very little oxygen and a trace of water-vapor. There were no signs of the famous canals, the surface with so many craters resembled the moon. Mariner VI on 30 July, 1969 approached closer to Mars and transmitted exceptionally clear pictures showing clouds, mountains, valleys, craters eroded by natural elements and registered temperatures from 24 to minus 237 degrees Centigrade; however this probe showed the absence of nitrogen, the presence of oxygen, hydrogen and carbon-dioxide; Mariner VII reached Mars a few days later and confirmed this analysis revealing also the presence of methane gas and ammonia near the south pole and showed temperatures from 24 to minus 90 degrees Centigrade, its exceptionally good photographs showed the Martian canals as resembling enormous and deep canyons 1200 km long and from 160 to 120 km wide. None of the 202 complete pictures and the 1,177 part pictures taken by Mariners VI and VII at distances ranging from a million miles to 2,180 miles showed any sign of life on Mars; however from such ranges pictures by the same craft would not have revealed any life here on Earth. The scarcity of water may be a serious limiting factor to life as we know it but the water supply may perhaps be seasonal. During the Martian Spring when the ice-caps melt, the darkened expanses turn greenish-brown

indicating vegetation watered by the melted ice flowing down river-beds. Giovanni Schiapparelli noted that the very intricate network of canals from the north pole lost in the southern deserts doubled in length when the ice-caps melted. Radar observations appear to show an oasis where two or more canals meet. The reflecting power of the Trivium Charontis suggests an immense expanse of water—probably a marsh. For the last hundred years many strange lights have been seen on Mars. On the night of June 17, 1873 according to Charles Fort a luminous thing was seen to emerge and separate itself from the disc of the planet Mars and explode in the sky of Hungary, Austria and Bohemia; a Dr. Sage saw the meteor apparently issue from Mars and the planet appear as if it was breaking up and dividing into two parts. This celestial intruder evokes the intriguing explosion in Tunguska on June 30, 1908 which devastated acres of Siberian forests; the absence of any meteoritic core suggests it may have been a spaceship which crashed. In 1962 an American scientist observed enormous luminous flares followed by the appearance of clouds veiling the zone similar to the flashes seen by Tsuneo Saheki on December 8, 1951 and his colleague, Tosaka, in July, 1954. Speculation arises as to whether these flares denoted atomic-bomb tests by the Martians since volcanic eruptions would hardly be so brilliant; the glow might possibly mark the terrible impact of large meteors unimpeded by the tenuous atmosphere crashing down on Martian soil to produce those lunar-like craters. The closer detail from Mariners VI and VII somewhat contradicted the impression from Mariner IV that Mars resembled the moon. Much of its surface now appears to be flat with only few craters.

Homer and Virgil mentioned two steeds of Mars; for many centuries they were lost. In 1636 a sketch of Mars showed a sphere inside a ring—in the sphere's center a great protruding body. Jonathan Swift in 1726 gave a remarkably accurate description of the moons in "Gulliver's Travels"; Voltaire in 1752 mentioned them in "Micromegas", and the notorious Marquis de Sade in his bawdy tale "The Mystified Magistrate" made the sorely-abused President of the Parliament of Aix say in 1772 that he had written six volumes on the satellites of Mars. The moons were not seen by William Herschel or Leverrier, both brilliant astronomers, which occasions surprise, as if the satellites were not there. Asaph Hall of the Washington Naval Observatory rediscovered both moons in 1877, Phobos ten miles in diameter, only

9

3700 miles above the planet makes a complete revolution in 7 h 39 m; Deimos, five miles in diameter at 12,500 miles, takes 30 h 18 m; both show characteristics of our artificial satellites. Phobos rising in the west and setting in the east appears to be decelerating for eventual crashdown in ten or twenty million years, though this has been denied; both with unusual metallic luster, also denied by some observers; may be hollow suggesting interstellar spaceships, space-stations or monuments to a Martian civilization long vanished. Why were these moons not discovered during Mars' closest approach in 1862? Were they not there?

Charles Fort in his whimsical way suggests that "an examination of infirmaries and workhouses and asylums might lead to some marvellous astronomical disclosures." He observes all too prophetically for our present extraterrestrial contacts, saying: "Suppose any human being ever should be translated from somewhere else to this Earth and should tell about it? Just about what chance would he have for some publicity? I neglected to note the date but early in the year 1928 a man did appear in a town in New Jersey and did tell that he had come from the planet Mars. Wherever he came from, everybody knows where he went after telling that."

In 1951 Dr. George Hunt Williamson claimed radio-contact with Regga and Zo, entities on Maser (Mars); two years later Geroge Adamski alleged a trip in a spaceship; one of its crew was Firkon, a Martian. Adamski in rare romantic vein lyricized another crew-member, Ilmuth, a tall brunette. "She also wore her hair in a cascade that fell to just below her shoulders, and it was a beautiful wavy black with highlights of reddish-brown." She wore a robe of pale, rich green and her sandals were of a copper hue." No wonder the Americans and Russians are racing to Mars! On February 18, 1954 Cedric Allingham near Forres on the north Scottish coast watched a flying saucer land. A man descended resembling an Earthman, by signs he indicated that he came from Mars and was photographed. On April 24, 1964 Gary Wilcox on his farm in Newark Valley, New York, saw a UFO descend, two human-like figures about 4 feet tall dropped to the ground from beneath it. Both were completely encased in silvery one-piece suits. Their heads were totally covered with the same fabric, no facial features were visible, the pair were filling trays with samples of soil. One visitor said in a deep voice not coming from his head that they were from the planet Mars and explained that although they had been obtaining their food from the atmosphere they had to find a way to rehabilitate their soil to grow crops.

Dr. George King states that Mars was inhabited by an advanced race who were the engineers and builders in the solar system, its culture far ahead of anything experienced on Earth. Long ago the Martians aided the White Magicians of Atlantis against powerful Black Magicians wielding nuclear-bombs. Pictures from the Mariner VI and VII probes only 3200 km from the planet's surface show Mars as being inhospitable, yet no more desolate than our own Earth from such altitude. On August 20, 1924 Mrs. H.C. Hutchinson, Denver, Colorado, a medium, claimed to have received messages from elder brothers on Mars who stated the Martians now lived underground. Their ancestors were the earliest colonizers of Earth; two million years ago they built Lemuria, Atlantis and cities in the Antarctic, instead of making love, healthy and intelligent Martian maidens propagate the race by parthenogenesis, somewhat frustrating for the men, who not surprisingly are flocking to reconquer Earth.

On January 1, 1801 Piazzi discovered a small wandering star 437 miles in diameter between the orbits of Mars and Jupiter, which he named Ceres, since then many hundreds, some very small, have been located. Astronomers wonder whether they are debris of a disintegrated planet. Some sensitives believe that long ago evil scientists of the planet Maldek exploded a super-hydrogen bomb and actually destroyed their entire world. The souls suddenly released on to the different etheric planes were not welcomed on the other cultured solar planets but were forced to incarnate on lowly Earth as the people of Lemuria, where conflict between white and black magicians eventually shattered their brilliant civilization. The Shilluks, a primitive tribe in South Africa, apparently saw two of the moons of Uranus about 2,600 million miles away yet did not even notice the asteroids less than a tenth of that distance. Galileo discovered four moons of Jupiter; why did he not detect the nearer asteroids? Hermes in 1937 missed Earth by only 485,000 miles, Icarus in 1968 came almost as close. Where were the asteroids before Piazzi found them? Why with all our wonderful instruments are so many others still being discovered? A most fascinating article "100 Years Behind in the Space Race" by an anonymous writer in Ray Palmer's "Flying Saucers", August 1969, wonders why hundreds of asteroids easily visible with binoculars were not discovered until this century, the orbits of many are surprisingly erratic, their accentricity

10

suggest intelligent direction not natural motion. The sudden approach of these celestial bodies of tiny size and their unusual orbital inclination leads to speculation as to whether they are space stations launched from Mars or possibly from Ganymede, a moon of Jupiter. Some asteroids have apparently vanished, new ones have suddenly appeared. Fantastic though it may seem there is reason to assume that for the last hundred years extraterrestrials are sending artificial satellites to surveil Earth.

Jupiter about 483 million miles from the sun is 1319 times as large as Earth but only 318 times its mass with astonishingly low density. The planet rotates on its axis in about ten hours and around the sun in nearly twelve years. Most of Jupiter apparently consists of hydrogen with some ammonia and methane around a layer of ice surrounding a rock-core at a temperature alleged to be minus 100 degrees C. Jupiter and Earth are believed to have been created about the same time; why has Jupiter's primeval atmosphere remained almost unchanged? If data from the satellites close to Earth prove so erratic, can we really believe our analysis of Jupiter and more distant planets many hundreds of millions of miles away? Space intelligences are said to allege that the sun does not actually emite heat and light which are phenomena produced by a primal positive force reacting with the secondary negative force of a planet. Chemical heat and light may radiate from atmospheric gases and volcanic activity, gravity is possibly combination of a universal pressure. George Adamski claimed that the asteroid-belt accelerates particles from the sun providing normal heat and light for Jupiter, Saturn, Uranus and Neptune, a secondary belt of asteroids beyond Neptune similarly provides heat and light for distant Pluto. As far as Jupiter is concerned are our astronomers really much wiser than those simple souls who thought our moon was made of cheese? Scientists are vastly intrigued by radio-noise and infra-red emissions from Jupiter. Dare we suggest that electrical vibrations reveal a wonderful civilization on Jupiter using far more electricity than we do? Are those sudden bursts of power from Jupiter attempts at communication?

Astronomers marvel at the famous Red Spot, 30,000 miles long and 7,000 miles wide apparently drifting high above the surface, sometimes hardly visible. Why was the Red Spot never noticed before 1878? Is it a space station launched by the Jovian super-scientists or can it be an intelligently controlled asteroid?

Dr. G.H. Williamson asserts that Jupiter is inhabited, being called Etonya, its capital city is Adee; in 1952 he claimed contact with an intelligence there called Ankar-22, who said Jupiter is the mental research center of this solar system. In 1952 fourteen-year old Ronnie Tucker complained of a mind-probe directed from Jupiter. Dr. George King states that already ages ago Jupiter had reached such a high state of spiritual culture that it was used as a reception-center for the Interplanetary Confederation. The twelve Jovian moons are too small and too far away for any reliable analysis. The largest, Ganymede, about the size of our own moon, is believed to have an atmosphere and even canals not observed until 1862 when they may have been built. A brilliant writer, regrettably anonymous, in the August 1969 issue of Ray Palmer's "Flying Saucers" discussing those Martian moons suggests: "Possibly Mars was colonized by emigrants from Ganymede who constructed the canals and launched the satellites. Can it be that Ganymede is our competitor in the space race?"

Why did the Greeks and the Romans associate Zeus with the planet Jupiter, worshipped by all the peoples of antiquity? Did space kings from Jupiter once rule Earth in a golden age destroyed by interplanetary war? Are the Jovians returning today?

Saturn, diameter 75,000 miles, 744 times the volume of Earth, revolves around the sun 886 million miles distant in 29 years; it rotates on its axis in a day of about 10 hours. The vast planet is believed to be composed mainly of hydrogen, methane and ammonia frozen at about minus 150 degrees Centigrade around a small core possibly of metallic hydrogen. Notwithstanding its immense bulk, low density makes its gravity only slightly greater than Earth's. The most characteristic feature of Saturn are its three rings even known to the Assyrians four thousand years ago and to the ancient Hindus who encircled "Sani" with a ring of serpents. How could the ancients see the rings around Saturn? Had the old astronomers telescopes? Did they inherit this knowledge from previous civilizations or from spacemen? Space intelligences are reported as saying the rings are the debris of a moon shattered by a comet, today we may suspect disintegration by a nuclear-bomb; scientists somewhat puzzled conclude they must be constituted of millions of particles of dust, oddly enough some observers have alleged a tenuous ring of dust around our own Earth. Two of Saturn's nine moons are said to be inhabited by beings in

11

astral bodies, startling perhaps to our conventional thought but not impossible from a cosmic viewpoint. Phoebe, the ninth satellite, discovered by William Henry Pickering in 1898, has an unusual retrograde motion evoking the Martian moon, Phobos; it orbits in the prolonged duration of 523 days 13 hours, eight million miles distant. Like Hyperion, the seventh moon, its orbit is highly eccentric. In 1905 Pickering discovered a tenth moon, Themis, 930,000 miles distant, in an orbit tilted at 39 degrees to the planes of the other moons; it has not been seen since. The unusual motions of Phoebe, Hyperion and Themis suggest that may be controlled artificial satellites, even vast spaceships.

Surface conditions on Saturn as analyzed by our astronomers would make life as we know it impossible there. Space intelligences have told various contacts that Saturn, seat of the Interplanetary Confederation, has a marvellous civilization in a sub-tropical paradise whose advanced beings do not need to eat but live on radiations emanating directly from the solar logos. In February, 1953 George Adamski enjoyed a highly controversial trip in a Saturnian mothership with an interplanetary crew including his friend, Ramu from Saturn, to within 40,000 miles of the moon, though the revelation by the pilot that parts of the moon were populated in a verdant oasis would be news to our cosmonauts. Adamski told a colorful tale of flying to Saturn in only nine hours on March 26, 1962 to attend a conference of cosmic masters. He was enchanted by a world of wonder radiant with gorgeous flowers and magnificent buildings. Howard Menger claims to be a reincarnated Saturnian and rhapsodizes over this dream planet. There he alleges that the heightened rate of vibrations elevates corporeal structures to an etherean plane, something which Adamski forgot to mention, assuming he ever knew. Dr. Carl Sagan relates an amusing experience during the last war as witness for the prosecution against a certain Helmuth Winckler, a Nebraskan, who alleged that Saturnians took him beneath the Bering Straits and later into a secret chamber in the Great Pyramid. In California Winckler found a special quartz which he sold as a cure for cancer, although it was not his to sell. Mr. Winckler diverted the court with his fantastic adventures, the jury were baffled nearly as much by Dr. Sagan's learned disquisition on astronomy. Science prevailed; Mr. Winckler, despite the film he concocted, was sent to prison for fraud. A stern warning to all would-be contacts: They are not all locked up!

Uranus, diameter 29,300 miles, rotates around the sun 1783 million miles away in about 84 years. Owing to its low density its gravity is similar to Earth's. The greenish-blue planet is inclined at the unusual angle of 98 degrees to the perpendicular of the plane of the solar system being apparently composed of methane at a temperature of minus 160 degrees Centigrade. The inhabitants, hermaphrodites, are feared as wizards. Five moons have an odd retrograde motion.

Neptune, diameter, 27,800 miles, rotates around the sun, 2792 miles away, in 165 years and is largely composed of methane much in liquid state at minus 170 degrees Centigrade; its inhabitants are similar to the Uranids. One of its moons, Triton, has the retrograde motion we associate with some artificial satellites; the orbit of the other moon, Nereid, is extremely eccentric.

Pluto, possibly the size of Mars, rotates around the sun 3,675 miles away, in 248 years, it is composed of methane at about minus 200 degrees Centigrade; its orbit is most eccentric, possibly due to attraction by yet another outer planet, Proserpine, claimed by Russian astronomers at the Kazakhstan Astrophysical Institute in 1960. The Inhabitants of Pluto are said to be brilliant perverts destined for inevitable doom.

Studies by astronomers quite obviously deny life to Uranus, Neptune and Pluto, however it is difficult to refute suggestions that thermocouple and spectroscopic data may be inaccurate for these immensely distant planets, especially as the same instruments apparently fail to detect life when only a few hundred miles from Earth. Perhaps chemical and vegetable light, atmospheric and volcanic heat, do render the outer planets habitable; people may live in conditions we simply cannot imagine. Dr. G.H. Williamson claimed radio-contact with Agfa-Affa and Zrs from Uranus, Zo from Neptune, Garr and Touka from Pluto. They told him of the further planet, Patras, Dr. George King reveres cosmic masters on Pluto; other sensitives claim revelations insisting that all the solar planets are inhabited. Truman Bethurm wrote of several meetings with Aura Rhanes, a beautiful blonde in a spaceship from Clarion, a planet on the other side of the sun which we cannot see.

For centuries strange lights, vanishing craters, volcanic domes, have mystified astronomers studying our moon. Some contacts tell of UFO bases and spacemen activity, certainly not confirmed by those chill and sterile photographs or our cosmonauts who have landed on that barren lunar soil. Who knows?

12

ANCIENT SECRETS OF MYSTERIOUS AMERICA

Our own Earth may still have secrets few suspect. Photographs taken on January 6, 1967 by ESSA-3 satellite and on November 23, 1968 by ESSA-7 seem clearly to show the existence of a hole at the north pole said to lead to the wonderful civilization of Agharta deep inside our hollow Earth, subterranean home of the flying saucers and the humanoids. Tales are told of UFO bases under the Antarctic ice, secret cities in the jungles of the Amazon and strange activities by flying saucers plunging into ocean depths.

Little reliance can be placed on the revelation of many alleged spacemen contacts; some are given by men of high integrity and great moral purpose, who are surely worthy of our confidence as those prophets of the Bible.

Our survey of the universe and the solar system now enables us to view our tiny Earth in perspective against the whole glittering cosmos. We can perhaps more fully question whether the "God" of the Bible, far from being the creator of all, was most probably an extraterrestrial similar to those spacemen visiting Earth today.

13

Chapter Two
The Origin of Man

The legends of spacemen warring with fantastic weapons destroying some wondrous civilization on Earth long ago, cosmic catastrophes ravaging our planet and plunging the few frantic survivors back to barbarism, evoke within our souls some atavistic memory beclouding our secret lives. The ancestral trauma of suffering inhibiting our subconscious minds is suddenly dispelled. Free and gloriously elated we gaze at the familiar world around us with new eyes; tired old Earth glows in heroic splendor, the fragments of ancient wisdom synthesize into a marvellous, exciting panorama inspiring the pilgrimage of Man with pregnant meaning. All we have learned appears inadequate as though down the centuries the truths of our universe were wilfully suppressed, leaving us conditioned by dogmas sadly out of date. Conventional histories recording the follies of mankind through merely seven milennia now seem trivial, their wars stupid setbacks on humanity's onward march to its glorious destiny; the squabbles of rival religions become sterile, those classical Authorities founding our Western civilization misled our Fathers as our modern culture confounds us today. As we survey the universe in the light of our new knowledge, we find ourselves making a complete re-appraisal of the past. No longer will we remain bemused by official disparagements from scholars with antiquated ideas, we demand our cosmic heritage to attune our souls in thrilling wonder to those Celestials from the stars.

The ancient Hindus taught that each universe manifests during a Day of Brahm lasting one hundred and fifty-four million, million years vanishing throughout an equally long Night of Brahm, then the Absolute imagines a new universe conditioned by experience of its predecessor, the cycle of creative activity and creative cessation continuing forever. Astronomers smile at such recondite speculation until they brood on their own choice between a sequence of cyclic universes expanding from, then contracting to, a single atom in eternal recurrence, or a state of continuous creation, where atoms are born from spatial energy to compensate for atoms elsewhere which have died. Physicists add a symmetrical universe of anti-matter where time appears to run backward; they postulate worlds within our own supporting the astral realms of the occultists. Truth is veiled beyond human cognizance; it is apparent that our universe has existed through unimaginable ages, galaxies could have lived and died before our own Milky Way was born. The universe exists to satisfy the Divine Mind. Life persists from Beginning to End.

Stellar evolution suggests that our sun is middle-aged; billions of stars are very much older. Astronomers observe that stars at the time of creation rotate very quickly, then later the rotation retards as if their original kinetic energy were partly drained by an attendant family of planets, sometimes corroborated by radio-emissions. An immense number of stars are thought to govern worlds of their own; the Milky Way must have millions of planets, many with civilizations millions of years old peopled by humans wise and foolish like ourselves. All races who have developed space-travel must master a more advanced

14

technology and probably exquisite intelligence far beyond communication to our own immature minds; however a few extraterrestrials may derive some amusement from our antics or feel inspired by some cosmic duty to land and teach us the arts of civilization. The theory of Relativity, if it is true for the vast chasms of space, limits motion to the speed of light 186,000 miles per second. In 1970 a team of scientists led by J.S. Allen and Geoffrey Endean of Oxford University came to the conclusion that the electromagnetic fields produced in the Crab Nebula by the explosion of a supernova are receding at a velocity of 372,000 miles per second. The report in "Nature" considered this observation to be an apparent contradiction of Einstein's theory.

Limitation is only a quality of mind. The Great Intelligences may have dreamed up techniques for speeding to the furthest galaxies quicker than thought. Intriguing evocations in the Egyptian "The Book of the Dead" such as "I, Horus, am yesterday", "I am tomorrow", "I course through space and time" all suggest that the old gods or spacemen may have teleported themselves through dimension beyond our imagination. The universe itself is a great mind; communication between its myriad cells seems certain.

Students of flying saucer phenomena now tend to support the teachings of the ancient mystics and yogis, also the ultra-modern "borderland" scientists, all agree that wondrous beings emanate from realms of finer vibrations beyond our normal perception. A vast literature down the ages from most ancient times tells of invisible worlds in astral realms inhabited by angels, devils, devas, faeries, nature-spirits, who often manifest on our physical Earth.

How and when human life appeared in our universe we shall probably never know. The American astronomer, David Buhler, of the radio-astronomy observatory at Green Bank in Virginia, following the discovery in space of abundant quantities of formaldehyde, presumes that the existence of methane and the verified presence of water and ammonia must provide the elements essential to the formation of life. Complex molecules formed from these basic elements could constitute living cells and descend on our Earth in clouds of gas; similar clouds might bring life to all the planets, the Milky Way and other galaxies.

The ancient Hermetic philosophers taught that Man materialized from spiritual realms descending to our grosser dimensions, perhaps the origin of the Fall of Man; however it is probable that sentient beings appeared somewhere vast ages before our Earth was born. The purpose of Life is to people the universe. In the remote past beings mastering immense technology moved from galaxy to galaxy disseminating through untold ages their wondrous civilization; eventually they reach our Milky Way and from its center in Sagittarius these celestials and their countless descendants throughout millions of years expanded their galactic empire to the outer limits, where they found a small star with a family of planets awaiting settlement. Earth may have been a transit base enroute to further planets, different races called here leaving those characteristic skeletons disputed by palaentologists and possibly accounting for the various racial groups populating our world today. Traditions assert that all the worlds in our solar system have long been civilized in a federation dominated by Saturn which like Jupiter and possibly Uranus once ruled our Earth in those golden and silver ages sung in the Greek myths. Cylinder seals discovered in Babylonia show nine planets circling the prominent sun in the sky lending confirmation to the chronicle of Berossus that the Sumerians were first taught by Oannes and other Akpallus whom we now identify with spacemen. The space-colonists probably brought animals and plants; it is said that the bee and wheat originated from Venus.

Psychics claim that wondrous beings on Sirius wage perpetual war with dark entities on Orion. Interplanetary conflicts probably rage in space beyond our cognizance. What if those super-novae which suddenly flare up and die are stars which some super enemy has rubbed out? Aeons ago the planet Maldek between Mars and Jupiter exploded into fragments called the asteroids; occultists allege its inhabitants became so wicked that the guardians of our solar system decreed the planet's destruction. The explosion of Maldek may have devastated neighboring Mars and impelled survivors to abandon the red planet in emigration to Earth as told in the legends of the Hopi Indians.

Mars was probably colonized long before Earth. The American astronomer, Carl Sagan, agrees with his Russian associate, Josef Shklovsky that once Mars was humid with abundant oxygen and water to support life. Explorers from the inner galaxy would settle on Mars where the ancient Martians constructed those famous canals and the artificial moons, Deimos and Phobos, in which people lived when the planet's surface and atmosphere became inhospitable, although recent studies challenge that fascinating theory. Photographs taken by Mariner

15

IV in July 1965 reveal faint lines, possibly canals with oases at intersections; one picture appears to show a quadrangular structure suggesting intelligent life; Mariners VI and VII in July and August, 1969 showed no canals, merely alignments of random dark patches, possibly deep canyons. They revealed no signs of life but from 3,200 kms these probes would find no evidence of life here on our Earth.

"Is the moon a product of human intelligence?"

In a fascinating article published in "Komsomolskaya Pravda" on January 10th, 1970 Mikhail Vessine and Alexandre Chtcherbakov reject the three hypotheses stating our moon once constituted part of Earth from which it was torn out; secondly the moon was formed independently of Earth but from the same cloud of dust and gas, thirdly it wandered from far outside the solar system finally to be caught by Earth's gravity. With daring logic the two scientists explain that our moon's low density compared with Earth's suggests it is an artificial satellite launched on a geocentric orbit by unknown beings endowed with intelligence, possibly a giant spaceship, abode of a civilization. The hollow sphere appears to consist of two shells containing an atmosphere, the inner 30 kms thick made of extremely hard metal, the outer about 4 kms thick composed of thermoprotective, resistant and inoxydizable rocks including chromium, titanium and zirconium, used on Earth in electric stoves. The large lunar craters and their surprisingly small depths were caused by meteorites striking the metallic shock-absorber and exploding sideways, not inward, causing extensive shallow holes and scattering debris far and wide. Inside the hollow interior were storerooms for propulsives, tools and materials for repairs, navigational equipment and observational instruments. Some lunar rocks are different and older than terrestrial rocks; this does not prove the moon was fabricated before Earth was formed but it is undoubtedly extremely ancient. The ship now probably uninhabited is becoming a wreck, the stabilizers no longer function, the poles are displaced, the face opposite Earth wobbles badly; the dark "maria" or "dried seas" seem to be patches of the metallic inner sphere stripped of its protective sheath later repaired with cement, the repair material and equipment underneath these localities explain the phenomena of "massons", zones of increased gravity discovered in eccentric orbits of our own lunar satellites. Gas sometimes seen escaping through craters is not due to volcanic activity but to leakages of atmosphere inside from fissures in the outer sphere.

This fantastic theory of our moon is supported by ideas that not only are Deimos and Phobos, moons of Mars, artificial satellites, but possibly the asteroids, the Red Spot of Jupiter, Phoebe, Hyperion and Themis around Saturn, and even the moons of Uranus and Neptune whose unusual motion arouses conjecture. The old legends of Greece tell of space wars with the Uranids, an ancient stellar race. Did the Uranids once inhabit our moon?

In his five-act comedy "Man In The Moon" the present writer describes a wonderful civilization inside the moon with 500 women and only 50 men. The lovelorn women capture the American and Russian cosmonauts then make themselves known to Earth. We wonder?

Theosophists insist that Man is older than the apes whose earliest fossils are said to be found only in comparatively recent geological strata. Man belongs to a kingdom distinctly separate from the animals. The first men were etherean beings whose attenuated forms in the course of ages became more condensed until they attuned to the slower vibrations of our physical plane and assumed solidity; such materializations descended to the entire visible universe; peopling not only Earth but all the planets.

In 1650 Archbishop Ussher calculated the age of our Earth from alleged evidence in the Old Testament and concluded it was created in 4004 BC although Archbishop Langland deplored such inexactitude and swore that creation occurred on October 23rd of that year at 3:30 p.m. in the afternoon. The French naturalist, Count Buffon, around 1750 heated two large iron spheres and from the time they took to cool gave the Earth a minimum age of 74,832 years. Lord Kelvin in 1862 hazarded an age of 20 million years but admitted somewhat unscientifically that it could be as much as 400 million years; in 1941 the American physicist, George Gamow, raised the age to 2,000 million years. Many astronomers believe that the universe is expanding from a Big Bang about 10,000 million years ago, others still support Fred Hoyle's Steady State, Continuous Creation theory. The sun is said to be 5,000 million years old and our Earth 4,500 million years, an age determined by the radio-active decay of uranium-238 into lead. This estimate is now challenged by Professor Erich Gerling of Leningrad and his colleagues, who by new techniques have found the rocks in the Kola Peninsula in Northern Russia to be at least 11,000 million years old; allowing more than 1,000 million

16

years for Earth to condense from a gas-dust cloud to a solid body. This ages Earth to more than 12,000 million years, apparently older than the rest of the universe. It is likely that soon ideological rivalry will prompt some Chinese scientist to surpass the Russian claim. The true age of our Earth is probably beyond ascertainment and like the age of Man much older than we think. Conventional theories may require revision.

The age of Man upon Earth is constantly advanced. Palaentologists now suggest that life may be a thousand million years old. Fleas have been found in Paleocene amber eighty million years old; perhaps some theologian would explain why the Deity felt disposed to create fleas sixty million years before He created Man? Fossil jaw-fragments found by Dr. Louis Leakey in 1967 at Rusinga and Songer in Kenya apparently belonged to Kenyapithecus Africanus, a man-like creature distinct from the ancestor of the modern ape, which lived during the middle Miocene period twenty million years ago long before the Ice Age. Man is carried back a million generations. Edgar Cayce, the renowned American seer, in his psychic reading 5748-1. May 28, 1925, revealed that ten-and-a-half million years ago human souls incarnated on Earth with a vastly different geography from today, they numbered a hundred-and-thirty-three million, their period corresponded with the humanoid skeleton discovered in 1958 by Dr. Johannes Huerzeler six hundred feet deep in an Italian coal-mine, which palaentologists date as ten million years old. What if these fossils were the bones of spacemen? Such new discoveries in the last few years have advanced the age of Man dramatically from one million to twenty million years. Suppose some enterprising palaentologist alleges human fossils a hundred million years old! What happens then? Must these wonderful theories of Man's age and ancestry be revised yet again?

Historians hint that God was so little impressed with His latest creation that for nearly twenty million years He condemned men to live little better than animals, then suddenly in the last hundred centuries speeded their evolution from caves to space-capsules. Scholars trace civilization to about 5000 BC, archaeologists in Turkey suggest 9000 BC, all assume that before then prehistoric men dreamed in the darkness of an immensely prolonged stone age. Obelisks and circles of stones erected all over the world, also those strange signs and elliptical forms of unknown objects painted with men and animals on the walls of caves in the Pyrenees dated 12000 BC, may not be sexual symbols as hitherto supposed but primitive representations of spaceships. Did God create the first man in the whole universe billions of years ago? Countless stars and myriads of planets may have lived and died before our sun was created. What is special about our own Earth, except the fact that we happen to infest it? Whether we believe in the special creation of Man by God or the creation of life by cosmic accident, it is surely nonsense to insist that life was restricted to an inferior planet revolving around a dwarf sun near the edge of the Milky Way just one of numberless galaxies. In a few centuries Man may repopulate Mars; could Martians have left their dying planet millions of years ago to people Earth? Foreseeing the inevitable destruction of our own Earth, indeed of the sun itself, advanced Earthlings in millions of years time will emigrate to another solar system, perhaps to another galaxy. Such a suggestion a decade since would have seemed science-fiction, today with our new knowledge it merits serious study. We are haunted by the suspicion that Man may not belong to Earth; perhaps he descended when our world was young like a God from the stars.

The return of the spaceships to haunt our skies, surely the most wonderful manifestation since the advent of Christ, evokes ridicule, a sad commentary on our twentieth-century cynicism; a hundred years ago our great grandfathers would have welcomed the spacemen with delight to settle the most violent controversy convulsing the Victorian Age. On November 24th, 1859 Charles Darwin, after twenty years reflection, published his "Origin of Species" asserting that Man had evolved from the same common ancestor as monkeys; the whole edition of 1,250 copies was sold out that first day. This historic work raised a storm which echoes still. Theologians believing God's special creation of Man in "Genesis", rushed sternly to attack, the scientists seduced by the theory of Natural Selection leaped in defence. For many years the battle raged; the Church, Art, Science, Society itself, took sides in bitter debate about Man's evolution, transforming contemporary thought, even leading to Marxist dialectilism revolutionizing our world today. Discoveries in geology and excavations in ancient Egypt and Babylon appeared to support materialist science in rejecting "Genesis" and the sudden creation of Man. Palaentologists searched the rocks for fossils and conveniently found what they were looking for; their labors were enlivened by aggrieved

17

theologians who swore the old bones had been put there by the Devil to deny the work of God, an argument which the irreverent British found funny. Botanists intensified research on plants, zoologists classified animals; soon the evolutionists produced ingenious charts tracing the ascension of life from a single cell on the primeval sea-bed to fishes then monkeys, finally to the noblest work of nature, Man himself. Religion suffered a crushing defeat until some preacher suddenly claimed that evolution was God's idea. He could have created Man at once but did not mind waiting more than four thousand million years until Homo Sapiens evolved; only God knows whether Man was worth this long wait. Now even He must wonder! Science won a tremendous victory. Darwin's theory dominates world-thought, evolution and natural selection are now accepted everywhere, except in Bible-punching Tennessee—there teaching men descended from monkeys might land a lecturer in jail.

As Darwin's enthusiastic disciples dethroned the old idols of religion and proclaimed the new deity of science, they reluctantly admitted that while this wonderful theory of evolution brought meaning to the progression of mankind, the "link" between ape and man was still missing. Today a century later the elusive "Missing Link" is not yet found. Recent fossil finds of curled, worm-like objects up to a few inches long discovered during the blasting of a new road just north of Lake Huron in Ontario were examined by Mr. H.J. Hoffman of the Geological Survey of Canada, who described them in the journal "Science". This discovery is alleged to prove that the first multi-celled animals must have appeared on Earth not about 700 million years as currently believed but more than 2,000 million years ago; the animal kingdom has apparently existed for roughly half our Earth's history. The fact that the chance finding of a few fossil worms can so dramatically, even outrageously, revolutionize our whole conception of the duration of animal and therefore of human life on our Earth demonstrates how most vital theories may be dreamed on the flimsiest evidence. Evolutionists unblushingly accept that Man's earliest ancestor was not the coelocanth still inexplicably swimming in our tropical seas but a worm crawling under Canada two thousand million years ago. The Tibetans are said to sift the soil rather than injure worms, how many British gardeners have qualms about killing their own grandfathers ten billion times removed? Scientists must be surely the most credulous of mortals, they

scorn all suggestions that Man came from space yet seriously accept evolution from worms. The sad state of our world may suggest that men think like worms but the only hope for all humanity is to act like the angels, our ancestors, the spacemen.

Biologists generally still follow Darwin just as physicists believe Einstein's doubtful theory of relativity. Shortly before he died, that great nuclear physicist, Robert Oppenheimer, wondered if the genius of Einstein had directed twentieth-century science on a false path, particularly as all attempts by scientists during the last forty years have quite failed to reconcile the two great theories of modern physics, Relativity and Quantum; similarly the new idea of the inhabited universe arouses speculation as to whether Darwin put our conception of the evolution of Man on a wrong track. Some critics suggest our Earth is not old enough for Man to have developed from protoplasm in the sea, if indeed Darwin's theory were correct, evolution of species appears to be so extremely slow that very many billions of years would be needed for a single cell to evolve to our exasperating selves.

Josef Shklovsky believes that the extinction of the dinosaurs about seventy million years ago was possibly caused by the explosion of a super-nova which greatly intensified the cosmic radiation influencing Earth ten- or even a hundred-fold, which would have serious genetic effects on animals and plants. Fluctuations in powerful cosmic rays would cause significant mutations in human species, raising of the level of ionization in the atmosphere might last tens of thousands of years with most profound effects on the evolution of all forms of terrestrial life. Instead of the gradual development of life on Earth through long ages preached by Agassiz and the nineteenth century geologists, scientists now believe that evolution advances by a succession of sudden shocks. In its long history our Earth has suffered collision with comets; changes in cosmic radiation along our planet's trajectory through space have influenced human genes bringing startling changes in species.

Some palaentologists now speculate that the origin and extinction of species may possibly be caused by the periodic disappearances and reversals of Earth's magnetic field. Dr. Bruce Heezen of Columbia University states that apparent reversals of the magnetic field occur at intervals from a half-million to one million years and take as long as 10,000 years for one cycle. During the process of reversing to zero, the Earth's protective shield

18

attenuates, allowing the bombardment of cosmic rays to kill off some species completely and to create in others new and dominant mutations. Studies of rock-cores from geologic strata indicate that major "semi-permanent" reversals of the magnetic field took place 700,000 years ago, 2,400,000 years ago and 3,500,000 years ago, while temporary reversals of short duration occurred 900,000 years ago and 1,900,000 years ago. At present the intensity of the magnetic field is decreasing, resulting in corresponding increase in the potency of cosmic radiation reaching Earth. Georgio Piccardi, Professor of Chemistry at Florence University, in a prolonged series of chemical experiments conducted with exquisite care, has proved that even in a few years variation in spatial tensions exercise considerable influence on matter and consequently on mind. This theory may be the basis of the ancient art of astrology. Educationists state there is reason to believe that our new generation today has a higher intelligence than its elders, which may not be difficult; the increased mental powers may be attributed perhaps to more potent cosmic rays. Earth's magnetic field may reach zero in 2,000 years when the intensified cosmic radiation may kill off some species and create supermen. Similar fluctuations in human intelligence must have occurred many times during changes in Earth's magnetic field modifying cosmic radiation in the past. Our ancestors a million years ago far from being the benighted cavemen we imagine may have been wondrous beings with a cosmic civilization beyond our dreams, in fact the marvellous transcendent culture of Lemuria.

Zoologists have dosed birds and animals with excessive radiation and like the atom-bomb's effect on the pregnant women of Hiroshima have produced strange mutations. Irradiated flies have changed color, a duck had three legs but monkeys still remain monkeys.

In "Timaeus 29" Plato declared:

"Let me tell you then why the Creator made this world. He was good and the good can never have any jealousy of anything. And because he was free from jealousy, he desired all things to be as like himself as they could be. This is in the truest sense the origin of creation and of the world."

Christian theology accepted the Platonic vision teaching that nature is the incarnation of divine ideas. At the beginning of the last century Lamarck supported by Kant repudiated the principle of the immutability of species and suggested a constantly changing Earth with changing living creatures including Man; this conception was demolished by Cuvier whose reconstruction of fossil animals made him believe in a succession of cataclysms followed by new forms of species. Darwin reconciled Lamarck's transformism with a mechanistic explanation for transformation of species; his theory of evolution failed to explain how such a wonderful work as the human eye could develop mechanically as by blind chance, Gergson therefore postulated creative evolution by *elan vital*, the creative power. Teilhard de Chardin a few decades ago rejected determinism and believed that evolution confirmed progress, the progress of nature to spirit, history to justice, humanity to superhumanity, a philosophy taught ages ago in India by the Gnani Yogis; this doctrine conflicts with the principles of heredity proved by Mendel supported by modern biological discoveries of chromosomes.

Science generally teaches that Man, heir to about 3,000 million years evolution, descended from a common ancestor with the monkey. The future span of life on Earth is limited to about another 10,000 million years, then covered with thick ice our Earth will revolve silently around the sun, then an unstable white dwarf star, which in 15,000 million years time will explode like a super nova vaporizing Earth to utter extinction. Ages later the universe itself will stop expanding and slowly contract to a primal atom, all in the state of entropy. After an immensely long quiescence the universe will start yet again.

Perhaps conventional ideas on evolution are still wrong?

The old conventional evolutionists knew nothing about atom-bombs, cosmic radiation or viruses, which may cause sudden changes of species. Biologists are breaking down the barriers between inorganic and organic matter and seem on the verge of creating life, even the miracle of the eventual creation of Man in test-tubes no longer appears remote.

Dare we suggest the bizarre fantasy that vast ages ago some cosmic genius in a distant galaxy created Man and in further experiments created animals too? Nonsense, of course, we must agree, yet the dreams of biologists of creating new species seem alarmingly real with each new thrilling discovery.

The ancient teachings of world ages and previous civilizations suggest that there have been several previous creations of Man; whether we, the latest, are the best is open to doubt. We too in turn shall be superseded, perhaps for a new mutation, the superman.

The purpose of evolution? The meaning of life? Can Man ever know?

19

Chapter Three
The Antiquity of Man

Above the portals of temples in the ancient world were carved the words "Man, Know Thyself". Today Man stands expectant on the threshold of space challenging the stars, conscious of his strange, exciting, wondrous destiny; our human race becomes reborn to the new cosmic age. Never was self-knowledge needed more than now. Already our cosmonauts look back and see the old familiar Earth shrivel to a small ball rotating forlornly like some lost toy; all the historic passions of mankind fade like a dream. Tomorrow's travellers may see their ancient home dwindle to a point of light then disappear, leaving them alone gloriously free under the glittering constellations lost in the timeless infinitudes of the universe. Centuries hence new mutations of Man with miraculous techniques speed on to Andromeda and the galaxies beyond, watching the billions of worlds in our Milky Way dissolve to a luminous veil then vanish, amid the stellar splendor of eternity that speck of dust called Earth drifts from memory. As strange constellations swing into sight studded with glowing stars, our cosmonauts soar to cosmic consciousness, their souls thrilling in fellowship for all the myriad forms of life throughout the living universe. Man will attune his mind to all Creation and know himself at last as the immortal son of God.

Today space-medicine is specially concerned with the effects which potent cosmic radiation, weightlessness or gravitational stress may cause on the cosmonaut's body, while psychiatrists explore the influence of the strange environment affecting his mind. Intensive training in space-simulators prepares the cosmonaut for the physical and mental hazards yet research overlooks the greatest problem, illumination of the astronaut's soul. Imprisoned in his tiny capsule, exiled from familiar Earth, the spaceman must experience a primeval loneliness chilling his very spirit; turning from the hidden depths of his own self to the vastness of space, he smiles at the friendly stars and senses in those lustrous constellations the presence of life. He speculates on the humans who live there, their lives, their ideas, and suddenly wonders how they would receive him, whether his own thought-pattern attunes to other planets, if the religions, philosophies and sciences of Earth are valid throughout the universe, perhaps the truths he was taught prove false? To some Intelligence from the stars he with his sophisticated knowledge might seem a superstitious savage. Under the glorious vault of eternity the astronaut thrills to a resurgence of soul as the cosmic wonder of Creation turns his thoughts from tortured Earth to the splendor of the universe, he will feel truth, in the silence he will know. When the traveller returns, spiritually reborn, he will see our world with new eyes, stripping the shams from society, skimming culture of its crudities, religion of its dogmas, science of its pretensions, he will yearn to impart to all humanity the wondrous inspiration of the stars. The doctors would diagnose space-sickness; any astronaut claiming truth from the stars might be considered mad.

Man's greatest embarrassment on confronting extraterrestrials may be his own ignorance. We Earthlings glory in our ego-centricity, fostered by

20

the false materialism which taints contemporary culture; five great religions contend for truth, science creates to destroy; men plod on their cosmic pilgrimage without purpose, no world-figure can now reveal the meaning of the universe. Despite the genius of so many scholars in diverse fields of human endeavor no cosmic wisdom inspires our world, to people of other planets our earthly ethics may seem barbaric. To communicate with extraterrestrials on their cultural level Man must expand to cosmic consciousness, attune his soul to all creation; Man must know himself; first he must revise his views of our own Earth.

It is popularly assumed that the scholars of antiquity during many milennia must have bequeathed for our benefit records documenting history since civilization began, just as our own century is accumulating a prodigious profusion of books to bewilder posterity. Apart from a few inscriptions in hieroglyphics or cuneiform the oldest written text actually extant to us may be a papyrus scroll from "The Book of the Dead" dated about 1500 B.C.; the absence of earlier records superficially suggests people could not read or write, that for twenty million years Man lived in ignorance, then suddenly in the last forty centuries evolved from scratching signs on stones to Sunday newspapers. Such an assumption seems illogical even stupid, yet academic opinion credits civilization with only a few thousand years; archaeologists of genius from cave-paintings and flints have conjured panoramas of prehistory which may be far from the truth. In ten thousand years time after wars and cataclysms, what picture would future scholars paint of our own century from broken pottery or buried bombs?

Wise men in the past left records for us, many in weather-eroded petroglyphs we cannot read, perhaps in evidence all around us, which we do not recognize. Julius Caesar accidentally burned thousands of scrolls in the famous library of Alexandria. The early Christians probably destroyed the 200,000 volumes contained in the great library built about 190 B.C. at Pergamum in Western Anatolia, giving its name to "pergamena" or "parchment"; in 213 B.C. the Emperor Che Hwang Te made bonfires of Chinese books as his Communist descendants do today; megalomaniac Roman emperors and fanatical Christians ruthlessly destroyed all pagan writing, as Bishop Landa in 17th century Mexico erased all the Aztec archives. Today much of what we accept as fact proves to be baseless illogical assumption;

astronomers who have never visited Mars swear there is no life there, historians who were not alive ten thousand years ago insist that men must have been uncivilized; such logic is surely false, our pundits accept it as truth and scorn any rebel who objects.

Original records from prehistory have long been lost through fire, flood or human ignorance, yet fragments preserved by classical authors suffice to show the vast antiquity of civilization. The Stanzas of Dzyan written in the sacerdotal language of Senzar imparted the teachings of the Atlanteans to the sacred volumes of China, India, Tibet, Egypt and Japan; their wonderful revelations inspired students of the occult down to our present day. Plato in "Timaeus" records that his famous ancestor, Solon, visiting Egypt in 590 B.C. was told by the priests of Sais about the destruction of Atlantis. Records in Indian temples describe the sinking of Mu in the Pacific. The Vedas, invocations to the gods written in Sanskrit about 1500 B.C., contain astronomical data valid many milennia earlier. The brilliant "Ramayana" significantly similar to the "Iliad" telling of the quest of Rama for his stolen wife, Sita, is dated 500 B.C. or even 3000 B.C.; internal evidence suggests times more remote. The most fascinating "Mahabharata" describes the Bharata war of 1400 B.C. It is said to quote records of 20,000 B.C., its startling accounts of war in the air with nuclear bombs suggest another race of men when Earth was young. In China the "Shu-King" refers to the Fourth Root Race, the Atlanteans; the Japanese "Nihongi" describes the gods descending to rule the cherry-blossom isles of Nippon. Manetho, priest of On, in "Aegyptica" explains that the first kings of Egypt were gods about thirty thousand years ago. Simplicius writes that the Egyptians had astonomical observations covering the last 630,000 years; Herodotus marvels that the Egyptians believed themselves the eldest of men; the priests of On said there were three hundred and forty-one generations of men from the first king to the last. Berossus believed ten kings (divine dynasties) reigned in Babylon 432,000 years before the Flood; the Sumerian king-list found in Assurbanipal's famous library at Nineveh states that eight kings ruled for 241,000 years then the Flood swept thereover. These ancient authorities surely quoted from records since lost; our own scholars refuse to accept them until these dates are confirmed by the space although they cheerfully agree chronologies concocted by historians today.

"Because the study of the past by means of

21

ancient manuscripts has almost reached its limits, archaeology has an important place in the reconstruction of history."

Henri-Paul Eydoux in his brilliant survey of great archaeological discoveries, "The Buried Past", expresses this somewhat bleak view of prehistorians that further knowledge of remote antiquity depends henceforth on the chance excavation of artifacts from the earth. When contemporary records do happen to exist, experts distrust them, especially if they shatter accepted ideas. Homer sang of golden Troy; scholars for centuries regarded the "Iliad" as merely a collection of minstrels' tales until a credulous German grocer, Heinrich Schliemann, believed every word of that epic and restored those topless towers of Ilium to history. Without his enthusiasm professors today would still be teaching that Helen's face that launched a thousand ships was some romantic dream. Young Arthur Evans, intrigued by the legend of Minos, excavated Knossos and revealed the wonderful Minoan civilization of Crete; the Han Annals reported ambassadors from Marcus Aurelius attending the Chinese Court, such claim was questioned, but in 1944 golden coins bearing the image of that great emperor were found at Oc-Eo on the Cochin China coast.

Most ancient documents turn out to be true despite our reluctance to accept them. So many excavations in the Old World and the New have proved the reliability of the old records, surely we should class the traditions of the past as true until research demonstrates them to be false. Men founded world religions on evidence questionable in courts of law, yet we hesitate to accept those references to Lemuria, Atlantis and the immense antiquity of Man made by classical authors, whose pronouncements on trivial topics are treasured as truth. If archaeologists in ten thousand years time cannot unearth our twentieth century, would that prove we never existed? Such speculation seems absurd, so does the attitude of our own scholars regarding prehistory; like the astronomers who dramatically accept life throughout the universe after denying it so long, the same scholars would jump with joy if just one scroll found in the sand proved the reality of those lost continents and the world empire of the space kings. Perhaps history like beauty lies in the eyes of the beholders?

A fascinating index to the age of Man on Earth is given by etymology. This traces the evolution of languages, particularly the derivation of the Aryan or Indo-European group from Sanskrit, which must have taken many milennia to develop into the national tongues spoken today. Churchward explains affinities between Mayan and Greek by descent from Mayax, the language of Mu, Empire of the Sun, once dominating the world. Sir John Morris-Jones noted remarkable similarities between Welsh and ancient Egyptian; echoes of the Lost Tribes of Israel are evoked by the astonishing links between Hebrew and a dialect of the Chiapenec Mayas, philologists teach that Sumerian, priestly tongue of old Babylon, had the same agglutinative structure as Chinese. Modern Finnish, Basque and Hungarian, totally dissimilar, seem completely unrelated to other tongues spoken today, jutting like prehistoric islands in a linguistic sea suggesting vast antiquity. If as "Genesis" affirms, before the Tower of Babel all men spoke one common language, then surely long ages must have elapsed to evolve the hundreds of different tongues dividing our troubled humanity today. The story of Babel parallels Hesiod's "Theogony" describing war in heaven, probably the conflict between the space kings and their rebel subjects on Earth confirmed in legends all over the world. The destruction of civilization, the isolation of survivors into separate communities and the difficulties of communication would eventually lead to the development of different languages. Obviously such evolution must have taken an immense time. If men did descend from a monkey-like ancestor, as we are told, then the wonderful English we speak today apparently evolved from the chatter of chimpanzees, the fantasy of countless years.

Suppose Earth was colonized by people from several planets? What if we inherited our different languages from spacemen?

Archaeologists judge a man by his dustbin and conjure ingenious pictures from the rubbish he leaves behind; from a few old flints and fossils our palaentologists imagine some hairy humanoid striking sparks to kindle a fire in his cave, when the bones might have belonged to the greatest genius of antiquity, a man who moved the world, or to a space king from Venus. Surely true civilization lies not in its outer shell but in its inner soul; the immortal dreams of Man shine in his thoughts.

Proof of Man's antiquity is found in semantics, the study of meaning; research into the world's oldest literature reveals a sublimity of thought transcending the materialist culture of our twentieth century. Despite our scientific wonders bedazzling the world, the human spirit seems to have degenerated from the lofty wisdom inspiring

22

the philosophers of the ancient East. In the library of Assurbanipal at Nineveh twelve tablets of cuneiform script were discovered containing three thousand lines, transcripts of texts before 2000 B.C., the Gilgamesh Epic, the wonderful story of the Flood anticipating by more than seven hundred years the version of Moses in "Genesis". The "Mahabharata" of 1400 B.C. includes material milennia older; among its colourful epics of bejewelled India glows the Bhagavad Gita, the sublime discourse on human ethics between Krishna and Arjuna, a wondrous quintessence of morality which inspired the noblest philosophers of India and Greece and our greatest minds today. How many thousand years of human experience were suffered to distil such eternal wisdom? The marvellous system of yoga, self-control of mind and body culminating in transcendental ecstasy, samadhi, was collated about 300 B.C. by the sage, Patanjali, from most ancient teachings. Now yoga exercises growing influence on our modern thought. In Egypt 1350 B.C. Akhnaton's great hymn to the sun in beautiful simple words invoked adoration of the One God of the living universe with a sublime insight unsurpassed by later religions. Five hundred years rolled by before Homer composed his "Iliad", a thousand years before Aristotle and Plato debated the philosophy of Greece, foundation of civilization today. Compared with ourselves in this twentieth century those great souls of the Bronze Age surely seem gods.

This literature from an age veiled in mystery makes us marvel at those wonderful minds, whose genius flames across milennia soaring in celestial splendor beyond the passions of centuries, the rise and fall of civilizations, the deeds of noble men and women flitting down the dusty corridors of time. Such inspiration from the gods transcends all the vicissitudes of mortal strife and speaks to our troubled century in words of sublime wisdom. What man today can pen immortal prose to captivate the scholars of A.D. 6000 as those great masters of prehistory enchant our own century? Has our strife-torn world any commanding soul to give the word of God to generations yet unborn, who must surely hunger for spiritual solace? The future will not look for inspiration from us tearing our Earth to suicide; men will gaze across the chasm of world wars and seek the limpid purity of the Upanishads. Scorning our modern materialism the idealists of tomorrow will study the secret wisdom of the Magi and politicians spurning the sorry frustrations of our century will ponder over

that golden age of long ago to rebuild our tortured world in truth and beauty. We today are mental pygmies compared with the giant intellects of antiquity; the Sanskrit texts tell of spaceships, laser beams, nuclear bombs, with sophisticated wonders surpassing our proud science; celestials lived and loved on Earth in flamboyant sparkling renaissance eclipsing our dull society today. How dare we patronize those peoples of the remote past and label their bones like higher apes? The cosmic wonder of those civilizations still gleams across long centuries of darkness to inspire our questing souls so desperately seeking truth today.

The evolution of mankind is a mystery still unsolved; social historians have compiled persuasive chronologies, pedantically documented, profusely illustrated, proving with impressive logic the ascent of Man from huts to bingo-halls, from spears to atom-bombs. Professors like politicians delight in proclaiming that we ourselves are nature's noblest work, the crowning glory of milennia of progress; all great men and women of the past, the bloody wars, the cruel sufferings, the flaming inspiration of genius, the patient resignation of poverty, all the tremendous influences of religion, art and science, have culminated in the supermen, who bestride our Earth today. Nature, the divine evolutionist, after milennia of breeding and countless failures, has at last produced her latest model of homo sapiens, the survival of the fittest, our proud selves.

But are we so superior? Were those demagogues of Athens and Sparta waging the Peloponnesian War lesser mortals than the politicians of America and Russia wrangling over the war in Vietnam? Britons today imagine Boadicea as a painted savage although her enemies according to Tacitus and Dio Cassius described her as a most cultured woman. They reported her patriotic speeches burning with idealism, inspiration, nobility of mind, which mark her as the greatest, if most neglected, queen to rule Britain. What queen or king will inspire Britons in two thousand years time?

Does humanity progress or degenerate? The saddest problem of our century may be Africa; after so many decades of beneficent British rule and enlightenment from missionaries, countries proud of their new independence seem to lapse back to tribalism and anarchy. Without the white man's enterprise the Bedovins would still roam the sands like Mahomet not dreaming of the oil beneath; the Hottentots hunt on the veldt ignorant of the priceless diamonds under their feet. Since Moses fought as general for the Ethiopians, the

23

black races have lived in a trance. Had the white man not opened their eyes they would slumber still. There is reason to believe that backward peoples are the degenerate descendants of mighty nations, the mumbo-jumbo of the witch-doctors remnants of a psycho-science inspiring Earth and the stars.

The evolutionists would have us believe that the Bronze Age poets of the Rig Veda, the builders of the Egyptian temples, the jewellers fashioning the diadem of queen Shubud of Ur, the astronomers of China, the architects of Tiahuanaco, developed from ape-men. If this be true, how many milennia rolled by before Man taught himself the wondrous conceptions of morality, the techniques of building, the craftmanship of precious metals, the glorious design of the heavens, the mathematics of town-planning, when during four thousand years of known history the Africans hardly moved from their mud huts? Even the few mutilated misconstrued relics of the remote past bequeathed to us demonstrate beyond doubt that Man can boast immense antiquity. During such vast ages many wonders must have happened, the old legends dream of that golden age in the dawn of time when the gods winged down to Earth to teach mankind, much of the wisdom of antiquity was surely inspired from other planets.

Archaeologists seek Man's origin in the mud, we search with shining eyes for our home in the stars.

Chapter Four
Lemuria

Geologists believe that two or three thousand million years ago after the surface of our Earth had cooled, all the land formed one single continent, Pangea, in a unique ocean, Panthalassia. Stress in the lithosphere split the Pangea into two branches separated by Tetis, a vast Mediterranean Sea: Laurasia comprising the present North America, Europe, Northern and Central Asia, also Gondwana embracing South America, Africa, the Antarctic, India and Australasia.

Throughout long ages Gondwana, then luxuriant with vast forests, ravaged by violent changes of climate and convulsed with subterranean pressure, lacerated by glaciers, eventually cracked in fault zones, possibly occasioned by oscillations in cosmic radiation and exposure to the solar wind of protons streaming from the sun which weakened Earth's protective magnetic field. Immense slabs of the crust slowly drifted apart on the viscous magma beneath; South America receded from Africa, in the south Lemuria existed for perhaps a hundred and forty million years until rent with explosion the continent subsided into the Pacific leaving the tops of its mountains as islands. The Antarctic long bloomed with giant vegetation to be pressurized into coal; the ancient Piri Reis map showing coastal contours, and sample cores of ice, suggest that the immense ice-cap may be only a few thousand years old, possibly caused by some comparatively recent cosmic cataclysm which suddenly altered the climate and violently displaced Earth's axis.

Eccentricities in the orbit of artificial satellites now show that our Earth has bulges and dents with areas of high and low gravities suggesting fountains of rising and descending currents of flaming rock related to convector cells between the plastic magma under Earth's crust and the central iron core. Studies of the ocean floors show huge ridges and depressions, seismographs record intermittent activity proving our planet is not rigid and quiescent as generally believed but subject to surprising change aggravated by internal pressures and the variable flux of cosmic rays, dangerously intensified by the million miles per hour breeze of protons from the sun. Changes in the sun itself induce through resonance sympathetic oscillations in the electrical tensions of Earth causing movement within our planet's sensitive structure. Perhaps the ancient art of astrology was more than the superstition we imagine? Geophysicists at Cambridge have discovered that at intervals in the past Earth's magnetic field has reversed, with north and south magnetic poles changing places. The last flip 700,000 years ago was accompanied by the extinction of some species of small marine creatures and possibly by the sudden deaths of many humans and animals leaving only a few men and women to start civilization again. It is speculated that a similar flip may have accounted for the dramatic and unexplained mass extinction of giant reptiles some 65,000,000 years ago. A most extraordinary discovery has come from magnetic surveys of the ocean floors. Over huge areas the sea-floor rocks appear to be magnetized in alternate stripes of normal and reversed polarity likened to a zebra by Sir Edward Bullard, Professor of Geophysics at Cambridge, in his 1967 Bakerian

25

lecture at the Royal Society. Tape-recordings indicate that in recent geologic times magnetic flips have become more frequent; this evidence supports Sir Edward's "dynamo" theory of Earth's magnetic field and suggests that the dynamo may be unstable. A symmetrical pattern of stripes runs on each side of the gigantic system of cracks running down the mid-Atlantic through the Pacific and elsewhere; these latest findings would appear to establish evidence for the lost continents of Atlantis and Lemuria.

The Nobel prizewinner, Paul Dirac, theorizer of the positron, suggested in 1931 the existence of a particle known as the magnetic monopole, north and south magnetic poles existing independent of each other as sub-atomic particles, contrary to the dogmas of conventional physics. Confrontations of these opposite particles would result in mutual annihilation. Monopoles possibly produced at the original creation of the universe thousands of millions of years ago and accelerated by tremendous magnetic fields in space may impinge on Earth among the powerful cosmic rays; a shower of north or south monopoles at the rate of only one per square centimeter per second could cancel Earth's magnetic field, even reverse it, causing sudden and cataclysmic mutations of human and animal species.

A conference held at Newcastle University in 1967 suggested that our Earth is slowly expanding like a balloon; on a globe half Earth's present size the continents would fit almost perfectly together; in its 4,500 million years history the planet may have doubled its volume. This expansion may be caused by changes in internal structure, although it is possibly due to a weakening of the gravitational forces holding Earth together, resulting also in expansion of Earth's orbit and a progressive minute lengthening of the year, originally theorized by Professor P. Dirac and apparently confirmed by ultra-sensitive quartz clocks. In the June 1967 issue of "Nature" Dr. F. Machado of Lisbon suggested that Earth's gravitational field may slowly pulsate, making Earth alternately swell and shrink through geological time; geological evidence apparently points to alternating periods of receding oceans with cooler climate (Earth expanding), and advancing oceans with warmer climate (Earth contracting). At present Earth appears to be in a state of maximum expansion and is due for a period of contraction.

Some sensitives allege that very soon our Earth will suffer immense convulsion, the poles will become displaced and our civilization destroyed.

What has been, shall be again! Spacemen surveilling our Earth for millions of years may have taught the peoples of continents now mouldering on the sea-bed.

Titanic cataclysms have happened before. Hans Hoerbiger's "World-Ice Theory", somewhat discredited by official Science but not disproved, postulates that in its long history Earth must have had at least three successive moons at various times caught by its gravity, each eventually spiralled closer to the surface whirling around the globe several times a day drawing immense tidal waves until each satellite in turn crashed on to our planet. During those intervening ages without any moon great civilizations arose only to suffer destruction from new cataclysms after Earth's gravitational attraction captured another wanderer in space. Familiar Luna, whose seductive smile allures our cosmonauts, appears destined one day to fall down on our remote descendants, unless like Zeus slaying the Cosmic Dragon, Earth's planetary engineers destroy the moon before it drops. For countless generations the oft-derided occultists have preserved memories of these great catastrophes in their ancient wisdom confirmed by legends from all the countries of antiquity, at long last science reluctantly confirms the apparent reality of those lost civilizations of the past.

Most ancient traditions agree that Earth's first civilization began in the far north long before the ice-cap froze the arctic wastes. Man's divine ancestors descended from the "Land of the Gods", "The Imperishable Isles", "Mount Meru", an abode of light and beauty beyond the north pole, vaguely extended to the northern sky, suggesting that Earth was colonized by spacemen.

The mysterious north fascinated the peoples of antiquity as a wondrous, sacred region inhabited by magicians conjuring the destinies of mankind, some deep race-memory from the remote enchanted past. The Chinese believed their emperor derived his power from the dragon god at the celestial north pole, symbolical of a space king; the imperial throne and the sun-temples therefore always looked southward while the worshippers bowed to the north; the Chinese revered the constellation of the Great Bear, like their northern neighbors in Siberia who also held the bear in superstitious awe as if the beast evoked some being in a spacesuit. The Papyrus of Ani, part of "The Book of the Dead" states that the shining ones and holy ones, who stand behind Osiris, are they behind the thigh of the constellation of the Great Bear in the northern sky; the entrance passage in

26

the Great Pyramid is said to have pointed to Alpha Draconis, the pole star at the time of its building, a fact of occult significance, possibly intended for visitants from the stars. As the prophet Ezekiel wept in exile by the waters of Babylon he raised his eyes to heaven and marvelled at a whirlwind coming out of the north in the likeness of a wheel bearing wondrous living creatures, who resembled men. The peoples of the Caucasus believed that the winged Simorgh or twelve-legged horse of Huschenk, legendary builder of Babylon and Ispahan, flew northward across the Arctic to a wonderful continent.

Zeus and Mercury winged down to the Greeks from Mount Olympus symbolizing the north; Odin with his retinue of Norse gods and fair Valkyries rode through the heavens to fabulous Asgard, the Britons associated the north with the people of the Bear, suggesting celestials of divine wisdom; the Red Indians and the Eskimos worshipped shining spirits in the northern skies, who descended in ships of light to bring them beneficence. Today a fascinating echo of these pagan traditions lingers with children all over the world, who pray to Father Christmas in his wonderland at the north pole to fly through the skies with reindeer and sledge answering their prayers with gifts. Such childish belief, more potent to the infant mind than any religion, may actually be a dim memory of those far-off days when benevolent beings did fly down from beyond the north pole. This universal fascination for the north astounds us until we suddenly realize that the UFO's sighted today usually appear from the north, presumably through the polar-vent in the Van Allen radiation-belts, shining startling and wondrous revelation on the old traditions.

The second cycle of mankind lived in Hyperborea beyond the north wind in the circumpolar continent now forming Greenland, Iceland, Northern Norway, Sweden and the Arctic coast of Siberia. The Greeks believed that beyond the fog-wrapped country of the Cimmerians bloomed a land of perpetual sunshine peopled by immortals in perfect happiness, whom Apollo loved to visit for six months every year. The Classical poets sang nostalgically of this blissful land of spring. Only a few great heroes ventured to Hyperboria, for this wondrous realm could not be approached by land or sea, only by winging the skies; there the air resounded with joyful singing and dancing, for sickness and sorrow were unknown; all those holy people basked in eternal youth. Such lyricism of Hyperborea like the

legends of the Golden Age echoes ancient memories, for in remote times the region was sub-tropical long before the ice age froze it to wilderness, suggesting some titanic conflict or cosmic catastrophe milennia ago. Geologists support the story told to Herodotus by the Egyptian priests that more than once our Earth has shifted its axis. Nostalgia for the north still lingered. Ages later Homer told of wandering Ulysses far from Troy cast ashore in the marvellous country of Phaeacia, said to be around modern Oslo, where he dallied with fair Nausicaa, daughter of king Alcinous, in a cyclopean palace gleaming with all the splendor of the Bronze Age. Today some scholars allege that this paradise beyond the north actually exists and with surprising conviction claim it to be Agharta, an advanced civilization in the interior of our own Earth, home of the gods and the spaceships.

"Divine kings descended and taught men sciences and arts for man could live no longer in the first land which had turned into a frozen corpse."

(Book VI. Commentaries on the "Book of Dzyan".)

After the cataclysm blasting Hyperborea and encasing the Siberian mammoths in huge blocks of ice, the third cycle of man was set on a mighty continent known to the occultists as Lemuria or Mu, which several million years ago covered most of the Pacific Ocean northward to the Himalayas, then bordering the great Asiatic inland sea, southward to Australia and the Antarctic, west to America, east to the Philippines, girdling almost all the Earth; throughout its long existence the land was racked by volcanic eruptions, finally splitting into islands submerging to the sea-bed. The first Lemurians, semi-human monsters of giant stature are believed to have existed during the age of reptiles and gigantic tree-ferns, a claim discounted by the palaeontologists, yet reports quoted by Charles Fort and others of blocks of wrought metal found inside coal-seams or embedded in solid rocks do suggest human activity during geologic ages long ago. Near Brayton on the Tennessee River were found footprints impressed in rock including those of a human heel-ball thirteen inches long. The Doheny expedition to the Grand Canyon in 1924 discovered a remarkable petroglyph depicting a dinosaur, tyrannosaurus rex, standing erect on his powerful tail with huge open jaws. Dinosaurs were swamp-dwellers; scientists assert that this canyon has not been under water for forty million years.

27

Iron seeping from the stones had formed a protective covering, impressive evidence of fantastic age. In the Havasupai Canyon nearby was found a rock carving of a giant human fighting a mammoth, also marked with immense age. In California and Arizona skeletons of giants twelve feet tall having six toes have been unearthed suggesting visitors from another planet or a most ancient race of Man millions of years ago.

The Stanzas of Dzyan state that the Sanat Kumara, the Logos of Venus, descended to Earth with his disciples in a huge spaceship to guide primitive Man to civilization.

"Then with the mighty roar of swift descent from incalculable heights, surrounded by blazing masses of fire which filled the sky with shooting tongues of flame, the vessel of the Lords of the Flame flashed through the aerial spaces. It halted over the White Island which lay in the Gobi Sea. Green it was and radiant with the fairest blossoms as Earth offered her faintest and best to welcome her King."

The Great White Island with its fantastic city, Shamballah, the most sacred psychic center on Earth a million years ago, flourished among luxuriant tropical forests in a wonderful civilization extending to Australia. Now the vast lake which once washed the barrier of the Himalayas, is parched to the Gobi Desert, called by the Chinese, "Han-hai", the "Dried-up sea". The blond Sons of God were magicians taught by masters from Venus, tunnels led from mystic Shamballah to sanctuaries all over Earth. In 1959 a Chinese-Russian expedition led by the noted Chinese palaentologist, Chou-Ming-Chen, discovered a calcined footprint in the present Gobi sands and traces of riverbeds and most ancient rock-walls. Legends say that below the drifting sands lie the treasures of a wondrous civilization.

Philip L. Selater, a zoologist, believed that the lemurs or dog-faced monkeys found in all lands bordering the Indian Ocean had fled from a vanished homeland, now the sunken ridge from Antarctica to India, which he called "Lemuria". References to this lost continent exist in the most ancient Asiatic literature, the Puranas written in a now-forgotten language ages later translated into Sanskrit recall gods and heroes of far prehistory. The magic names of "Sveta-Dwipa" (the Sacred Land) and "Hiranya-Dwipa" (the Golden Land) the Persian "Shah Namah" (Book of Kings) still echo that ancient civilization in the south remembered by the Sumerians as "Dilmun" and in the Tibetan "Bardoo Thodol" describing those legendary lands. On isolated Pacific islands people tell the same story of their ancestors dwelling in a great and wonderful continent which long ago sank below the sea.

The first peoples of Lemuria were said to be androgynes, bi-sexual beings, who in some obscure fashion reproduced themselves; after several million years they evolved into males and females following natural reproduction. Plato recalls this most ancient tradition in his "Symposium" 189; he quotes the great comic poet, Aristophanes, as explaining that Earth's first beings were androgynes, men-women, "terrible was their might and strength, they had proud thoughts and made an attack on the Gods". After reflection Zeus discovered a way to curb their insolence. He split them in two; thereafter each half male and female was fully occupied searching for its mate.

Throughout long ages the stature of the Lemurians decreased from twelve to about seven feet. They generally resembled our red Indians though their skin had a faint blueish tinge. The typical Lemurian had a disproportionately large head with a very high forehead in the center of which was a large protrusion like a walnut known as the "Third Eye", evidence of highly developed psychic powers cultivating telepathy and sixth-sense awareness of cosmic consciousness dormant in men today.

The teachers from Venus would reveal to initiates in Lemuria the cosmic truths imparted to them by great souls from Sirius, who were probably inspired by illumined beings from more advanced galaxies; their sublime wisdom was to form the secret doctrines of India and Tibet later preserved in the mysteries of Egypt, Babylon and Greece and the esoteric teachings behind most religions of East and West. The great spatial intelligences divined that God, the Absolute, though perfect needs deeper perfection so is dreaming into existence an endless series of universes, each conditioned by the character of its predecessor, that he might learn vicariously from the experience of all creatures, humans, spirits, on all planets in all the planes of His creation. Man needs God, most wondrous of all, God needs Man, otherwise He would not have created him. The most illumined intellects claimed that the Absolute is constantly creating and holding in His Mind countless universes in different stages of evolution throughout an endless sequence of cosmic days and nights.

The Absolute begins each cosmic day by

28

involving mind through myriads of forms to the grossest vibrations of matter, when involution is complete, evolution begins; through numberless ages matter evolves to finer and more complex forms gradually attenuating to pure spirit returning to God, Who then broods over the experience during a cosmic night when nothing exists. After a vast period of inactivity in this sector, the Absolute creates a new universe, then rests for ages and ages beyond the comprehension of Man.

The educated peoples of Lemuria realized from the discoveries of their own scientists, enhanced by the revelations of their Venusian masters, that Earth was not the center of creation nor the sole concern of God but only a grain of dust in a vast space-time universe with universes of different dimensions co-existing within our own, all paralleled by a possible universe of anti-matter. The Lemurians would have been puzzled, even outraged at the suggestion that the Creator Himself imagining the infinite series of universes would somehow enter His own cosmic dream, descend to our tiny Earth whose very atoms are manifestations of God, and participate in the politics of some primitive tribe to whom centuries later He would send His Son for crucifixion. Such a suggestion would not have made sense. Mindful of the spacemen in their midst, the Lemurians might have admitted the possibility of a Venusian interesting himself in enlightening some backward people; even so, it is doubtful whether they would have prophesied that any extraterrestrial would incarnate on Earth to be tortured to death to save mankind, when it seemed so obvious that Man could be saved only after countless incarnations by seeking illumination from the God inspiring his own soul.

Exoteric religion of the masses possibly worshipped their wonderful Venusian teachers as gods and somewhat vaguely credited them with creating the universe, thus the cult of the sky-father, "Who art in heaven", became inextricably confused with the worship of God, the Absolute, in Whom we live and move and have our being. This confusion between God, the creator, and "God", the spaceman, has muddled theology and religion ever since, only now in our space age do we realize the difference.

Belief in God, the divine mind, inspired the Lemurians to a purity of thought beyond the dogmas of formal religion, a sublime conviction that they were heirs to a great and glorious universe in fellowship with every insect and star. Life was joy, death a blessed rest in astral realms until the soul became born again for new experience. Life had dynamic meaning, the children of Mu treasured every moment of precious existence attuned to the wondrous spiritual vibrations emanating from their creator, symbolized by the sun. The Lemurians believed that body and mind were not the real self, but only instruments for the soul. They were taught to cultivate a delicate refinement of mind in an exquisitely developed body, to experience and enjoy the most subtle pleasures in attunement to the cosmic mind. Men were the color of the rising sun, perfectly formed like gods, women fair and graceful with psychic perceptions giving feminine insight transcending the logic of science, nudity went unashamed, though all delighted in exotic colors expressing vivacious personalities. Sex was spiritual at-one-ment with the divine androgyne, marriage a sacred bond entered only after months of severe trial; divorce was unknown. Since death meant ascension to nobler realms, the Lemurians decided their time of transition and could die when they wished, a birth was often greeted with sadness, since a soul had descended from a loftier plane for experience on Earth. Life for the Lemurians was far from perfect; the world in which they dwelled was ravaged by cataclysms, they suffered natural pain and disappointments; but people knew who they were and why they lived. Their souls rejoiced in glorious adventure on their cosmic pilgrimage reincarnating through life after life on Earth and other planets ascending to God.

Our own space-scientists find themselves tantalized by glimmerings of new knowledge revolutionizing many conventional beliefs. It is likely that the Lemurians visiting Venus and other planets acquired a strange and wondrous wisdom undreamed by us today. The solar system may have belonged to the galactic federation, whose great intelligences possibly communicated with even more advanced beings in other galaxies learning new facts about the universe unsuspected even by them; the Lemurians may thus have attained access to knowledge unattainable by Man for millions of years unless we too seek other planets. Lemurians may have differed from modern Man more than we differ from Martians; we today know only what we know, frankly we do not appear to know very much. It is doubtful whether on our Earth today there exist a half-dozen people capable of intellectual communication with spacemen. The alleged conversations with extraterrestrials, whether reported by Moses or

29

Adamski, show Earthlings completely eclipsed. Tales of adepts in antiquity operating on mental planes to work magic evoke the witch-doctors in primitive societies today, who occasionally startle our sophisticated selves by controlling the weather, suggesting that the ancients mastered a psychic science we may now be rediscovering. Physicists theorize worlds of matter in different frequencies of vibration co-spatial with our own, analogous to the etherean and astral realms long preached by occultists; students of cosmic rays now postulate a universe of anti-matter in which time appears reversed, a faustian universe with beings travelling, as it were, from our future. The astronomers intrigued by quasars find themselves confronted by a completely new type of matter. Today no single mind can fully comprehend our latest conception of the universe; all this esoteric knowledge and much more still undiscovered may have been known to the Lemurians in their age-long history.

"They (the Lemurians) built huge cities. Of rare earths and metals they built. Out of the fires (lava) vomited. Out of the white stone of the mountains (marble) and the black stone (of the subterranean fires) they cut their own images in their size and likeness and worshipped them."

(Stanzas of Dzyan.)

Houses, mainly of redwood, were tall and rectangular built with wide projecting roofs to cast maximum shade, since the brilliance and heat of the sun intensified by the warmth from the volcanic soil posed considerable problems to the Lemurians, already troubled by the earthquakes eroding their empire. Gigantic palaces and temples of unusually hard stone withstood the ravages of time, remains of cyclopean buildings still sprawl in forlorn desolation in the wilds of the Americas, India and Asia, colonies of Lemuria not convulsed by the cataclysm. Gold and silver were plentiful and used for ornamentation, not for coinage; diamonds by their profusion being no more precious than glass. The most valuable adornments were rare brilliantly colored feathers. Buildings in the towns were not congested; their sunlit architecture gleamed amid luxuriant tropical vegetation; transportation was mainly by water. The Lemurians were great mariners, who founded settlements all over Earth, characterized by cyclopean stonework; they gradually built a world-wide empire of the sun, whose peoples spoke a common language, Mayax, an agglutinative tongue, root of Sumerian and Chinese.

The scientists of Mu inspired by their teachers from Venus studied vibratory forces, developing radionics based on solar and cosmic energies bringing light and heat to homes and minor industries; their profound insight of jewels familiarized them with the astonishing properties of semi-conductors and laser-beams, the Lemurians were also noted for their cold light burning in lamps for centuries.

Ships and aircraft were motivated by a form of nuclear power; Lemurian scientists probably learned from extraterrestrials the secret of utilizing cosmic energy for spaceships, which they apparently bequeathed to ancient India.

Colonel James Churchward, who devoted his life to studying temple records and relics of ancient civilizations in the East, discussing airships of the Hindus 15,000 to 20,000 years ago, refered to

". . . .a drawing and instructions for the construction of the airship and her machinery, power, engine, etc. The power is taken from the atmosphere in a very simple inexpensive manner. The engine is somewhat like our present-day turbine in that it works from one chamber into another until finally exhausted. When the engine is once started it never stops until turned off. It will continue on if allowed to do so until the bearings are worn out. These ships could keep circling around Earth without ever once coming down until the machinery wore out. The power is unlimited, or rather limited only by what metals will stand. I find various flights spoken of which according to our maps would run from 1000 to 3000 miles."

Traditions suggest that in ages past space travel existed between Earth and Venus, although terrestrial civilization was far eclipsed by the wonders of that lovely planet; later world-wide legends agree that Earthlings rebelled against their space overlords and waged aerial warfare with devastating weapons. Ancient stones found in Yucatan and India bear glyphs inscribed with crosses, circles and swastikas recognized by initiates as universal symbols for cosmic forces; all infer that the Lemurian scientists were in some fields more advanced than our own and mastered fundamental radiations which our physicists are just discovering. With such powers at their disposal it seems likely that the Lemurians enjoyed radionic inventions beyond our cognizance. Space-flight, aeronautics and nuclear-warfare require many ancillary logistic, medical and electronic techniques, only now as we marvel at the glorious

30

promise of our own space-technology can we imagine the fabulous wonders of Mu after thousands, perhaps millions of years of civilization inspired by golden Venus.

Intuition into cosmic laws gave the Lemurians sensitive awareness of nature; they cultivated Earth like a botanical garden and established a sympathy with animals, which they regarded as group-souls awaiting incarnation as humans.

Dr. George King, who claims inspiration from cosmic masters, reveals that Lemuria was split into two different camps, the white magicians and the evil black magicians; in ominous emulation of the wicked scientists of Maldek between Mars and Jupiter who hundreds of thousands of years earlier exploded their planet into the asteroids. The black magicians probed the titanic powers of the atom and eventually destroyed Lemuria. Before the destruction the chosen were evacuated by spaceships from Mars and Venus like their descendants milennia later from Atlantis, and possibly like initiates near the end of our present century who may be rescued by spacemen when our own civilization faces nuclear extinction.

Lemuria's destruction was probably a gradual process lasting ages. The continent was slowly consumed by subterranean fires and subsidence with a final cataclysm leaving only the mountain-peaks to garland the South Seas with islands. Foreseeing impending doom initiates in the secret wisdom migrated to Atlantis, America, India and China, where they preserved the cosmic teachings of their Venusian masters in mystical brotherhoods publishing exoteric doctrines comprehensible to the masses as popular religion.

Stone tablets and cliff carvings in North and South America still show the wide-spread influence of Lemuria. The mineralogist, William Niven, found among shattered houses and temples covered by ash, hundreds of petrified glyphs referring to "Mu, the Motherland, The Lands of the West". Intriguing tablets depict the winged circle, which thousands of years later in Egypt and Babylon became associated with the sky gods, surely spacemen. Colonel James Churchward studied American written records such as the Troano manuscript, an ancient Maya book written in Yucatan between 1500 and 3000 years old, also the Codex Cortesianus probably from the same

temple; he also referred to a record from an old Buddhist temple of Lhasa and to records found by Le Plongeon in Yucatan; all seemed to confirm statements in the Sanskrit classics mentioning that glorious empire of the sun destroyed in the Pacific so long ago.

The Popul Vuh, the sacred book of the Quiche Mayas, speaks of an infinitely ancient civilization which knew about the nebulae and the whole solar system stating that the first race of men were capable of all knowledge, they examined the four corners of the horizon, the four cardinal points of the firmament and the round surface of Earth.

In still mysterious California around Mt. Shasta persist strange sects, who claim to be actual descendants of survivors from the sunken continent; their communities are shrouded in secrecy; they allege visitations by silver ships from space and hint at communication through long tunnels with Lemurians living a wondrous civilization deep inside our own Earth. Some of the space-inspired Lemurian wisdom reached Europe via Atlantis; the main influence probably came through India, Egypt and Babylon. The Naacals, holy brothers, are believed to have brought the sacred writings of the motherland to India about 70,000 B.C. Later teachers founded colonies in upper Egypt and Sumer, whence their wisdom inspired the traditions of Babylon, greatly influencing Judaism and the early books of the Bible, the religious heritage of the West.

The mythologies and chronicles of India, Tibet, China, Japan, Egypt, Babylon and the Pacific islands all tell of spacemen in the ancient East, supermen from the skies, divine dynasties ruling our Earth in a golden age. War in the heavens was waged with fantastic weapons, cataclysm, barbarism, then the rebuilding of civilization under the guidance of spacemen worshipped as gods.

Recent discoveries in European prehistory are flooding new light on the Bronze Age, though the few written records cannot match the fascinating literature of old Asia; study of the classics suggests comparable evidence of spacemen in the ancient West, when our world was blessed by celestials from the stars.

Magic twilight veils our old West with mystery, its secret enshrined in lost Atlantis.

Chapter Five
Atlantis

The soul of the ancient West broods in mists of enchantment enshrouding dim antiquity; beyond the clamor of modern Europe steals the plaintive cadence of some magic past, faint echoes of faery lands forlorn, the surge of perilous seas, then stillness after the storm. Twilight empires loom in grandeur; the glint of golden kings, visions of alluring queens, temples touching a sunlit sky; suddenly the ocean foams in flame, all dissolve in troubled dreams to fade in forgotten mystery tantalizing our minds beyond recall. For moments of muted wonder we gaze across the glare of our materialist world to realms of haunting witchery, an elusive splendor illuming secret longings. As we thrill at recognition, illusion slowly drifts away to leave us desolate.

In the ancient East those lands of the sunrise fill our hearts with surging joy at the miracle of birth, we watch again the golden dawn warm sleeping Earth to life and feel that glorious radiance milennia ago awaking mankind from age-long slumber to build those glittering civilizations of the Orient flowering in exotic beauty and spiritual wisdom beloved of the gods. To all the peoples of antiquity the West was veiled in deepest mystery, realms of immemorial magic transmuting some ancient memory in the destiny of men. Beyond the Egyptian sunset brooded Amenti, kingdom of the dead; those secret shores beckoned the souls from Babylon, there the Greeks beheld the Isles of the Blessed; today the old West still casts its poignant spell, chastening our spirits with cataclysms unseen. Across the chasm of unremembered milennia we sense some nameless tragedy, the shadow of Atlantis.

For countless generations the word "Atlantis" has evoked magic in the hearts of men; priests have mourned its spiritual wisdom degenerating to wickedness, philosophers have moralized on its divine kings, poets have extolled its fabled perfection; all the virtues, all the vices, all the splendors of a brilliant civilization when Earth was young banished from memory like a dream. Such a golden age, the secret yearning of Man's inner soul, seems more than illusion, intense longing makes the mirage real. We sigh at the splendor of Egypt lost in the sand, the greatness of Babylon buried in mud, the glory of Greece shattered to ruins; all preach in muted eloquence the fleeting triumphs of men. Atlantis—its towers, temples palaces, navies, armies, its myriads of men and women thronging those marble courts through many milennia, all have vanished like ghosts, leaving not a stone behind. Fantastic wonder now empty nothing, as though those marvels had never been, yet Atlantis enchants imagination to glow in our souls more magic than ever. In the mirror of some future age so we see our own civilization vanish into oblivion? Are we haunted by some heavy guilt calling down destruction? What nameless sin sank proud Atlantis? Can our century learn before it is too late?

Thousands of books have been written proving the reality of Atlantis, thousands more denying its existence. Can the minds of men down dusty ages be held captive by the same vain dream? Spiritual awareness is the most solid of facts. Where was this city of wonder?

The remarkable fact that the east coast of South America so neatly fits into the West coast of Africa inspired Alfred Wegener in Germany about 1910 to propound his famous theory of continental drift, reviving the idea suggested by Sir Francis Bacon as long ago as 1620. Plausible though it appeared, Wegener's theory met opposition from certain geologists and did not find general acceptance until 1964 when Sir Edward Bullard at Cambridge claimed that these two countries fit precisely at their submerged continental shelf according to the most detailed comparison by computer. Truth now lies with computers; scientists seem completely enslaved by their mechanical minds. Socrates would be surprised! Human intellect after ages of glory surrenders to machines.

Wegener's theory apparently denies the existence of Atlantis, however some geologists doubt the findings of Sir Edward Bullard's obliging computer and speculate that America and Africa were originally joined by a backbone of mountains; seismic convulsions caused splits at each side leaving the sundered mighty islands to recede slowly from each other across the magma beneath. The stranded mountain-range, now the submerged Atlantic Ridge, was left to become Atlantis.

The transience of human destiny on tiny Earth lost in the trackless immensity of space finds fleeting significance in that fabled continent, where for a million years men and women triumphed and suffered, scaling the heights and plumbing the depths of mortal experience with all the passions and pains of history forever unknown. This exotic, brilliant civilization communed with the stars, conjuring the gods themselves to tread our Earth; now of wonderful, idyllic, depraved Atlantis only the music of her magic name echoes down dark ages to remind us today that soon we too shall fade from memory.

Occult traditions assert that at the zenith of its magnificence a million years ago, the continent of Atlantis extended from Iceland down to South America; maps actually exist showing how catastrophes in 800,000 B.C. and 200,000 B.C. progressively reduced the land to two islands, Ruta and Daitya. A convulsion around 80,000 B.C. left only part of Ruta, known as Poseidonis, said to have been finally submerged in 9564 B.C., when the British Isles were still joined to Europe and the Sahara formed part of the Atlantic Ocean. Early inhabitants, the Rmoahals, black-skinned giants, roamed the dense forests contending with gigantic animals; after climatic changes and glaciation Tlavatlis, a shorter, reddish-brown race, settled

mainly among the mountains. The Toltecs, the classical Atlanteans, originated in the area of modern Mexico; they were magnificent copper-colored people averaging eight feet tall, their stature gradually diminishing through the ages; their noble features resembled the ancient Greeks, their psychic faculties were keenly developed and many adepts attained lofty spiritual and mental powers bringing Atlantis a world-wide golden age shortly after the earlier civilization of Lemuria in the Pacific, torn with volcanic eruptions, sank below the sea.

Time on the cosmic scale is only relative, a somewhat meaningless conception since there are hardly any co-ordinates within our own experience to which time in terms of the universe may be related. Civilizations may have risen and fallen on worlds which died long before Earth was born; some of those myriad stars in the sky may bask in cultures beyond our comprehension. Atlantis, so impossibly remote to our minds, may be mourned by the Venusians as dying only yesterday. Atlantis at its zenith glorying in wonders of which we can only dream, surely attracted visitors from space, perhaps those same celestials who wenched and warred in the glittering India of the "Ramayana"; esoteric Hindu traditions assert that Rama's epic defeat of Ravan, Lord of Lanka in Ceylon, represents the victory of the "Sons of God" over the Atlanteans. The Stanzas of Dzyan, written in the ancient sacerdotal language of Senzar, describe how the Lords of the Flame descended to inspire the long civilization of Lemuria, it was certain that initiates from that drowned empire of the sun emigrating to new Atlantis would pray assistance from those wondermen in the stars. All old occult records mention the kings of light, sovereigns of the divine dynasties, who obeyed the cosmic hierarchy, possibly the solar federation, or even a galactic empire and promoted the development of the fourth root race of Atlanteans, successors to the lost Lemurians.

Our minds today conditioned to the stark concepts of science become bewildered and intolerant of ancient, esoteric terms; we fail to realize that when our own cosmonauts land and meddle in the affairs of some primitive planet, the unsophisticated natives marvelling at those shining spaceships may worship the Americans or the Russians as "Kings of Light" or "Lords of the Flame" just as the deluded Incas of Peru venerated Pizarro and his plundering conquistadores like gods.

The basic impediment to acceptance of

33

spacemen is probably our imperfect comprehension of the past; conditioned to the present we cannot attune our mind to the alien thought-patterns of our ancestors, whose environment, experience and traditions differed vastly from our own. People tend vaguely to assume that somewhere exists a supreme authority who decides what is and what is not in papal pronouncements final and infallible, that this divine wisdom is solemnly preserved by custodians of truth, the religious and scientific establishments. The stormy history of mankind, the struggles against intolerance, the sufferings of martyrs in religion and science, the diversity of beliefs battling for domination of men's minds today, prove plainly that in Earthly affairs truth apparently degenerates to merely a matter of opinion forced by custom or even oppression. With lofty omniscience official opinion rejects spacemen and ridicules Atlantis enjoining the public to deny their existence. Rebels now realize sadly that no mortal Man has monopoly of truth. Aristotle, the universal genius of the classical world, mesmerized the minds of men, impeding progress for two thousand years; today we guess that this great philosopher knew nothing of the ancient civilizations of the East and was obviously ignorant of our own tremendous technology transforming the Earth; today his profound intellect could hardly pass a university entrance-examination, his knowledge would be two thousand years out of date. Our learned professors would probably fail Aristotle on ancient Greece, which they would claim to know better than he did; after all Shakespeare would not need a university education to understand his own plays. Surely in two thousand years time our most brilliant scholars might be completely lost amid the new knowledge current then, space-travel will have brought intercourse with our planetary neighbors, submarine archaeology, perhaps the discovery of more buried scrolls, could resurrect Atlantis in glories eclipsing Babylon.

Five centuries ago the establishment swore our Earth was flat although thousands of years earlier Pythagoras taught it was round; only a decade since astronomers preached of a sterile universe, now somewhat belatedly they proclaim it thrills with life. Does it really matter what we think? Our thoughts are only transient fancies flitting across the cosmic truth. History we cannot change but understanding of Man's past can shape his future. Only by accepting Atlantis may we learn from its fateful lesson.

Believers in Atlantis snubbed by science may find encouragement in the revolution of thought regarding our own moon. The ancient books of Dzyan mention the lords of the moon descending to Earth; people in antiquity worshipped celestials on the moon; Dante sighed at those inconstant souls languishing in their lunar paradise; that strange mystic, Gurdjieff, taught that the moon is still an unborn planet gradually growing warmer until it becomes like Earth with a satellite of its own. Astronomers ridiculed these bizarre beliefs, insisting that our moon is a barren inhospitable world devoid of air, where nothing happens. Alas for such illusions! On November 3rd, 1958 Nicolai Kozyrev at the Crimea Observatory photographed reddish volcanic explosion in the Alfonse crater, soon confirmed by observers in Britain. American Ranger pictures revealed the moon's surface to be rock, not thick dust as generally thought; on December 26th, 1966 the Russian Luna 3 equipped with a mechanical hand scooped up fragments from the moon and telemetered analysis to Earth. Academician Alexander Oparin states that a form of primitive life may be lurking beneath the moon's surface protected from extremes of temperatures, underground water might also have survived the scorching days and freezing nights. Mikhail Vessine and Alexandre Chtcherbakov with fascinating reasoning almost persuade us that our moon is an artificial satellite. No Selenites greeted Neil Armstrong when he planted the Stars and Stripes on their moon on July 21st, 1969. Perhaps like our scientists they do not believe in spacemen and dismiss any reports of Apollo craft as mythical UFOs?

Immense research by oceanographers examines the hitherto neglected sea-bed; already surprising discoveries reveal a fascinating submarine world of mountains, valleys, chasms, volcanoes, lands which once smiled at the sunlit sky, where people lived and loved long ago. Soon science itself with its latest sonar and radar devices may detect the sunken temples of Atlantis, then suddenly all those old tales will ring true.

Whether science ever does accept Atlantis seems somewhat irrelevant. If by chance a submarine mining ore from the ocean-floor grabs the shell-encrusted gates of Poseidon, Atlantis is proved; should it pick some stone instead, is Atlantis denied? Discovery of authentic ruins may convince sceptics that Atlantis, like Troy, was not just the dream of Plato; but who cares what science says? Can opinion in the present affect the past? Does it worry us to wonder whether people in ten

34

thousand years time believe in a mythical London at the bottom of the British Sea?

The subaqua explorer, Dimitri Ribikoff and the archaeologist J. Manson Valentine, have discovered a submerged city off the island of Bimini, the Bahamas. At a depth of six meters a complex of walls several hundred meters long was photographed. This report in the "Gazetta del Popolo", October 20th, 1970 stated that according to a group of experts from Miami University directed by Doctor Cesare E. Milani, it was a question of fortifications dating back to ten thousand years ago. In some circles it is claimed that the spectacular discovery made off Bimimi could contribute to reopen the quest for the existence of Atlantis, the mythical continent mentioned by Plato.

In March 1882 Captain David Amory Robson, master of the "Jesmond" sailing from Messina, Sicily, to New Orleans, was astonished to observe two hundred miles south-west of Madeira that the sea appeared dark and muddy; the surface was littered with dead and dying fish including species unknown. To his surprise he saw an uncharted island, rocky and barren, steaming in the sun as though newly emerged from the sea. Captain Robson landed with some of his crew and amid the basalt cliffs covered with marine growth they found flint arrowheads and small knives; returning the next day the seamen discovered a rough chamber with walls of squared, unmortared stone, probably an ancient tomb containing spearheads, axeheads and a sword, figures of birds and animals made of stone or pottery, two large urns containing fragments of bone and a recognizable part of a human skull. Near the tomb was a statue six feet high from a solid block of stone weighing a ton, which was ferried out to the "Jesmond". Inscriptions on the pottery were said to resemble Egyptian or Hebrew. The statue was brought to England, possibly with the intention of its donation to the British Museum who never received it. All trace is lost: perhaps the statue now graces some Tyneside garden. Lawrence D. Hills who recounts this tale in "Lands of the Morning" refutes all suggestions of hoax. Unfortunately the story could not be checked, since like so many submarine islands Robson's island soon sank again below the sea.

A museum in Bagdad displayed some bric-a-brac more than a thousand years old classified by archaeologists as a "ritual object" until a German engineer realized it was actually a Voltaic cell. If we dredged some jug from Atlantis, people would swear it was bought at Woolworth's. Students of the occult who talked of entities dwelling on cold, dark stars were ridiculed as crazy; now our radio-astronomers discovering unseen constellations emitting radio-waves instead of light are knighted and loaded with honors. These same scientists still consider occultists as crazy just as they scoff at water-diviners, whose twigs find water which the geologists miss. Telepathy long practised by adepts but rejected as impossible by scientists is now being seriously studied by the Americans and Russians as a means of communication by thought-waves with their spaceships and submarines; this occult art, like hypnosis, is becoming respectable. Perhaps other psychic practices may soon find acceptance.

If science has nothing to say on Atlantis, then surely scientists should listen with respect to the revelations of occultism, this most ancient of arts, which offers a plausible, brilliant picture of that wonderful civilization in the West. Down the ages solitary students living in obscurity have jealously preserved their ancient lore with secrecy, fearing the megalomania of kings, the intolerance of the Church, the ignorance of the rabble, whose hostility condemned all culture before the year 0 A.D. The secret wisdom was guarded down the centuries by the sages of India, Babylon and Egypt; their priests imparted the sacred knowledge to initiates like Solon, Pythagoras and Plato, enshrining it in mysteries inspiring the noblest souls of history; the dogma and ritual proffered as religion were exoteric shows to please the mob, the esoteric inner meaning of the mummery was reserved for seekers for truth. Those who speak do not know, those who know do not speak!

Today our Earth spirals to a new octave of evolution; astrologers say that humanity is passing from this materialist age of Pisces to the aery realms of Aquarius to enter a new great cosmic year lasting twenty-five thousand years, an event of occult significance. Such speculation hardly matters in these days of spaceflight; evolution is speeded, science transformed. Now Man leaves his ancient home and soars to the stars, the old wisdom is needed more than ever to fertilize the new.

Fascinating panoramas of Atlantis are evoked by astral clairvoyance, alleged spirit communications, reincarnation or dreams, sources scorned by the scientists ignorant of the fount of their own inspirations. Advanced scientific and philosophic thinking expands Einstein's theory of relativity to esoteric speculations fringing the occult. The

35

Russian mathematician and mystic, P.D. Oouspensky, postulates a seven-dimensional universe, where past, present and future exist in eternal now. The transient present is illumined by our consciousness traversing the universal-continuum imagined as a cosmic egg; sometimes stimulated by drugs or mental discipline a person's consciousness transcends conventional limitations and in astral body journeys into the future or the past perceiving events as they actually happen. This recondite theory baffles common understanding and conflicts with usual conceptions of our space-time universe, yet it could explain authenticated cases of precognition or retrocognition confounding our materialistic science. Occultists know that nothing ever perishes, they believe that every scene, act, thought and thing that ever existed or occurred are preserved unaltered on a higher plane of matter. These Akashic Records are mirrored on the astral plane and are accessible to advanced intelligences who have developed time-clairvoyance and can view these future or past events like we watch television. Scientists scoff at such bizarre claims though they cheerfully admit that many of the stars in the sky may no longer exist; perhaps they exploded long ago before their light travelled to us. What could be more occult than astronomy studying stars which may not be there?

Communications from alleged spirits confound scientists and laymen alike; many are soon exposed as frauds yet the literature of occultism does offer extraordinary revelations of the past, later confirmed by authentic historical evidence suggesting that in some mysterious way beyond all understanding reliable factual information of the past may be imparted to us.

In 1883-4 near mystic Mt. Shasta in California, a boy of eighteen, F.S. Oliver, sensed the inspiration of an entity called Phylos, the Thibetan, who educated him by mental talks and then dictated his fascinating auto-biography "A Dweller on Two Planets" narrating his adventures in Atlantis and on Venus. Sometimes this young amanuensis would cover eighty letter-size sheets a night penned by lamplight, often in darkness; oddly enough much of the work was written backward, the sentences rightly last coming first, so fast and mixed that Oliver made little sense of it. Phylos had this erratic script revised twice, later it was edited by a literary expert, then published by the Borden Publishing Company, Los Angeles. In archaic language Phylos describes with wonderful detail the glory of Atlantis, its laws, religion and way of life, the golden age and the decadence which doomed that great continent. Exquisite scenes are set on Venus depicting the lofty idealism of advanced souls basking in the omnipresence of God, the Father, reminiscent of Adamski's discourse with the cosmic master in the spaceship. Our modern minds are fascinated by wondrous inventions; space travel with anti-gravity, television, transmutation of metals, conveyance of heat and power without wires, tidal energy, electric-odic powered cars, airships, brain-washing by magnetism, sidereal death-rays and an electron-telescope, only now conceived by our own astronomers. Such technology surpassing our own all vividly described by a country-youth in the wilds of America long before he saw a motor-car! We think of those Sanskrit classics painting a similar picture and see Atlantis.

Reincarnation slowly dawning again in the consciousness of the West, where once it was taught by the Druids to the Colts, has long been the fundamental belief of all the peoples in the East. The Lemurians inherited from their Venusian teachers this wonderful doctrine of metempsychosis, ascension through life after life until the soul attains perfection, union with God. Initiates from the empire of the sun imparted the cosmic wisdom to their disciples in India, China and Atlantis. Later Atlantean missionaries instructed adepts in America and Egypt, their priests inspired the Eleusinian mysteries of Greece, whose brothers included many of the Greek and Roman philosophers. The Gnostics believed that Christ actually preached reincarnation; His true teachings were distorted by theological disputes until their inner meaning was lost. Despite savage persecution, most of the greatest minds of the Middle Ages found reincarnation the only answer to the cosmic questions of life and death; today amid an apparent materialism many world-figures secretly admit to conviction that Earthly existence is only one incident in countless lives gaining purity of soul on our pilgrimage to perfection.

Our conscious mind is only a fraction of the immense unconscious mind recording all that happens in our lives. A few rare sensitives can recall most ancient memories, others in hypnosis, dreams or psychic shock live again their pains and passions talking in tongues of forgotten lands when the world was young. Rudolf Steiner, disciple of Goethe and founder of Anthroposophie, claimed occult inspiration; he wrote a detailed history of Atlantis describing the conflict between the Spiritual beings and Luciferians, the white and

36

black magicians, whose perversion of occult forces brought cataclysm to Atlantis. Foreseeing their doom, initiates escaped to inspire the civilizations of Egypt and Chaldea.

A remarkable psychic, Edgar Cayce, born on a Kentucky farm in 1878, startled scientists, physicians and clergymen by his amazing "readings" in self-imposed trance concerning people and places he had never seen in physical body. For more than forty years he gave wondrous help and comfort, performing inexplicable cures. It is strangely significant that Edgar Cayce who had never read the "Critias" of Plato nor the revelations of Phylos should when unconscious site Atlantis in the middle of the Atlantic and describe its electrical technology in almost identical terms as the "Thibetan's" communications fifty years earlier. Atlanteans travelled through the air and under the seas, photographed objects at a distance, utilized X-rays, recorded sounds and sights on video-tape, obtained laser-like powers from crystals, devised a terrible weapon from cosmic rays and apparently discovered anti-gravity propulsion. The "Firestone" from which initiates produced power from fusion or fission with radio-active forces was detailed by the "sleeping prophet" in 1933 twelve years before the explosion of the first atomic-bomb. Misuse of the dark forces of nature by arrogant priests and increasing volcanic eruptions accelerated the shattering of the continent into islands which throughout many millennia submerged until about 10,000 B.C. Poseidonis, convulsed by earthquakes, sank in flames down to the sunless deep. Cayce vividly described how initiates, foreseeing the catastrophe, migrated to Egypt in the east and America in the west to continue the Atlantean civilization there; he prophesied that frequent earthquakes were already heralding the re-emergence of Atlantis during the cataclysms destined to convulse our doomed twentieth century.

Interest in Atlantis was revived a hundred years ago by Helena Petrovna Blavatsky, born in 1831 at Ekaterrinoslav, Russia, of a noble family; after an early unhappy marriage she travelled extensively all over the East seeking mystics in India and Tibet who imparted the ancient wisdom of antiquity lost to our Western world. With Colonel H. Olcott, Madame Blavatsky founded in 1875 the Theosophical Society. Denounced as a charlatan by the Church, scorned by scientists, spurned by her own followers, today she is chiefly remembered for her books "Isis Unveiled" and "The Secret Doctrine", works of incredible erudition, written

so she claimed under telepathic dictation from her Eastern masters quoting most ancient occult wisdom to prepare humanity for the new age. It is easy to ridicule Madame Blavatsky and her followers, to stress their occasional frauds and exaggerate their quarrels. Today when the teachings of the Church appear more doubtful and the dogmatism of science more suspect we find the wisdom-religion of the occultists strangely appealing and surprisingly relevant, linking our tormented world today with lost Atlantis.

The Atlanteans believed the universe to be the manifestation of a great thought, a conclusion agreed by the ancient Hindus and our own modern scientists; the planets of the solar system owed allegiance to the lords of the sun, symbolized by the sun itself in a cosmic wisdom-religion said to be followed by spacemen today. Lords of the Flame from Venus who millennia earlier had brought civilization to Lemuria again descended to aid Atlantis, ruling as a dynasty of divine kings remembered in legends all over the world; belief in the divinity of kings has persisted in human consciousness almost down to our own irreverent days. The Venusians radiated a golden aura visible to the highly developed psychic perceptions of the Atlanteans, perpetuated later in the haloes of saints and the crowns of kings. As inferred in Genesis the spacemen consorted with the "daughters of men" and begat giants; the early Atlanteans were of great stature and possibly identical to the Rakshasas chronicled in the "Ramayana". It is said that before the emergence of Mu there existed a great continent in the North Pacific called Adoma, A-dom is a Lemurian word meaning "race of men from the red earth". The name "Adam" is generally believed to have come from the Hebrew "Adom" meaning "red" suggesting that "Adam" was a generic term for the red-skinned Atlanteans who in their golden age lived in the Garden of Eden; later they tasted from the tree of knowledge the forbidden fruit, that is to say, they developed sorcery, said to be the occult reason why Atlantis was destroyed, forcing "Adam" or the Atlanteans into harsh and bitter exile. An ancient tradition preserved by Cosmos Indica-Pleustes recorded that Noah formerly inhabited the island of Atlantis; if so, Noah was an Atlantean, a titan who fought the gods or Venusians in the heavenly war described in the Greek classics, although the Bible suggest that Noah was a follower of God, Who warned him of the coming flood, as "God", probably a spaceman, warned Lot of the destruction of Sodom and Gomorrah.

37

Atlantis was ruled by its priest-king in a theocracy dominating every aspect of life, a social system continued in ancient Egypt and Peru, persisting until the last decade in Tibet. The cosmic religion taught reincarnation, death was welcomed as a blessed rest before rebirth, resurrection in astral realms inspired men long before Christianity. The priests practised psychism like our modern spiritualists, certain sensitives foretold the future, others studied people's auras to diagnose and cure disease, radionic and color-healings resembled spiritual and psychiatric techniques adopted today. The Atlanteans apparently did not burn coal, utilize the power of steam or invent the internal-combustion-engine motivating our own technology; their society and civilization were therefore quite different from our own; Atlantean science was based on vibratory forces we are now discovering. Sound and resonance could be used to kill or cure, as we are finding ourselves; in ways unknown to us vibrations could be utilized to counter gravity as a force of levitation to build mighty temples or propel street-cars, aircraft or spaceships. Static electricity, generally neglected in our present age, was somehow harnessed for transport, industrial or military use by the Atlanteans and may explain the worship of lightning by the Greeks, Etruscans, Druids and Tibetans, who knew of its ancient application; only the greatest adepts like Numa Pompilius could control the electric forces to discomfort their enemies, although the Ark of the Israelites was probably an electric battery whose power struck profaners dead. Nuclear physics proves that all things emit radiations, the priests of Atlantis studied the occult powers of plants and minerals in conjunction with emanations from the stars, the reason perhaps why medicine in antiquity became mingled with astrology.

Precious stones were credited with powers for good or evil, evoking talismans and fatal gems bringing good luck or misfortune to influence notorious personages in history. Aaron, high priest of Israel, according to Exodus XXVIII, wore a breastplate of jewels containing the Urim and Thurrim, two devices enabling communication with the "Lord", probably a spaceman. Today we know that crystals and jewels are semi-conductors, bases of miniature radios and laser beams. The Atlanteans probably mastered electronic techniques for communicating with their far-flung empire and the near planets, abode of their teachers; priest-scientists probed the occult secrets of nature with all the genius of our own

nuclear-physicists and discovered the terrible sidereal force called mash-mak or vril, etheric vibrations of fantastic power whose destructive blasts annihilating armies explode in the "Mahabharata". Last century John Worrell Keely of Philadephia is believed to have re-discovered this primordial force but was mysteriously prevented from developing it, otherwise world-history during the last seventy years would have been shatteringly changed. This titanic weapon may have been the lightning of Zeus, the hammer of Thor, recalling the war in the skies between the gods and the giants, spacemen versus Atlanteans.

Intercourse with celestials from other planets promoted the study of astronomy; all spacemen are not benevolent, the old legends suggest that the ancients kept radar-like watch on the heavens, dreading invaders from space. Legends assert that in Ireland, king Conn mounted the battlements of royal Tara fearing hostile intruders from the skies, while ill-fated Montezuma is said to have got up two or three times a night to look for visitants winging down from the stars; an excuse harrassed husbands might use tonight, though their wives would suspect some other motive.

All the peoples of antiquity feared evil "spirits" hovering in the air and scrutinized the skies with a care which we even in these days of sputniks cannot imagine. The Dogon in Mali knew of the Dwarf-companion of Sirius, Shilluks in South Africa recognized the two moons of Uranus. A Japanese fairy tale of the "Nippon Mukasi Banasi" collection anticipated Einstein's theory of relativity with its time-dilation paradox and mentioned a man returned still young from a trip to heaven only to find no descendants in his home apparently centuries later. Such fantastic knowledge must surely have originated from some great civilization, perhaps Atlantis.

The Atlanteans worshipped the physical sun as symbol of the supreme being and erected circles of giant monoliths or trilithons in complex arrangements showing the rising of the sun on certain dates, also the orientation of Sirius and other important stars. For many milennia stone circles like Stonehenge were built all over the world as astronomical observatories, probably with religious or interplanetary significance. Stanzas of most ancient Asiatic literature mention a towering personage, the astronomer and magician, Asurmaya, said to be an Atlantean, to whom the sun god himself imparted knowledge of the stars, oddly suggestive of the Babylonian sun god, Shamash instructing Hammurabi, or Jehovah inspiring Abraham. The Atlantean astronomers incorporated their immense wisdom in the structure of the Great Pyramid which they probably built about 80,000 B.C.

The airships of Atlantis were constructed of thin wood or electrically welded alloy lighter than aluminium and propelled by the etheric force generated in a strong heavy metal chest recalling Pandora's famous "box", which when opened caused dire affliction suggesting lethal vibrations or radio-activity. These aircraft bore an extraordinary resemblance to the vimanas or the beautifully-painted two-stored celestial car furnished with windows and adorned with flags in which victorious Rama escorted his wife, Sita, on their aerial trip from Ceylon toward the Himalayas. The Sanskrit classics described ships which flew to the planets and stars evoking Atlanteans and spacemen.

The golden age of Atlantis lasted for thousands of years, bringing great beneficence to all Earth still basking in the glory of celestials from space. Man evolves by suffering. God must destroy to create, again raising Man to ever higher octaves of evolution. Cosmic law decreed that as the Lemurians of the third root race perished for their successors, the Atlanteans, the fourth race, so they too must surrender to the Aryans, our own fifth race of Man. Preachers hope for heaven on Earth, philosophers dream of Utopia, socialists strive for their welfare state, forgetting that human nature hates perfection, preferring pride of the spirit and lust of the flesh to the selfless peace of the soul. The Atlanteans forsook their idealism and sought the exciting pleasures of perversion inspired by the powers of darkness contending for the soul of Man.

The occult Stanzas of Dzyan moralize sternly:

"Then the Fourth became tall with pride. We are the kings, it was said, we are the gods. They took wives fair to look upon.....They bred monsters, wicked demons, male and female....They built temples for the human body. They built huge cities of rare earths and metals they built.....the first great waters came. They swallowed the seven great islands. The holy saved, the unholy destroyed. With them most of the huge animals.....few men remained."

Ancient traditions suggest that Enoch, ancestor of Noah, was an Atlantean. The "Book of Enoch", believed to be far older than the Mosaic account of "Genesis", describes how the "sons of god" mated with the "daughters of men" siring giants; these fallen angels taught men sorcery, seduced the women with jewellery and sinned in unnatural pleasures, mocking in their pride "God" Himself. Enoch, inspired by celestials visited wondrous regions of the heavens, probably travelling to other planets. The patriarch was borne on a whirlwind to the West, surely to Atlantis. Enoch records a cataclysm "when the ends of the Earth got loose", the last convulsion of that drowned continent. Enoch "walked with God", his son, Methusaleh, begat Lamech, who according to the Genesis Apocryphon in the "Dead Sea Scrolls" complained before the birth of Noah that his wife, Bathenosh, had consorted with one of the angels descended from heaven.

"Behold, I thought then within my heart that conception was (due) to the watchers and the holy ones.....and to the giants....and my heart was troubled within me because of this child....Bathenosh, my wife, spoke to me saying....I swear to you by the holy Great One, the king of (the heavens) that this seed was planted by you.....and by no stranger or watcher or son of heaven."

This "old, old story" is older than we thought! Celestial commercial-travellers were no different from their descendants today, keen to combine business with pleasure. Bathenosh would surely have blushed had she realized her indiscretion would occasion saucy comment ten thousand years later, proving once and for all that truth will out. While unlike her husband we should gallantly give Bathenosh the benefit of the doubt, it is highly significant that Noah was chosen to survive the flood and to found the new age, suggesting he might have been sired for this mission by some celestial.

The Atlanteans delved into the dark side of nature, maleficent adepts conjured elementals, evil thought-forms like the tulkus materialized by Tibetan magicians; they summoned spirits from lower astral realms to work their will and appeased sinister powers by blood-stained rituals, degenerating to human sacrifice and murder. The subsequent records of ancient China, Babylon and Mexico teem with tales of demons, black magic and bloody sacrifice; in the Middle Ages the Church waged bitter war on witchcraft. Paracelsus and Montfaucon de Villars in his "Le Comte de Gabalis" wrote of sylphs and salamanders; ultra-modern physicists now theorize parallel worlds with beings in other dimensions, while many borderland researchers are beginning to believe that the extraterrestrials originate from

39

etherean realms, inner space.

Cosmic adepts reveal the titanic mental battle on Atlantis between the white magicians and their black adversaries. Perverted scientists invented "Indra's dart", an atomic-bomb, and an atomic-ray "The Brahma weapon", annihilating forces so vividly described milennia latter in the "Drona Parva". Martians, friends of the white magicians, foresaw the cataclysm on Atlantis and landed five great spaceships called "Cities of Shan" to rescue the chosen. Atomic war broke out in all its horror, convulsing Atlantis in radio-active ruins down to the sea-bed. A tale sadly topical today!

The distruction of Atlantis and the rescue of the illumined by spaceships from Venus and Mars are wonderfully described in those ancient Stanzas of Dzyan revealed in "The Secret Doctrine".

"And the 'great king of the dazzling face', the chief of all the yellow-faced, was sad, seeing the sins of the black-faced. . . .He sent his air-vehicles (vimanas) to all his brother-chiefs with pious men within, saying 'Prepare, arise ye men of the good law, and cross the land while (yet) dry."

"The lords of the storm are approaching. Their chariots are nearing the land. One night and two days only shall the lords of the dark face (the sorcerers) live on this patient land. She is doomed, and they have to descend with her. The nether lords of the dark eye are preparing their magic Agneyastra. But the Lords of the dark eye are stronger than they (the elementals) and they are the slaves of the mighty ones. They are versed in Ashtar (Vidya, the highest magical knowledge). Come and use yours."

"Let every lord of the dazzling face cause the Vimana of every lord of the dark face to come into his hands, lest any (sorcerers) should by its means escape from the waters, avoid the rest of the four (karmic deities) and save his wicked (followers or people.)"

"Then the great king fell upon his dazzling face and wept. When the kings assembled, the waters had already moved. . . .but the nations had now crossed the dry land. They were beyond the water-mark. The kings had reached them in their Vimanas, and led them on to the lands of fire and metal (East and North). . . .Stars (nuclear missiles?) showered on the lands of the black faces but they slept. The speaking-beasts (radio?) kept quiet. The nether-lords waited for orders but they came not, for their masters slept. The waters arose

and covered the valleys from one end of Earth to the other. High lands remained, the bottom of Earth remained dry. There dwelt those who occupied, the men of the yellow faces and of the straight eye. When the lords of the dark faces awoke and bethought themselves of their Vimanas in order to escape from the rising waters, they found them gone."

Professor Ludwig Zeidler of Poland believes the destruction of Atlantis was caused by a large cosmic body which struck our Earth 12,000 years ago, shifting it 30 degrees on its axis; the sudden change of climate froze the Siberian mammoths in ice.

Hans Hoerbiger, the Austrian cosmologist, taught that Atlantis flourished during a long age without any moon in the sky; about 11,500 B.C. our present satellite wandered from space and was caught in Earth's gravity, activating volcanoes and raising immense tides near the equator to engulf Poseidonis.

The Austrian geologist, Otto H. Much, conjectured a planetoid crashing down on Atlantis in 8,496 B.C. causing fantastic shocks all over the globe; his theory is cogently supported by Peter Kolosimo, the brilliant Italian scholar, who quotes the Gilgamesh Epic, Mayan, Hawaian and Chinese legends, all telling of the culture hero, Noah, warned by a god to build an ark and save humanity from the floods.

St. John the Divine in Revelations VI, v 12-14 may recall some race-memory of the destruction of Atlantis when he describes the end of the world; there were earthquakes, the sun became black, the moon as blood, the stars fell from heaven, mountains and islands were moved out of their places on the great day of God's wrath.

Surely the Atlantis cataclysm was recalled by Jesus as He sat upon the Mount of Olives foretelling the future to His disciples:

"But in those days, after that tribulation, the sun shall be darkened, and the moon shall not give her light."

"And the stars of heaven shall fall and the powers that are in heaven shall be shaken."

"And then shall they see the Son of Man coming in the clouds with great power and glory."

"And then shall He send His angels and shall gather together His elect from the four winds, from the uttermost part of heaven."

Many people believe that the Last Days are upon us now. Soon cataclysm will convulse our Earth, destroying our own civilization. The heavens will open; shining spaceships will wing down to rescue the chosen as long ago in lost Atlantis.

40

Chapter Six
Poseidon

"Now first of all we must recall the fact that 9000 is the sum of the years since the war occurred as is recorded between the dwellers beyond the pillars of Hercules and all that dwelt within them, which war we have now to relate in detail. It was stated that this city of ours was in command of the one side and fought through the war, and in command of the other side were the kings of the island of Atlantis, which we said was an island larger than Libya and Asia once upon a time but now lies sunk by earthquakes and has created a barrier of impassable mud which prevents those who are sailing out from here to the ocean beyond from proceeding further."

Our minds conditioned for nuclear war slowly day-dream!

. . . .Explosions in space blacked out radar. Rockets from North, East and West foxed the missile defences, bombs of anti-matter crashed down on the doomed continent. Earth shook, ocean roared. Submarine volcanoes belched forth floods of fire. Rent with flame shattered America sank below the sea. Nine thousand years later four philosophers in a Moscow park are discussing that ancient land of capitalism which their heroic ancestors destroyed. Since that holocaust the Atlantic is barred to shipping by a wall of mud. . . .

For an agonizing moment we imagine the destruction of the United States which atomic war makes possible, then we realize this stark account was related to Critias discoursing on lost Atlantis in Plato's Academy at Athens. So dreaded is such cataclysm in our present century that we promptly accept its occurrence in the past. Scholars scoff at the reality of Atlantis as once they ridiculed Troy; today with our nuclear knowledge we wonder?

The ancient West was veiled in mystery. To all the peoples of antiquity beyond the Pillars of Hercules, our modern Gibraltar, stretched waters of desolation washing on yon unseen shore the twilight land of death. Today men challenge the moon, tomorrow the stars; the noblest characteristic of Man is his conquest of the physical world, domination over all difficulties, raising the human spirit even higher in sublimity of soul. The wonderful, colorful, passionate history of ancient times shines with a brilliant galaxy of statesmen, scholars, soldiers, sailors, heroes hearkening to the call of destiny, whose valiant deeds illumine long centuries to inspire men today.

For thousands of years men knew less of the Atlantic than we know of the moon, though in classical times the ocean could have been crossed in contemporary ships, today men cross in rowing-boats. We launch space-probes to Mars yet only rarely in antiquity did mariners dare brave the Atlantic. Ancient Sumerian tablets describe how prince Naram-Sin about 2000 B.C. sailed presumably around the Cape of Good Hope to that "Land beyond the Western Sea". Evidence of the Sumerians and the Phoenicians is found in South America. About 600 B.C. Pharaoh Necho 11 despatched a fleet from the Red Sea to circumnavigate Africa, outraging Herodotus who swore the voyage incredible. Egyptian carvings dated about 30 B.C. have even been found in Wollongong, 50 miles south of Sydney, showing

41

that one of Cleopatra's ships ventured to Australia. Kolaios sailed from Samos about 600 B.C. and was blown by storms through the Pillars of Hercules into the Atlantic. Life on a real ocean wave seemed to unnerve this ancinet mariner for he sold his ship in Cadiz. Three centuries later the Carthaginian Admiral Hanno sailed to the Niger and in 320 B.C. the Greek traveller, Pytheas, circumnavigated Britain. Lucian, the great Sophist, in the second century A.D. in his wonderful "A True Story" anticipated our science-fiction and told a fantastic tale about setting out from the Pillars of Hercules across the western ocean to wooded islands on the other side; before he and his crew could land they were whirled by a storm aloft to the moon and captured by invaders from the sun. Lucian had never been known to tell a lie, if only we could believe him! Apart from the adventurous Vikings not until Columbus did mariners cross the Atlantic, nor did any redskin paddle his canoe to Europe.

What mighty taboo, what powerful block in human consciousness, for so many centuries prevented brave men from daring the Atlantic? What trauma blinded men's minds blotting out all memory of the west? This dark abyss daunting the most valiant soul is to us more illuminating than any literature. Out there some colossal tragedy numbed the unconscious of all mankind; the west was that bourne from which no traveller returned, before yon realm of the setting sun floated tangled trees, a sea of mud, marking the grave of that doomed continent, Atlantis.

"Do you think that you can reckon the time which has elapsed since cities first existed and men were citizens of them? It must be vast and incalculable? And have not thousands and thousands of cities come into being during this period and as many perished?"

Plato in his "Laws, 676" showed that the Greek philosophers were fully aware of the cycles of history even though they apparently lacked our own knowledge of those great civilizations of the past. Documentary evidence describing Atlantis is found in the "Timaeus" and the "Critias" by Plato, whose references to the submerged continent intrigue and exasperate students today more than ever. Plato might have written a full record of Atlantis not left to us; most of the literature in antiquity was lost in fire and flood or destroyed by megalomaniac kings. Occultists believe that initiates secreted time-capsules containing the history of their doomed continent, later when the time is ripe like the Dead Sea Scrolls these may be revealed.

Plato, born in Athens in 429 B.C., claimed descent on his mother's side from Solon two centuries earlier, the great law-giver of Greece. He sat at the feet of Socrates and after his master's execution visited Egypt, Sicily and southern Italy acquiring wisdom, then returned to teach in those shady groves of Athens dying at the remarkable age of eighty-two, still immortalized by his transcendent philosophy. With his famous pupil, Aristotle, Plato may be justly said to have civilized Europe. Over the vestibule of his house he set the inscription "Let no one enter, who is unacquainted with geometry!", which must have kept out many friends. Plato wrote no academic thesis or philosophy but discoursed in dialogues of entrancing elegance and luminous purity of style teaching that our physical world is merely an imperfect reflection of those supersensible realms divined by poets. The "Timaeus" and "Critias" consist of dialogues among Timaeus from Locris in southern Italy; Critias, distinguished as an orator, poet and dramatist, Hermocrates, leader of the Syracusan force against the Athenian expedition to Sicily, and Socrates, though the latter is disappointingly silent, also presumably Plato himself; they are sequels to his famous "Republic". For centuries scholars regarded Plato's description of Atlantis as brilliant literary fiction, somewhat surprising since its terse informative prose contrasts starkly with the persuasive rhetoric of his philosophic works. Plato suddenly leaves those aery disquisitions which delighted his disciples to recount factual history with a wealth of detail worthy of Herodotus. He plainly states that his ancestor, Solon, one of the Seven Sages of Greece, journeyed to Egypt about 600 B.C. and was assured by the priests of Sais, noted for their knowledge of ancient times, that their goddess Neith, identified with Pallas Athene, whom we may perhaps consider as a space personage, had founded the city of Athens nine thousand years earlier. The priests, versed in their vast accumulation of papyri texts, added that Athens was attacked by invaders from a great island in the west, the valient Athenians saved Europe and the Middle East; in a single day and night of storms Atlantis was destroyed. The Egyptians told Solon that the story was written on pillars which were still preserved; in 310 B.C. the Greek philosopher, Crantor, related that he had seen in Egypt a column on which was written the history of the great island submerged in the ocean.

42

Atlantis was not evoked by Plato to allegorize morality like the "Utopia" of Sir Thomas More nor did its theocracy promote the Platonic "ideal state". As historian rather than philosopher Plato resurrected a civilization quite different from his own day resembling the Bronze Age in western Europe and the sun-cultures of Mexico and Peru unknown to Athens. That magic, mellifluent, musical "Atlantis" enchanting us even today could not have been dreamed by Plato; this wonderful word is not found in any Indo-European language, "a" or "atl" in Toltec and Berber signifies "water", "Atlan" means "amid the water". "Aztlan", the fatherland of the Aztecs was depicted in old Mexican drawings as an island with mountains encircled by concentric rings of walls and canals similar to the citadel of Plato's Atlantis. A city named "Atlan" with a good harbor existed on the isthmus of Darien, when Columbus discovered America, it is now an unimportant village, Aclo. It surprises us to learn that "Thalassa", the Greek for "sea" is not a Greek word at all nor is it related to the Indo-European family of languages, arousing intriguing speculation as to possibly affinity with the toltec "Atl" evocative of Atlantis. Had Plato's account been fiction, he would surely have called the island by some Greek name impressing his audience. Plato would take "Atlante" from Solon's unfinished epic poem, "Atlantikos", based on Egyptian papyri translated by the priests of Sais; before writing his story he checked all relevant traditions and consulted Ekhenates, teacher of Democritus.

The "Critias" in terse guide-book prose describes the island of Atlantis with a realism attractive to our tourists today. Plato's impressive account rivals that brilliant description of Babylon by Herodotus delighting all antiquity. In the center of the whole island there was a plain which is said to have been the fairest of all plains and very fertile, surrounded by mountains celebrated for their size and beauty studded with prosperous villages, lakes, rivers and meadows, offering abundant food for the many animals wild and tame. Seafarers from Atlantis explored Earth and their enterprise built a vast empire dominating western Europe, Italy and Libya, whose bountiful treasures enriched the motherland. The virile Atlanteans, glorying in mastery of the world with the same imaginative conception and technical genius which built the Great Pyramid, fashioned their own sacred island with busy ports and wide harbors for their navies and merchant fleets and constructed broad, concentric canals linked by bridges leading to the

citadel. The entire outside wall was covered with tin, the innermost encompassing the citadel flashed with the red light of orichalcum, probably copper. The city shone with palaces of massive stones colored white, black and red, set amid fountains from hot and cold springs, which watered public baths and luxuriant trees of wonderful height and beauty. All these magnificent buildings glowing in the tropical sun were eclipsed by the great temple dedicated to Poseidon and Cleito, covered with silver and orichalcum, its pinnacles gleaming in gold, surrounded by an enclosure of gold. Such a wondrous metropolis embellished by sculptures and works of art through many milennia must surely have inspired all its inhabitants and imbued the Atlanteans with the proud feeling that they were truly the children of the golden sun god. The plan of Atlantis is said to characterize the design of old Mexico, Carthage and many ancient cities all over the world; some sensitives allege that all copy the splendid capital of Venus, implying that our civilization was inspired from space.

Plato continues with a brief description of civil administration under the ten kings, the army and navy and Poseidon-worship, then to the exasperation of all posterity his brilliant account abruptly ends.

Raphael in his Vatican fresco "The School of Athens" put "Atlantis" into the hands of Plato's friend Timaeus, presumably to show that this enshrined the most sublime wisdom of Plato.

Though Plato's tantalizing record of Atlantis is the most detailed bequeathed to us, it is not the only historical reference to that lost continent. The distinguished scholar, Egerton Sykes, states that there are over a hundred and fifty classical references to Atlantis. Heinrich Schliemann of Troy fame quoted a papyrus in the museum of old St. Petersburg describing a forlorn expedition despatched by Pharaoh Sent of the second dynasty to discover Atlantis, another papyrus in the same museum referred to the kings of Atlantis. Schliemann claimed to have discovered amid the ruins of Troy bronze vases and pottery engraved in Phoenician hieroglyphics signifying "From King Chronos of Atlantis", a similar vase is said to have been found at Tiahuanaco.

The Chinese cherished traditions of an island or continent called Maligasima destroyed owing to the evil of its giants; king Peirium escaped like Noah and his descendants peopled China with divine dynasties. The Hindu Puranas give a description of wars on continents and islands situated beyond western Africa in the Atlantic Ocean. Sanskrit

43

records suggest that the "Mahabharata" actually chronicles the conflict between the Atlanteans and the first Aryans, remembered in Persia as the struggle waged by the wicked giant Devs against the wise Peris. Proclus quotes Marcellus, who wrote a history of Ethiopia mentioning the great island of Atlantis destroyed in ancient times by a violent storm. Aelian in "Varia Historiae" tells of a marvellous tradition related by Silenus, son of a nymph, to Midas, king of Phrygia, as mentioned by Theopompus of Chios writing about 320 B.C.

"Besides the well-known portions of the world, Europe, Asia, Lybia (Africa), there is another which is unknown, of incredible immensity, where immeasurably vast, blooming meadows and pastures feed herds of various huge and mighty beasts, and men in these parts are twice the height and in the age of their years of men here."

These vast meadows could relate to the prairies and pampas of North and South America; Silenus might have been a spaceman or even an American Indian, who by chance had crossed the Atlantic. Traditions from Gaul quoted by the Roman historian, Timagenes, and Diodorus Siculus, mention warlike giants from the western ocean invading Hyperborea, the lands of the west. Dionysius of Halicarnassus suggests that Hercules after his tenth labor, capturing the oxen of Geryon on Erytheia, Red Island, perhaps originally the fabulous land of the sunset glow (Atlantis?), placed somewhere near the Pillars of Hercules, invaded Europe. Hercules was the greatest commander of his age; with naval and military forces he swiftly conquered Spain and Italy, founded Herculaneum near Pompeii and received divine honors from the people of Italy. This invasion of Europe by the giant Hercules in dim antiquity may be a confused memory of the war between Atlantis and Athens.

Supporting evidence for the existence of Atlantis may be discerned in the doctrines of the Druids, the folklore of America and Peru, particularly in that repository of ancient Mayan wisdom, the Popul Vuh.

In A.D. 14,000 historians vaguely recalling our Hitler War may tell of ten million men from the lost continent of America invading Europe in titanic conflict; no doubt they will be ridiculed by scientists arguing that America never existed, the legend of that wicked continent was a tale told by philosophers.

Students in varied research associate to support the reality of Atlantis. Last century Ignatius Donnelly, member of congress and sponsor for Sir Francis Bacon's authorship of the Shakespearean plays, made an impressive comparison of the languages, customs and cultures in ancient times on both sides of the Atlantic, publishing in New York, 1882, his erudite revelation, "Atlantis, the Antediluvian World", which took academic circles by storm and founded modern Atlantology. By a wealth of cogent facts and masterly arguments Donnelly proved the truth of Plato's story, his marshalled evidence corroborated the destruction of Atlantis in a cataclysm about twelve thousand years ago. Fossils recently discovered in America show that the ancestors of the horse originated in the western hemisphere and must have crossed to Europe by a land-bridge in ancient times; botanists find many plants existing on the east coast of the Americas and on the west coast of Europe and Africa yet missing on the Pacific coast. Bananas originated in tropical Africa and Asia, they cannot be transplanted like geraniums or roses nor have they seeds or roots easily transportable; it is difficult to understand how bananas can be common to Africa and the West Indies without having been cultivated in some land in the Atlantic.

Fascinating links between Ancient America and Sumeria were established by the brilliant researches of A. Hyatt Verrill and his wife, Ruth; Harold Wilkins disclosed startling revelations of secret cities in South America which allured to his death the ill-fated Colonel Fawcett. The great archaeologist, Marcel F. Homet explored the primeval forests of the Amazon and on a vast plain in Brazil discovered the Pedra Pintada, an immense rock painted with cosmic symbols similar to hieroglyphics of ancient Egypt and drawings on the prehistoric dolmens of stone age Europe and North Africa. It may be significant that today U.F.O. activity and landings of spacemen seem to favor South America. The mythologist, Lewis Spence, in shrewd analysis of Celtic legends and American folklore offers valuable support to Donnelly's findings. H.S. Bellamy applied the cosmic ice theory of the Austrian cosmologist, Hans Hoerbiger, and in persuasive exposition suggested that Atlantis was destroyed in the immense floods raised when Luna, our present moon, was captured by Earth's gravitation. Comyns Beaumont postulated a great comet devastating the west in prehistoric times, while Immanuel Velikovsky assembled overwhelming evidence of cosmic collisions devastating the Middle East.

Scholars differ in their interpretations of Plato's account. Jurgen Spanuth equates Atlantis with the island of Heligoland dominating a Bronze Age

44

empire, which appeared to be the land of the Phaeacians visited by Ulysses, so vividly described by Homer. The great war waged by the Atlanteans was believed by Spanuth to represent the invasion of the North Sea peoples across the Mediterranean aimed at the Middle East; the northern hordes were smashed in 1195 B.C. by Rameses III in a memorable battle near the Libyan border. Professor Berlioux, who occupied the chair of geography at the university of Lyons, said that in a distant epoch caravans coming from Memphis and Thebes met at Cerne, capital of Atlantean Africa, the fleet which came from the "American" lands. From one end to the other of this long trail there was trade, also cultural exchange, then one day the flow ceased and was interrupted for centuries. A tremendous war had overwhelmed the empire of Atlantis and a geological cataclysm had completed the destruction. Researches made by Louis Rinn in the Atlas mountains of Morocco on the ancient language of the Berbers and their sacred characters or "taffinari" show that an authentic brown-skinned race similar to the Celts, Medes and Iranians are still divided in milennia-old rivalry between peoples of the north and south, their traditions and culture evoke Atlantis. Dr. Angelos G. Galanopoulos, professor of geophysics at the university of Athens, suggests that Plato's Atlantis was really the small island of Santorin, one of the Minoan islands, which erupted and disappeared below the Mediterranean around 1500 B.C.; the same eruption polluting the atmosphere possibly caused the plagues of Egypt at the time of the Exodus. He states that a tidal wave destroyed the Cretan civilization known to the Egyptians as Atlantis. Scholars with plausible arguments have sited Atlantis in South America, Sweden, Palestine, Nigeria, North Africa, Cyprus, Ceylon, Spain and the Sahara, each rejecting his rivals with learned disdain. Psychics inspired by occult sources scorn these conflicting theories and insist that the lost continent was in the Atlantic.

Colonel James Churchward, noted for his erudite researches into ancient Mu, claimed to have found an old Greek record stating that when Atlantis disappeared there were three thousand Athenian soldiers stationed there, probably an army of occupation. He revealed that in one of the oriental temples there was a long history of Atlantis written 20,000 years ago, this revelation is somewhat devalued by his surprising omission to quote the text which must have surely revolutionized our knowledge of Atlantis and prehistory, too.

For many centuries scholars have concluded that the Atlantis story was meant by Plato to be a morality, though the moral lesson, if any, seems somewhat obscure; scientists today dismiss the account as fiction by the Greek philosopher devoid of fact like his Discourses. Perhaps the most impressive comment is the rapt attention paid by Socrates and his disciples to the words of Critias, who told the tale. Socrates was hated by Critias, one of the Thirty Tyrants, who impeached him for corrupting the Athenian youth and for his fearless arguments against false teachings, condemning the old man in 399 B.C. to drink the fatal cup of hemlock. Socrates, this champion of truth, never contradicted one word of the talk on Atlantis, he had probably heard it all before and knew it was true. If Socrates accepted Atlantis, who are we to disagree?

The most intriguing revelations of Plato's story may be his references to the kings of Atlantis, regarded by the Greeks as gods evoking suggestions of spacemen.

"But before I begin my account there is still a small point which I ought to explain, lest you should be surprised at frequently hearing Greek names given to barbarians. The reason of this you shall now learn. Since Solon was planning to make use of the story for his own poetry, he had found on investigating the meaning of the names that those Egyptians who had first written them down, had translated them into their own tongue. So he himself in turn recovered the original sense of each name and rendering it into our tongue wrote it down so. And these very writings were in the possession of my grandfather and are actually now in mine and when I was a child I learnt them all by heart."

The terse description of Atlantis intrudes into Plato's polished prose suggesting that Solon's tale was interpolated into Plato's manuscript. Plutarch complained because the Atlantis story suddenly broke off leaving so much unsaid. This criticism was not voiced by Socrates or his companions, arousing speculation that perhaps Plato did quote the complete account of the lost continent in his "Critias" but his manuscript like so many writings in ancient times was badly copied by ignorant scribes or partly destroyed. Esoteric teachings of Atlantis preserved by initiates of Egypt probably inspired the Eleusinian mysteries; Pythagoras and all the great mystics including Apollonius of Tyana sternly refused to commit their wisdom to writing, Jesus Himself never wrote one word for posterity.

45

Aeschylus was accused of profaning the mysteries by revealing in his dramas certain secret rituals; it is understandable therefore that many of the ancient traditions of Atlantis would be censored from popular literature. We today are kept in ignorance of much of the secret history of our own troubled times; perhaps this is wise since the stuff we are forced to hear seems bad enough. Exasperating though it must be to students of Atlantis, the initiates of Greece probably venerated the lost continent as origin of their gods and veiled its destruction from vulgar gaze.

"Likewise as we previously stated concerning the allotment of the gods, that they portioned out the whole Earth, here into larger allotments and there into smaller, and provided for themselves shrines and sacrifices; even so, Poseidon took for his allotment the island of Atlantis and settled therein the children whom he had begotten of a mortal woman in a region of the island. . . .There stood a mountain that was low on all sides. Thereon dwelt one of the natives originally sprung from Earth, Evenor by name with his wife, Leucippe, and they had for offspring an only begotten daughter, Cleito. And when this damsel was now come to marriageable age, her mother died and also her father; and Poseidon being smitten with desire for her, wedded her. . . .And he begat five pairs of twin sons. . . .And to all of them he gave names, giving to him that was eldest and king the name after which the whole island was called and the sea spoken of as the Atlantic; because the first king who then reigned had the name of Atlas. And the name of his younger twin brother, who had for his portion the extremity of the island near the pillars of Hercules up to that part of the country now called Gadeira after the name of that region was Eumelus in Greek but in the native tongue, Gadeirus. . . .which in fact may have given its title to the country. And of the pair that were born next he called the one Ampheres and the other Evaemon; and of the third pair the elder was named Mneseus and the younger Autuchthon; and of the fourth pair he called the first Elasippus and the second Mestor; and of the fifth pair, Azaes was the name given to the elder, and Diaprepes to the second. So all these, themselves and their descendants, dwelt for many generations bearing rule over many other islands throughout the sea and holding sway besides as previously stated over the Mediterranean peoples as far as Egypt and Tuscany."

The Egyptian priests, men of immense learning, versed in most ancient traditions now lost to us, told Solon that the gods once divided the whole Earth among themselves; their own religion taught that long ago Osiris and Isis descended from the skies in a sun-ship bringing wheat and the arts of civilization to our world. During the golden age other celestials, Horus, Set, Hathor and Thoth, aided mankind, then Set in envy murdered Osiris, whose death was avenged by Horus in the titanic war in the heavens recalled in "The Book of the Dead". The name Osiris is un-Egyptian, it may be of Atlantean or even extraterrestrial origin. Solon accepted the priests' story, he believed that in the beginning the gods did rule our Earth, probably his own teachers had told him so. The Greeks esteemed Solon as one of the Seven Sages, one of the wisest men in all antiquity; he would surely be familiar with the works of Homer and Hesiod singing of the gods and heroes of ancient times. Solon became famed as a lawyer and about 590 B.C. completely remodelled the constitution of Athens, later he travelled widely in Egypt, Lydia and around the Mediterranean, his advice was sought by kings. The sage truly said that no man could be deemed happy until his life was finished in a happy way; remembrance of Solon's warning saved king Croesus from being burned at the stake by Cyrus of Persia, who made him his friend. The Cypriots named one of their towns, Soli, in his honor, poets long esteemed Solon's elegaics for their moral precepts and practical wisdom.

In 593 B.C. when Solon was contending in the stormy politics of Athens, a few hundred miles to the east a young Jewish priest, Ezekiel, sitting by the river Chebar in Babylon, saw the heavens open and a bejewelled wheel with wondrous men descended beside him. The "Power and Glory" of the "Lord", the spaceships haunting Palestine and Babylon, must sometimes have hovered over Mount Olympus, home of the gods. Solon could scarcely know that his contemporaries in India, Tibet, China, Japan and Mexico, believed in divine kings from the skies. One of the greatest minds of the ancient world, the sage lived until the age of eighty honored to our present day. If Solon believed in the living gods and in Atlantis, surely we should reconsider his story with respect!

Diodorus Siculus thought the first king of Atlantis was Uranus; since the Greek "Ouranos" means "sky", he possibly signified spacemen,

46

confirming the ancient Stanzas of Dzyan, which described the earliest rulers, progenitors of the divine dynasties, as lords of the flame from Venus. Solon stated that Atlantis was given to a god represented in Greek by Poseidon, grandson of Uranus and brother of Zeus, presumably by his father, Chronos or Saturn. This symbolism associated with the golden, silver and iron ages and the wars in heaven mentioned in classical mythology may conceal three separate epochs with invaders from space. Poseidon, the Roman Neptune, held dominion over the sea and dwelled in a wonderful palace in the ocean depths; he rode a glittering chariot drawn by brazen horses with golden manes almost identical to the golden car of Indra in the "Rig Veda" of old India; his trident, a three-pronged spear raised storms and shook Earth like Indra's dart, which blasted like a nuclear-bomb. It is intriguing to speculate on the origin of Britannia and her trident on British coins; does this confirm Britain's link with Atlantis? The Chinese believe that Earth was ruled by a dragon with a wondrous palace at the bottom of the sea who often flew breathing smoke and fire to his lair in the clouds, reminiscent of those UFOs today plunging to the ocean depths then speeding to the skies. Poseidon just like the sons of god described in "Genesis" mated with mortal women and produced a vast progeny. After marriage to Amphititre, daughter of a Titan, he seduced the great Earth goddess, Demeter; it was rumored that one of Poseidon's sons was Bellerophon, who wrought fantastic deeds on his flying steed, Pegasus. With Apollo Poseidon is said to have built the walls of Troy but favored the Greeks in the Trojan war; he was believed to have created the horse, races were run in his honor. "Poseidon" or "Potei-Dan" has been construed as meaning "Lord of Wisdom"; he was associated with dragons and horses, particularly with flying-horses, symbolism for the sky people.

Greek mythology has long been regarded as folk-tales of a primitive people making gods in their own image rollicking in love and war larger than life, totally removed from reality. Today awareness of the inhabited universe, suspicion that spacemen landed long ago to rule on Earth in a golden age followed by war in the heavens, then cataclysms, told in legends all over the world, make us wonder whether the symbolism of Poseidon conceals some glorious revelation transforming antiquity. Admittedly many interpretations are possible, were elucidation obvious truth would have shone for all to see; now we may view

Poseidon in the light of our modern knowledge and evaluate his fascinating relevance to Atlantis.

Poseidon rising from the sea to civilize the Atlanteans evokes Oannes, the being with the body like a fish, who according to Berossus appeared from the ocean to teach the early Babylonians all the arts of civilization. In esoteric language the sea often symbolized the depths of space, to primitive minds a man in a spacesuit might resemble a huge fish. Today observers sight UFOs plunging into or soaring from the sea; some writers believe that extraterrestrials have long had bases on the ocean bed, perhaps these in ancient times were pictured as the palaces of Poseidon. The fascinating submarine dwellings of commander Cousteau and the future plans for villages underwater, where people with lungs surgically modified could actually breathe like fish, make the fantasy of oceanic supermen startlingly possibly.

An interesting analogy may be found in the "Book of Job", Chapter XLI, once attributed to Moses, though the author is still unknown. The "Lord", who was surely not the creator of the universe but a spaceman, as Moses himself discovered during the "exodus", describes to lamenting Job a strange aquatic creature called "Leviathan" in language curiously familiar to UFO literature. The monster's face had doors surrounded by terrible teeth, light shone when it sneezed, its eyes were like the "eyelids of the morning", smoke rose from its nostrils, sparks and flames leaped from its mouth. Its heart was like a millstone, its body closely covered by scales rivetted together, invulnerable to blows from swords, arrows or darts. It made the ocean boil, causing a path to shine after it. Such description closely resembles the classical Chinese dragon and a formidable monster mentioned in "The Book of the Dead", both believed to symbolize a spaceship. The Leviathan cannot have been a whale or a crocodile for the "Lord" explained how it beheld all "high things" and was "a king over all the children of pride", surely implying it surveyed the world from the air. Biblical scholars have long been puzzled by the Leviathan and compared it with the equally intriguing seven-headed Canaanite Lotan in myths current about 1500 B.C.; today we are struck by its resemblance to the descriptions of spaceships given by those terrified peasants in Brazil. Varuna, the primeval Indian god known to the Greeks as Uranus, is now believed to represent a galactic race, the first spacemen to land on Earth probably as a transit-base; later Sanskrit writings describe him as riding the Leviathan, probably

47

symbolism for a spaceship.

Jonah spent three days and nights in the belly of a whale then instructed by the "Lord" was landed in Babylon (like Oannes) to convert the people of Nineveh. Perhaps he was taken in a spaceship like Adamski and while it submerged in the seas he received instruction from a cosmic master to preach to Nineveh? About the same time in the eighth century B.C. murals in Assyria depicted Shalmaneser 11 accompanied by winged counsellors, presumably spacemen.

Arcadian cults believed that Poseidon married Demeter, who gave to her favorite, Triptolemus, a chariot of winged dragons and grains of wheat to scatter the blessings of agriculture across the Earth. This tale evokes the tradition that in Snowdonia exist the ruins of the ancient British city of Emrys with Cyclopean fortifications, known as the ambrosial city of "Dinas Afferaon" or the "higher powers"; here in the ancient days of sun-worship were concealed dragons which were frequently harnessed for the children of the Welsh goddess, Keridwen. On the other side of the world in ancient China, the dragon kings fought wars in the skies with fantastic weapons. Such evidence is extremely tenuous and open to widely conflicting interpretations yet in the light of world-wide legends and our modern insight into extra-terrestrialism there does seem to be some relation between dragons, spacemen and possibly Atlantis.

Poseidon married the mortal, Cleito; their son, Atlas, became King of Atlantis. In Greek mythology Atlas was brother of the hero, Prometheus; together they led the Titans in the war in the heavens against Zeus, paralleled in folk-tales all over the world, which may be interpreted as a revolt by the giants or Atlanteans against the spacemen. Perseus, son of Zeus, flew through the air on winged sandals, he also slew the Gorgon, Medusa, and with her head changed Atlas into stone, the Atlas mountain in North Africa, a remarkable parallel to the Irish flashing Eye of Balor which annihilated all fixed by its gaze, the malignant rays of the gods of old Mexico, and the magic rod of Hermes. Confused and cryptic though such legends be, they coincide with occult teachings that the Atlanteans wielded a terrible sidereal force called Mash-mak and the power of vril described in the writings of occult initiates. For his eleventh labor, Hercules, son of Zeus, stole the golden apples from the Hesperides, daughters of Atlas, who lived in the extreme west, killing the guardian dragon, Ladon. Writers of science-fiction

celestial who destroyed an Atlantean spaceship and seized some wonderful weapons from Atlantis. An outrageous suggestion, yet no more fanciful than the idea of the world's strongest man venturing to the far west and slaying a dragon just for three oranges.

Solon mentioned a son of Poseidon called Mestor, the name of a king of Argos and of Mycenae about the time of the Deucalion flood; this may perhaps be confirmed by an inscription said to have been found by Heinrich Schliemann on the lion gate at Mycenae relating that Misor was the child of Thoth, son of an Atlantean priest, who fell in love with the daughter of king Chronos, escaped, then wandered to Egypt where he built the first temple at Sais and taught the wisdom of Atlantis. Some sensitives with cogent dissertation suggest that the Atlanteans built the Great Pyramid.

The Egyptian priests told Solon that about eleven thousand years ago a mighty power landed on the Atlantic coast and waged wanton aggression against the whole of Europe and Asia until defeated by Athens and her allies. Theopompus related that Silenus informed Midas, king of Phrygia, that the lands of the west were invaded by ten million men from a great continent in the Atlantic. Even allowing for exaggeration and mistranslation down the centuries, it seems obvious that any nation which attacked Europe, Asia and Libya must have assembled immense forces. We with our own experience of the second front during the Hitler war when a million men invaded Europe, realize the logistics involved, the masterly planning, the navies, the shipping, the armies, the equipment, the supplies, the generalship, strategy and tactics necessary to launch such onslaught. The Atlanteans conquered Libya, then a prosperous, populated country as far as the Egyptian frontier, stormed the coasts of Spain and France, swept the Mediterranean and overran Italy, then gathered their vast power in a mighty single battle for Egypt and Greece. At the very extremity of danger heroic Athens led her allied hosts in smashing victory and in dazzling offensive drove the routed enemy from the occupied countries back to Atlantis. Shortly afterward the island was convulsed by earthquakes and disappeared beneath the sea. Shades of Alamein, Stalingrad, D-day and the epics of the Hitler war! We need no imagination to picture this titanic conflict between Atlantis and Europe, we vividly remember our two mighty wars between the west and Germany.

48

Occult sources suggest that the Atlanteans possessed aircraft, nuclear bombs and laser-rays as mentioned in the Sanskrit classics. Solon describes the forces of Atlantis in terms of his own times, triremes, archers, slingers and cavalry. This contrast is understandable. In the sixth century B.C. neither the Egyptian priests nor Solon had any cognizance of aeroplanes or annihilating weapons; they knew Atlantis assembled immense armaments, which they interpreted in the concept of their own forces; they were discussing a war nine thousand years earlier; more details may have been given in that part of the manuscript unfortunately lost to us. We wonder more than ever at the weapons wielded by victorious Athens? Who knows what fantasies lie veiled in the past?

Although the Atlantean invasion of Europe is not recorded in the new ancient manuscripts now left to us, physical proof may perhaps be established by the sudden appearance of the magnificent Cro-Magnon man, whose impressive broad and lofty forehead, splendid cranial capacity and tall stature made him equal if not superior to Homo Sapiens today; about 10,000 B.C. this remarkable being, far more advanced than the brutish Neanderthal man, suddenly arrived in south west Europe as from another planet, more probably from Atlantis. The marvellous paintings adorning the caves in Altamira and the Dordogne show the artists had imaginative vitality and a wondrous delicacy of line revealing an exquisite, aesthetic sense requiring age-long development. The Cro-Magnons in facial contours strongly resembled the red Indians and employed many of the same social and religious practices, apparently believing in reincarnation, worshipping the sun and gods in the sky. The Basque language, totally isolated from the Indo-European tongues of present-day Europe, has intriguing grammatical affinities with red Indian dialects spoken on the opposite shores of America suggesting a common origin midway in Atlantis. Irish annals declare that the warlike Formorians colonized Ireland before the flood, the Celts are believed to have inherited their stature, coloring and occult powers from their Atlantean ancestors, when Britain was an outpost of the Atlantean empire.

In his fascinating researches into Chaldaic literature, that profound scholar, Y.N. Ibn Aharon, deduces from the "Zohar", "The Book of Enumerations" and "The Book of Formations", ancient works in Aramaic, that the Chaldeans believed Man originated on Earth 31,000,000 years ago, a claim supporting Lemuria. The Elohim on High were interplanetary beings, who settled on Venus 18,000,000 years ago, landed on our moon, then Earth and instructed the Atlanteans. About 11,000 B.C. confederations existed in Africa (Talantu-Atlantis), the Pacific (Rada) and Asia (Dravidya) with mixed nations in America and the Mediterranean. Divine kings, priests of the wisdom, ruled the world in a brilliant civilization based on a psycho-science utilizing electro-magnetism, sonics and radionics. The Chaldeans taught that in most ancient times a race of extraterrestrials, the serpent men, Nakhash-Na warred with the Titans; they may have been the Uranids usurped by Cronus. The serpent which tempted Eve in the Garden of Eden to eat the forbidden fruit probably symbolizes a serpent man from space teaching occult wisdom, black magic, thus encompassing the destruction of Atlantis and bitter hardship for Man.

H.S. Bellamy expounding Hans Hoerbiger's world ice theory construes the "Book of Revelations" as describing the destruction of Atlantis. St. John's poetic description of "God" sitting on a celestial throne amid lightnings and thunderings, attended by angels casting millstones into the sea while Heaven and Earth shook in flaming Apocalypse does suggest some world-cataclysm.

The suggestion that spacemen visited Earth about 10,000 B.C. received apparent confirmation from a novel and totally unexpected source. Legends all over the world tell of celestials, divine dynasties and war in the skies, particularly the folk-tales of China and Tibet, where fact and fiction mingle in exotic fantasy bewitching our wondering minds today, without disclosing any date when extraterrestrials actually descended among men. The Russian expert, Vyacheslav Zaitsev, who has spent thirty years collecting evidence supporting his thesis that intelligent beings from outer space have had contact with our Earth, quotes the German magazine "Das Vegetarische Universuum" commenting on the startling report in 1965 by a Chinese archaeologist that spaceships landed here 12,000 years ago.

During twenty-five years exploration of the caves in the Bayan-Kara-Ula mountains in the border of China and Tibet archaelogists found a total of 716 stone discs like gramophone records, each disc had a hole in its center from which a double groove spiralled its way to the circumference, the grooves were not sound-tracks but unreadable patterns and hieroglyphics. After two decades of research the Chinese archaeologist

49

presented his shattering theory of extraterrestrial visitation. The shocked Peking Academy of Pre-History banned publication but later the professor and his four colleagues published their intriguing thesis "Groove Writing Relating to Spaceships which as Recorded on the Discs, existed 12,000 years ago".

This most fascinating account by Mr. Zaitsev explained that the lofty caves in the Batan-Kara-Ula mountains are inhabited by the Ham and Dropa tribes, frail, stunted men averaging four feet two inches in height, about whom very little is known today. One of the Ham hieroglyphic texts was eventually diciphered and apparently read

".... The Dropas came down from the clouds in their gliders. Our men, women and children hid in the caves ten times before the sunrise. When at last they understood the sign language of the Dropas, they realized that the newcomers had peaceful intentions. . . ."

Another hieroglyphic of the Ham tribes deplored the destruction of their own spaceships during a dangerous landing in the lofty mountains and their failure to build new ones.

The stone discs were sent to Moscow for examination. Scientists were astounded to find that they contained a large amount of cobalt and other metals; the discs vibrated in unusual rhythm as if they carried an electric charge or formed part of an electric-circuit.

In corroboration Mr. Zaitsev quoted Chinese legends describing small gaunt, yellow-faced men, who descended from the clouds; these visitants possessed enormous heads and puny bodies rendering their appearance grotesque to the local people. Speleologists exploring some of the Bayan-Kara-Ula caves excavated graves 12,000 years old and found the remains of human beings with huge crania and underdeveloped skeletons. The inner walls of the caves are covered with drawings of the rising sun, the moon and the stars, spangled with dots suggesting spaceships apparently approaching a mountainous region of Earth.

This most illuminating study by Vyacheslav Zaitsev publicizing the revolutionary discovery of the unnamed Chinese archaeologists supports the Sanskrit classics, which so entrancingly describe the flying-cars used by the gods and kings of old India in their golden age long ago. The large heads and small bodies of the Dropas at once evoke familiar recognition by UFO students today. On 14th August 1947 Professor Rapuzzi Luigi

Johannis, a well-known Italian painter and writer, near Villa Santina in Fruili among the mountains north of Venice, was literally shocked by two dwarfs, heads caricaturishly large, wearing translucent overalls, who climbed aboard a huge disc and soared to the sky. Many humanoids are reported by frightened peasants in South America, resembling those famous little men with pumpkin heads and brains "at least three times as big as ours", who astonished M. Maurice Masse, a farmer at Valensole in the French Alps on 1st July, 1965. The astronomical pictures in the Bayan-Kara-Ula caves parallel the inscriptions in the caves of Bohistan, India, showing Earth and Venus 13,000 years ago joined by an arrow, also petroglyphs in a cave near Ferghana in Uzbekhistan.

Photographs taken from the two-manned Gemini 4 spaceship, which recorded a successful space-walk and encountered UFOs more than once during its 62 orbit flight around the Earth from June 3-7, 1965, showed an amazing sun-mark in Mauretania southwest of the famous Tassili cosmic frescoes. This clear picture was taken from an unbelievable altitude of 100-200 miles in the air providing evidence which Japanese students interpret as pictures of a cosmic base visited by UFOs in the past.

The Stanzas of Dzyan, Plato's "Timaeus" and the Bible mention the lords of the flame, the gods, the angels, who descended to Atlantis. Is it too fantastic to suggest that when the spacemen were rescuing initiates from the doomed continent one or two of their ships crashed in the Chinese mountains? The survivors marooned in an alien world far from civilization mated to produce their descendants, the now degenerate Ham and Dropa tribes.

In 1945 Richard S. Shaver, a Pennsylvania war-plant welder, told a fantastic tale claiming twenty years occasional contact with an underground race of deros, descendants of the Titans and Atlans, who fled down to gigantic caves when Atlantis was destroyed about 12,000 years ago. Believers in the hollow Earth theory tell of a wonderful civilization miles underground, alleged to be the origin of the UFOs surveilling the surface. Science ridicules suggestions of this subterranean world called Agharta yet sensitives insist that the Atlanteans built long tunnels from the Pyramids, the Mediterranean and the Andes to realms underground.

The Soviet scientist, N. Zirov in "Nauka i Zhizn" (Science and Life), July 1965 describes how the Atlantic land-mass barred the warm

50

currents of the South Atlantic from the coasts of Europe then covered with ice. The Swedish biographer, Rene Malaise, and the French geologist, J. Boucart, dredged two samples from the Mid-Atlantic Ridge, the sample from the western slope was ordinary oceanic mud, that from the eastern revealed glacial origin, evidently transported by icebergs. After the submergence of Atlantis the Gulf Stream washed western Europe banishing the ice age about 10,000 B.C. confirmed by our climatologists. In 1913 Pierre Termier dredged a piece of tachylite, lava evidently formed in the atmosphere above sea-level; later diatoms of algae were discovered native to freshwater lakes. Recently Americans dredged from a submerged peak a ton of strange calcareous discs 15 cms in diameter and 4 cms thick, partly smooth, partly rough, with a central hole, apparently artificial; radio-carbon tests showed them to have been formed above the surface about 12,000 years ago.

Geologically Atlantis was a young continent composed of basalt unlike the original ancient land-masses of granite. Russian geologists state that solid basalt eventually sinks into liquid basalt and under immense pressure in sea-water changes into strata of minerals with different densities causing inevitable subsidence. Atlantis was doomed by its own rock-structure of unstable basalt.

The mystery of the ancient west which haunted the noblest minds of antiquity confounds us more than ever in our space age. The wonderful secret still lies enshrined in those alluring, sea-green ruins of lost Atlantis.

Chapter Seven
Ancient America

The land of the sunset beyond the western sea fascinated the ancients, legends mourning Atlantis, that magical island drowned long ago, wondered whether those grey waters washed the far shores of some lost continent, realm of the gods. All the peoples of antiquity believed that departed souls crossed dim seas of dusk to some mysterious country in the west, whence no traveller returned, there to bask in the fields of the blest. To the west across the dark sea drifted the souls of the Egyptians for judgment in Amenti; the Babylonian hero, Gilgamesh, sought immortality across the deep waters of death. Procopius in "De Bello Gothico", Lib, IV-20, repeated the widespread traditions that the souls of the dead solemnly marched across Gaul to the Channel coast whence the ghostly Charon would ferry them over the Styx to Brittia to wander onward ever seeking yon spectral shore in the west. Celtic myths told muted tales of islands of splendor beloved by the gods manifesting to men, then that glorious civilization rent suddenly with fire sank down to those sunless caverns of the deep. The Goths called the northern ocean "Marimarusa", the "Sea of the Dead"; for centuries a mystic twilight veiled the west, only plaintive echoes murmured of the magic past and wonders of that land far away.

America is popularly supposed to have received its name from the mariner, Americus Vespucius, actually Alberico Vespuzio, son of Anastasio Vespuzio. Had the Italian sought immortality by christening the continent after himself he would surely have honored his family by calling it "Vespuzia" just as "Columbia" was called after

Christopher Columbus. In Central America the word "Americ" signified "great mountain" evoking "Meru", the sacred mountain in Hindu tradition, said to be the center of seven continents; ancient America was linked with India through lost Lemuria. The early voyagers probably believed "America" to be the native word for the land itself, so they too would use it. Vespuzio's comrades instead of "Alberico" would nickname him "Americo". Italian cartographers gleaned information about the new world from many sources and would surely adopt the native name for the country and call it "America".

Some native tribes called their land "Atlanta" Echo of Atlantis.

So much of the literature of antiquity is lost that it is difficult to determine exactly what the ancients knew of the "land in the west". First dynasty Egyptian inscriptions about 5000 B.C. (?) refer to the "land beyond the western sea" as "Urani Land", the Urani, "people of Ur", evoke Ur in Sumeria, birthplace of Abraham; there is said to exist evidence that before 3000 B.C. Phoenicians sailed from Lagash in the Persian Gulf to America. Centuries later, Menes, eldest son of Sargon, 2275 B.C., bade a voyage from Sumer to the sunset land "where he was poisoned by an insect and buried there". In May 1969 Thor Heyderdahl of "Kon-Tiki" fame with six other men sailed from the Moroccan port, Safi, for the Caribbean in a papyrus boat, an exact copy of Egyptian ships of 1800 B.C. thereby proving that crossings of the Atlantic by the ancient Egyptians were possible, even probable. Papyri tell of red beings met by the

52

Sumerians when sailing up a great river. The astonishing similarity between many Peruvian and Sumerian words, almost identical buildings, religions and ceremonies, suggest intercourse between South America and Babylon in ancient times. Legends of a white god roaming North and South America teaching and healing people suggest that Cretans from Knossus may have reached America during the Second Millennium B.C.

Tantalizing references in the classics hint that some Greeks and Romans were vaguely aware of the existence of America. Plutarch in "De Facie in Orbe Lunae" writes:

"To the west of the ocean there are many islands peopled by men of red skins and beyond these islands there is a vast continent with great navigable rivers."

Aelian in "Varia Historia" mentions "an unknown continent of vast blooming meadows and pastures"; the learned Seneca in "Hippolytus" talks of "a land on the remotest confines of the world separated by ocean's tracts" and in "Medea" prophesies:

"There will come an age in the far-off years when ocean shall unloose the bonds of things, when the whole broad Earth shall be revealed when Tethys shall disclose new worlds and Thule not be the limit of the lands."

Lucian and Diodorus Siculus describe islands far across the western ocean, which may have been the West Indies.

The Greek philosophers knew Earth was round; Eratosthenes and Strabo probably demonstrated its sphericity by means of a ball, their logical minds would surely reason that the Eurasian land-mass in their own hemisphere was symmetrically balanced by a similar continent on the unknown side of the world.

In the town library at Nancy, France, was a globe in brilliant color six inches in diameter, whose recorded history dated back to AD 1531 although it was centuries older; this global map showed the whole continent of North and South America apparently in prehistoric times. The general contour as far as could be determined from such a small scale was roughly similar to modern maps with the startling differnece that California now a peninsula appeared as an island, possibly the eastern edge of submerged Lemuria; swamplands in the Sacramento valley, sea-shells found in the soil and the strand-lines along local hillsides prove that long ago California was separated from the mainland. This remarkable map must have been thousands of years older than those intriguing Piri

Reis maps, said to date from 3000 B.C. or even earlier. The 16th century Turkish admiral and cartographer, Piri Reis, copying ancient maps showed California joined to the American continent, ice-free Greenland as three large islands, since confirmed by a French polar expedition, mountain-ranges in Canada, the exact course of the river Atrato in Yucatan, the Falkland isles not officially discovered until 1592, the Andes adorned with llamas and the exact contour of the Antarctic before its ice-cap. Such accurate mapping of the coastline and of details far inland suggests observation from the air by aircraft of a former civilization or by spaceships; the cartographers obviously possessed great mathematical skill presupposing advanced technology. The map on the Nancy globe showing a separate California clearly proves that thousands of years before the Piri Reis maps were originally drawn highly technical experts made aerial surveillance of the Americas.

Astronomers believe our Earth to be 4,500 million years old, geologists estimate that about eight hundred million years ago North America formed part of Laurasia and South America part of Gondwana. Theologians teach that God created the universe for the manifestation of Man, who appeared on Earth shortly after its creation without having to wait countless ages to evolve from the slime of the sea to a sentient being, a process to tax even God's patience. Extraterrestrials from other stars in our galaxy could have landed here and colonized our world hundreds of millions years ago, their bones long since dissolved to dust. Dr. L.S.B. Leakey has found in Kenya jaw-fragments of a man-like being living twenty million years ago; palaeontologists suggest the creature was savage yet he could have been wiser than Socrates. Prehistorians still teach that despite America's vast age it remained a virgin continent cut off from the rest of the world until about 20,000 B.C. when small groups of Asiatic nomads trudged across the Bering Straits from Siberia to Alaska then slowly took their stone age culture down the long coast to Patagonia. Anthropologists accept that during the last ten thousand years Man despite many setbacks has evolved from caves to spaceships but illogically insist that for the previous twenty million years human evolution was presumably suspended, men lived in a trance. There is ample evidence to suggest that down the ages Man has not progressed but degenerated. If men did live in Africa millions of years ago, surely contemporary men must have

53

lived in America. The spacemen who landed in the ancient east would also land in the ancient west.

The creation myths from North and South America show astounding similarity to those from Europe and Asia suggesting some central origin long ago, the simple tales often conceal great wisdom anticipating the teachings of theology and science today. The Omaha Indians believed that in the beginning all things were in the mind of Wakinda, all creatures including Man were spirits, they descended from the sun, then to the moon, finally to Earth, supposing that our planet was colonized by spacemen. The Winnebago Indians of Wisconsin evoked Genesis stating that the Earthmaker wished for light and it became light, he again wished for Earth and it came into existence; he took a piece of Earth, breathed into it and created Man. The Yakuts in California thought a supernatural being called Kodayarma with the coyote alighted on the primeval ocean, the coyote said "Let this become sand" and it became sand. The Indian tribes of the eastern woodlands believed in an All-Father like Zeus and Odin, on the northwest coast they imagined an old chief living in a house in the sky, the "Father in Heaven"; in the great forests the Indians believed in the Great Manitou, a supreme, formless, all-embracing spirit, called by the Pawnees of the plains "Tirawa Atius", the unknown power. The Iroquois, Hurons and Wyandots taught that the first people lived in the sky before the Great Turtle created Earth on the face of the waters; the Pueblo Indians believed that the god, Awonanwilome, existing in primeval darkness, thought into existence fogs bearing life-germs and from his own flesh made earth and sky. The Algonkians told a sophisticated creation myth about Gluskap killed by his evil brother Malsuni, then magically restored to life, reminiscent of Osiris and Set, he created the world from the bones of his mother, conquered the stone-giants and wrought great wonders; the Caribs said the Sky Father and Earth Mother came together and generated humanity. The "Popul Vuh", the original "Book of the People" written in the Quinche language of Guatemala, a transliteration of an ancient native chronicle, stated that in the beginning all was in suspence, all calm, in silence, motionless, the sky was empty, over the tranquil sea nothing existed only the Creator, the Maker, Tepeu, Gucumatz, the forefathers were in the water surrounded with light, they together created Earth and formed men out of wood, parallel to the Scandinavian belief of men made from trees. The Awawak Indians of South America believed men were created from stones, a remarkable affinity with the Greek legend of Deucalian and Pyrrha.

New discoveries in geology show that there have been many violent changes in continents and seas, climates and cultures, apparently explained by a shifting of Earth's axis and displacement of the poles, as recorded by Herodotus, who dated the last great cataclysm as about 11,000 B.C., contradicted by Immanuel Velikovsky, whose revolutionary thesis "Worlds in Collision" proves catastrophes in 1500 B.C. and 800 B.C. Evidence of those titanic disasters devastating our planet remembered in legends still exists all over the world, especially in North America. In his masterly study "Earth in Upheaval" Velikovsky marshals impressive data proving the fantastic cataclysms convulsing the continents in historical times witnessed by Man; the chronology he gives may be open to challenge, some catastrophes may have occurred thousands of years earlier causing the destruction of Mu and Atlantis; whatever the precise date, it is obvious that more than once the whole American land-mass and its people suffered earthquakes, floods and changes of climate, which must have shattered all civilization and plunged the stricken survivors back to barbarism from which they slowly emerged. In Alaska several miles of frozen silt contain the fossils of millions of mammoths, mastodons and animals now extinct, skin, hair and flesh mingled with uprooted trees, as in the Ivory Islands off Siberia, stone artifacts at great depths showed that Man lived in America in Pleistocene times and hunted elephants and sabre-toothed tigers. Immense erratic blocks of granite torn from Canada and Labrador weighing thousands of tons were piled high on mountains in New Hampshire, Massachusetts, Wisconsin and Connecticut; block limestone strata in Ohio and Michigan were packed with splendidly preserved fish, the skeletons of whales are found in Vermont and Montreal. Deep canyons of the St. Lawrence and Hudson Rivers stretch for hundreds of miles into the ocean indicating that land had become sea in post-glacial times; sea once flooded the great plains from Mexico to Alaska; in Nebraska are buried the smashed bones of thousands of rhinoceros, clawed horses and giant swine violently destroyed. In Montana for hundreds of miles mountains have been suddenly thrust up, vast flows of lava covered two hundred thousand square miles of Washington, Oregon and Idaho with layers hundreds even thousands of feet thick suggesting scores of separate ejections during the Cenozoic

54

Age of mammals and Man. Along the Atlantic coastal plain from New Jersey to northeast Florida are thousands of marshy depressions, bays filled with sand and silt, these oval craters inexplicable by geologic action are now believed to have been caused by meteoric impact, a comet probably struck from the northwest; in Labrador the Chubb circular meteoric crater covers an area of four square miles, probably made by an asteroid four thousand years ago; this is six times as large as the famous Arizona crater attributed to a comet. Soundings and analysis of sediments prove that the Mid-Atlantic Ridge is volcanic, the lava spread comparatively recently, not long ago there were land and beaches in Mid-Atlantic suggesting Plato's Atlantis. Paleomagnetism shows that the magnetic poles were reversed, violent changes of climate caused ice ages, millions of people and animals were killed, continents became changed, civilizations destroyed. A veil of twilight mystery shrouded North America, amid the cyclopean ruins of the cataclysms few monuments remained to record the mighty past.

Although scientists divide our Earth's past into geologic ages and teach that cataclysms have changed lands into seas and seas into lands popular opinion guided by Genesis vaguely reckons only two distinct periods, before and after Noah's flood. The Indians and Aztecs had more accurate knowledge, they agreed with the Hindus, Greeks, Scandinavians and Irish that four previous world ages had flourished and been destroyed. The Pawnees taught that when the end of the world was coming the moon would darken, the sun become dim, the north and south stars dance in the sky, Earth would be destroyed in meteor showers, probably race-memories of the same cosmic cataclysms recorded in the ancient east; they tell how Tirawa Atius placed giants on Earth, who grew proud and had to be destroyed in great floods, a legend repeated by the Creek Indians, they recall cannibal giants, deluge, monsters and only few people saved. The Navajos call our present world the fifth world, they suggest men travelled from world to world as though in space but they may really refer to our own Earth through five ages in time. The Mayas had a most profound conception of time and apparently believed in eternal recurrence when creation would come to an end, then return to its beginnings taught by the Yogis, Greeks and our own scientists. The Nahuas on the high Mexican plateau relate in the "Annals of Cuanhitlan" that our present era of the fifth sun is in decline, all creatures suffer

continual trials by the gods, and if any species fails it is destroyed, a remarkable anticipation of the teachings of palaentologists today. The Mexican native historian, Ixtlilxochitl, in his "Historia Chichemeca" described only four ages, the first age was Atonatiuh, (water-sun) when all men perished in a great flood; the second age, Tlachitonatiu, (Earth-sun) ended with violent earthquakes when the Quinames, the Aztec-Titans, were destroyed, probably the cataclysm engulfing Atlantis. The third age, Ecatonatiuh, (wind-sun) decimated the human race by terrific hurricanes reducing the few survivors to the level of monkeys. We are still living in the fourth age, Tlatonatiuh, (fire-sun) due to be destroyed by fire, a fate prophesied by alleged spacemen, who warn of the imminent intrusion of a second sun into our solar system causing planetary conflagration. The French ethnologist, Jacques Soustelle, renowned for his brilliant studies of the Mayas as for his stormy politics, believes that our civilization is the fifth of a series and is certain to follow the previous four. Human destiny rises and falls in cycles, the wretched Indians of Yucatan starve among the ruins of a once prosperous past.

The ancient Quiches believed their first fathers were sorcerers and wizards; the "Popol Vuh" states they were "good and handsome men" who saw "the large and the small in the sky and on Earth".

"They were able to know all, and they examined the four corners, the four points of the arch of the sky and the round face of Earth."

Such knowledge of the heavens and the sphericity of Earth suggests these first men could travel in space; their wisdom was so vast that the Creator and Maker in displeasure said, "It is not well what our creatures, our works, say; they know all the large and the small." The gods took counsel and clouded the sight of men destroying their wisdom and knowledge, to confound their judgment the Creator while men slept made for them beautiful women. The "Popol Vuh" in Guatemala used almost identical terms as Genesis III v. 22.

"And the Lord God said 'Behold the Man is become as one of us to know good and evil and now lest he put forth his hand and take also of the tree of life, and eat and live for ever.' "

God had created Eve from Adam's rib as he slept. It is intriguing to note that Hesiod in Greece thousands of miles from Guatemala wrote that in the golden age men lived without women, a parallel

55

to Adam before Eve; legends reveal that the first inhabitants of Earth were the Uranids, an ancient stellar race colonizing our planet, who resembled those omniscient "first fathers" mentioned in the "Popol Vuh".

According to Hans Hoerbiger's questionable glacial cosmogony when the last moon loomed close to Earth, its powerful gravitational attraction produced giantism in vegetation, animals and Man himself; during the period without a moon with attenuated cosmic radiation human stature decreased until the capture of Luna, our present moon about 12,000 B.C. promoted growth again. Hoerbiger's theory does not explain the existence of pygmies who are believed to have inhabited Earth for thirty million years although they may have developed when there was no moon in the sky. Dr. J.K. Jessup apparently had access to recondite sources concerning spacemen and other mysteries, he wondered if the pygmy is related to the giants as the present horned toad is related to the dinosaur. Eyewitness allegations of extraterrestrials landing today tell of startling differences in stature, perhaps the giants and pygmies originated from different planets.

The Navajos and the Mayas believe in four previous world ages, implying that they know of the first cycle of mankind around the north pole and of the second cycle inhabiting Hyperborea, the circumpolar continent where the spacemen would probably land after approaching Earth through the northern vent in the Van Allen radiation-belts. Such knowledge proves that the Amerindians possessed most ancient traditions even dating from the Carboniferous Age of giant vegetation and reptiles when Central and South America formed part of the vast southern continent of Gondwana. The Zuni Indians have race memories of reptilian monsters, a tyrannosaurus contemporary with Man was drawn on a rock in the Hava Supai canyon, Arizona; metal tools were found deeply embedded in coal-seams as though they had fallen among the trees before the coal was compressed. On June 11th, 1891 at Morrisonville, Illinois, the "Times" recorded that a Mrs. S.W. Culp breaking a lump of coal discovered as the lump fell apart embedded in a circular shape a small gold chain about ten inches in length of antique and quaint workmanship; the chain was an eight-carat gold and weighed eight pennyweights. Professor R.W. Gilder discovered in Nebraska and Kentucky traces of a Tertiary civilization suddenly destroyed by the great ice age.

The third cycle of Man known to the Amerindians was associated with Lemuria, Mu, the great continent in the Pacific, whose high eastern coast is believed to form the western seaboard of North America. This section of Earth's crust is a notorious fault-zone, for millions of years earthquakes have ravaged the area, some experts prophesy widespread destruction there this century. For an immensely long period Lemuria slowly sank, before final submergence the Lemurians had close links with South America, whose vast Amazon inland-sea and canals led to the Atlantic and the islands of Atlantis. The Grand Canyon of Colorado suggests that some cataclysm once convulsed the region; western America, remnant of Lemuria, is therefore one of the oldest lands on Earth, home of one of the earliest races of Man attaining a high civilization, which must surely have attracted the spacemen; petroglyphs carved near mountaintops suggest communication with visitants from the stars.

Rosicrucian traditions teach that a remnant of Lemuria still exists little changed as California, said to be the oldest civilized land on Earth, full of ancient mysteries. Legend ascribes the name "California" to the beautiful queen Califa who long ago ruled this romantic golden island near to the Garden of Eden. Today such alluring tale finds reality in Hollywood whose glamour surely conjures visions from the magic past. Is it more than coincidence that "Los Angeles" means "the angels" or "The spacemen"; does some mystic power from the skies still inspire this land of many strange cults? The story of queen Califa and her wonderful island in the west was told by troubadours in Spain during the Crusades and had evidently descended from antiquity, such romance must have thrilled young Columbus gazing seawards dreaming of a new world which seduced the sea-dogs across the Spanish Main with all that potent magic now beckoning our cosmonauts to those mountains of the moon.

On rocks at Klamath Falls in neighboring Oregon, once a colony of survivors from Lemuria, are inscribed thousands of hieroglyphics suggesting the symbols attributed to Mu with vague affinity to Sanskrit and Greek, marine deposits prove the mountains were once under water indicating immense age. The Modoc Indians who lived there generations later believed the ancients were men of great learning and called this region "Walla-Was-Skeeny", an incomprehensible name until its sound suddenly resembles "Vallis Scientiae", Latin for "Valley of Knowledge", a startling discovery paralleled by the many Latin

56

and Greek words bejewelling the local dialect. More intriguing links between ancient America and Rome were provided in 1833 by the finding of a Roman coin at a depth of 30 feet near Norfolk, Virginia; in 1882 a farmer in Cass Co., Illinois, picked up a coin of Antiochus IV with an inscription in Greek, and in 1913 a Roman coin was discovered in an Illinois mound. Charles Fort mentioned that stone tablets engraved with the Ten Commandments were said to have been found in North American mounds. Coins of Marcus Aurelius have been unearthed in Cochin China, perhaps it is not too surprising that Roman coins should have also reached America.

In his fascinating book "Lemuria" written in 1931 Wisher S. Cerve recalls that for many decades a great white light occasionally rises above the forests in the valley of Santa Clara, clearly seen from San Francisco bay; this evokes that mysterious fire seen since ancient times across the Pacific in the bay of Yataushiro-kai in Kyushu, Japan, which has never been understood and appears there on a specific day or toward daybreak on the first day in August. Japanese researchers wonder whether this unknown fire is lighted from space and controlled for some purpose by the spacemen.

When Earth was young its population numbered few people, especially if its first inhabitants were colonists from other planets, a possibility which our future space-expeditions should support. Traditions confirmed by comparative linguistics tell of a single primordial language, said to be the solar tongue Solex Mal, spoken before the destruction of the Tower of Babel symbolizing the giants' rebellion against their space overlords, followed by catastrophes and dispersal of peoples all over the world. Language does change but only slowly; Plato could understand the Greek of modern Athens even the alleged democracy there, vast ages must surely have elapsed for the single world-language to develop into the 2,796 different languages spoken today. Though oral languages greatly differ, the symbols on petroglyphs in many countries apparently agree, suggesting a world-wide picture-writing understood by ancient peoples everywhere. The earliest literature bequeathed to us are the Sanskrit "Vedas", the Egyptian "The Book of the Dead" and the Sumerian "Gilgamesh Epic" ascribed to 3000 B.C. probably much earlier; in wisdom, sublimity of thought and poetic expression these works remain unsurpassed even today. If, as the evolutionists insist, language has evolved from primitive sounds, can we possibly estimate the ages it must have taken for the monosyllables of a savage to perfect into the sublime poetry of the "Upanishads"? Unless culture was brought to Earth by teachers from other planets it would surely require millions of years before men could develop the profundity of thought, literary genius and expressive vocabulary to compose those classics of the past. Much ancient wisdom is couched in signs we cannot read, eroded petroglyphs scattered forlorn all over the world, proof of the vast age of Man exists all around us not in objects but in ideas.

The existence of a world-wide civilization destroyed long ago may be established by many signs insignificant perhaps in isolation but which together form a wonderful mosaic depicting a brilliant, tragic culture in ages past; much could be written on this glorious epoch in prehistory but here it must suffice to prove its reality. Theologians and mythologists agree that the earliest religion was sun-worship associated with gods from the stars, also fertility cults symbolized by representations of the phallus, yoni and serpent. Archaeologists discover ancient worship of the sun from the Amazon to Africa and Japan, remnants of the cosmic religion taught by spacemen. It is usually assumed that monolithic blocks or towers found all over the world represent the male phallus and that stone circles or circular temples represent the female yoni, sexual symbols of the most ancient fertility cult; speculation now arises as to whether the obelisk was really intended to copy a rocket or spaceship and the circle signifying a flying saucer, a novel interpretation which may be more plausible than it seems. Solomon's famous temple was said to represent the plan of a spaceship seen by David, literally the "House of the Lord" means the "dwelling of the spaceman" which to the Israelites would appear as a ship from space. Perhaps our archaeologists are wrong in interpreting stone age symbols as referring to the phallus and yoni, what if instead they copy the spaceships, evidence of those illumined beings from the stars?

The ancients are believed to have inherited a psycho-electrical science with fantastic powers from their space teachers or from wondrous civilizations long vanished. Traditions hint that milennia ago black magicians developed sidereal weapons more potent that our hydrogen-bombs whose explosion shattered civilization, displaced the magnetic poles, modified the protective radiation-belts causing intensified cosmic-rays to mutate species and change climate convulsing

57

Earth in immense disaster. Later generations condemned all science as black magic and persecuted those who practised the secret arts periodically burning their books, secretly dreading perhaps that scientists would again cause cataclysms. Fragments of the ancient wisdom were preserved for thousands of years by initiates who concealed their lore in the cabbalistic language of alchemy, those quests for the Philosopher's Stone and the manufacture of gold now interpreted in the terms of modern physics reveal secrets of nuclear reactions, radio-activity and transmutation of metals just achieved by our own scientists. Metallurgists in ancient times studied the occult properties of metals which they distilled by techniques unknown today, astrologers determined the influence of radiations from the stars on human destiny, much arcane wisdom was cloaked by numerology and the symbolism of the Tarot, manipulation of natural forces is still practised by shamans and witch-doctors to kill or cure, acupuncture performed by Chinese doctors probably descended from a most ancient medicine with a different conception of Man. All this knowledge alien to our modern thought-patterns reveals a tantalizing glimpse of that golden civilization mentioned in the Sanskrit classics when celestials visited Earth and Earthmen flew to the stars.

The earliest manuscripts of ancient Europe and Asia chronicle garbled race-memories of world-empire ruled by celestials with fantastic powers who taught sun-worship; the giants rebelled, after titanic war in Earth and sky cataclysms changed the climate, frantic survivors migrated across continents, such tremendous events could not be confined to Eurasia, they must surely have influenced the Americas. No literature survives from ancient America, the "Popol Vuh" from Guatemala, the Aztec codices and Maya stoneglyphs are comparatively recent, they probably copy older records; legends from Canada to Patagonia tell substantially the same stories which our modern minds may misinterpret. Records probably exist in forms we fail to recognize. Centuries hence information will be stored in miniaturized computers suspended in satellites, historians conditioned to such technology may not understand books written today should any survive. Our own civilization ends in the dustbin, our rubbish is promptly destroyed, bull-dozers obliterate our churches for gasoline pumps, what will future archaeologists

find in our cemeteries, soon displaced by crematoria burning us all to ash, of our twentieth century what will remain?

The great initiates of the past are said to have distrusted writing lest their wisdom be misused for evil, they transmitted their teachings orally to their disciples; such primitive method cannot cope with complex ideas. The ancients must have used devices to record and transmit their knowledge still unknown to us; legends suggest that records for posterity were stored in time-capsules we have yet to discover; this is hardly fantasy for we ourselves are recording data for milennia to come on microfilm and sensitized tape secreted in sealed caskets at the bottom of wells. The entire Library of Atlantis might be electronically recorded on a couple of tin-cans which we in our ignorance would toss back in the sea.

Startling evidence of lost civilizations may exist all around us which our minds cannot recognize. John Michell in "The View Over Atlantis" (Sago Press, London, 1969) describes how all over the world men utilized some remarkable power to cut and raise enormous blocks of stone in circles of erect pillars, pyramids, underground tunnels, cyclopean stone platforms, often as astronomical instruments, linked by a network of tracks and alignments marked by stones, mounds and earthworks. This system of natural magic involving the use of polar magnetism and solar energy found particular expression in ancient China where the landscape itself was modified to align with "a network of invisible canals, along which flowed the dragon current with the influence emanating from the heavenly bodies". Mr. John G. Williams of Abergavenny with most remarkable research has traced an ancient system of scamb-lines with power potentials connecting prehistoric landmarks all over Britain, often coinciding with leys, ancient tracks, focal points of magnetic force, generally sacred sites now occupied by churches. Strange power still emanating from prehistoric stones has been detected on photographs taken by Mr. Williams, proving that radiations from that electrical civilization in the most remote past still persist today. The prehistoric leys significantly appear to coincide with the flight-paths of UFOs.

The veneration of mountain-tops by tribes in North and South America suggests that the American continent has zones of power, a national grid of electrical even psychic radiation from the most remote past, perhaps from magical Atlantis.

58

Chapter Eight
Spacemen in
Ancient North America

Though North America in Ancient times apparently did not bask in those golden cultures enchanting the Mayas, Incas and Tiahuanacans, its peoples claimed great antiquity. Caves and mounds all over the American continent reveal human remains mingled with the bones of animals; in 1866 Professor J.D. Whitney discovered the Calaveras human skull at a depth of 130 feet in auriferous deposits buried under lava more than twenty million years old of the Tertiary period on the western slopes of the Sierra Nevada, California; however the hoax of the Piltdown skull in Britain obviously questions its authenticity. In a Carboniferous layer at Cow Canyon, Nevada, the imprint of a human foot was found stamped in clay of the middle Tertiary era, long before the accepted appearance of Man. The fossil imprint of a sandal discovered near Delta in Utah astonished American geologists, for on the inside were two miniscule trilobites dated before the Cambrian period, the oldest of the Paleozoic era about 250 million years ago. Fossilised human tibia are embedded in quartzite near Eureka, Nevada; Alabama and Kentucky abound with pebble-tool sites, evidence of Man two million years old. In 1889 at Nampa in Idaho, Mr. M.A. Kutz drilled a 300 feet deep artesian well through layers of soil, lava, quicksand and clay, among the material sucked up by the pump appeared a tiny female figure only 1½ inches tall, apparently made from a plastic material baked or burned with fire. While hoax is possible, experts suggest that iron-oxide cementing quartz grains on the body indicates that the image dates from early Quaternary times being

the work of advanced Neolithic culture. This figurine parallels the celebrated "Venus of Willendorf"; a statuette found in oolithic limestone at Willendorf in Austria.

At American Falls, Idaho, bones of extinct bison are found with round holes incised in them, presumably by Man about 43,000 years ago; this find equals the discovery by Russian palaentologists in 1962 of a well-preserved bison at Yakuzia in Siberia; in its forehead was a circular hole believed to have been caused in ancient times by a projectile from firearms similar to our own. The animal did not die from the wound; examination showed that the injury healed. Did the hunters who shot the bison in Siberia also hunt in Idaho? Were they spacemen? A Delaware myth describes how the god of Indians on a mountain-top at Big Bone Lick, Kentucky, fired thunderbolts destroying a herd of huge animals except their leader who bounded away to the Great Lakes; this may be a race-memory of extraterrestrials hunting on Earth. In 1968 the Belgian zoologist, Bernard Heuvelmans, and the well-known American biologist, Ivan T. Sanderson, investigated a remarkable Neanderthal "man" preserved in a block of ice, said to have been found in the Bering sea, presumably originating from Siberia or Alaska. The "man" about six feet tall, normally proportioned, appeared Caucasian, of some white race, his body was almost entirely covered with long brown hair. The investigators were astonished to find that the back of the "man's" skull was shattered and the right eye destroyed as though by bullets from a high caliber

59

firearm. Scientists remain somewhat sceptical; the circumstances admittedly seem dubious but hoax has not been established. Can the "prehistoric man" have been shot by the hunters, possibly spacemen, who shot those American and Siberian bison so long ago?

James Churchward studied hundreds of rock-writings in the southern states and found signs of great civilizations in areas now desolate, confirmed by local legends. He concluded:

"We have positive proofs that the whole of western North America was peopled by highly civilized races during the latter part of the Tertiary era and before the geological glacial period. Those first civilizations of America came from a country called Mu."

The glaciers of the ice ages scoured most works of ancient Man from America, but a few ruins still remain to preserve the remote past. Beyond the Arctic Circle in 1939 the explorer, Stefansson, discovered a city of eight hundred houses, El Lutak, its strangely Semitic name known to the Eskimos as Ipiutak; the inhabitants had the fair hair and blue eyes of the Cro-Magnons with a sophisticated culture like the Mayas. Ancient artifacts in Ontario suggest a highly cultured race in Canada 17,000 years ago; worked flints are found in Alaska more than a hundred feet below the surface, evidence of immense age; partly-burned bison bones at Folsom near Lubbock, Texas, reveal the presence of Man about 9,900 B.C. In New England elegantly wrought drinking-vessels were blasted from solid rock, relics of exquisite craftsmanship ages ago. Across the central and southern states run chains of mounds similar to the pyramids of Egypt and Mexico; their geometrical construction would require considerable engineering and mathematical knowledge. Inside the tumuli are found copper and lead axes, bracelets, rings, silver ornaments, copper-plated with silver, oxydized iron and steel necessitating advanced metallurgy with techniques for obtaining intense heat. Ignatius Donnelly associated the Mound Builders with Atlantis, but James Churchward believed that before the sinking of Atlantis the Mississippi area was a shallow inland-sea; when Atlantis sank about 11,500 B.C. the waters drained into the Atlantic ocean; centuries later the Mound Builders came from Mexico; cosmic symbols on artifacts found in the mounds apparently originated in Mu. The mounds may have been built as fortifications against savage races threatening from the north, many were serpent-shape, similar to the serpentine mounds

near Stonehenge and in Brittany; the cult of the serpent has religious significance and is also associated with the serpent men, beings with great wisdom from space. The Mound Builders possessed knowledge of cosmic forces and their application with a psycho-electrical science different from our own, possibly taught by spacemen. This talented race suddenly disappeared like the Khmers of Cambodia; they may have been overwhelmed by invaders from the north or destroyed by cataclysms. Prehistoric peoples all over the world built lofty mounds and anxiously scanned the skies. Did they fear destruction by comets or hostility from spacemen? Such fantasies were not so fanciful as they might seem. Orthodox archaeologists who cannot accept Lemuria and Atlantis believe that all Amerindians, Mayas and Incas were descendants from small tribes of Asiatics who wandered across via the Bering straits and the Aleutians about twenty thousand years ago, then slowly roamed from north to south to build the great civilizations of Mexico and Peru. This theory appears to be challenged by traces of Sandia Man perhaps fifty thousand years old; sculptures of elephants, cliff-drawings of men attacking prehistoric monsters, flints and tools found under the bones of animals long extinct prove that Man must have inhabited America from most ancient times.

In his erudite work, "The Rise and Fall of Maya Civilization" Page 43, J Eric S. Thompson, the distinguished archaeologist, admits "The whole problem of early man in America is extremely complex and is still far from solved." A conclusion which all the experts ruefully support! Mr. Thompson continues:

"No specialist in the field supposes that America was populated by immigrants from across the Atlantic or from across the Pacific, although the possibility of late influences having reached the New World from Polynesia cannot be ruled out. (It is even less likely that at any time voyagers from Peru or elsewhere in Latin America sailed to Polynesia.)"

Such dogmatic assertions completely ignore the researches of James Churchward and Ignatius Donnelly and flout the famous Kon-Tiki expedition of Thor Heyerdahl, who in 1947 drifted on a balsa raft from Peru to Raroia proving that Amerindians migrated to Polynesia, a thesis expounded in Heyerdahl's masterly work "Amerindians in the Pacific". His theory seems equally valid in reverse, Polynesians could have landed in America. Today Sir Francis Chichester,

60

Sir Allan Rose and other yachtsmen circumnavigate the world in small boats; it is logical to assume that mariners from Egypt, Babylon and China would sail the Pacific to the lands in the west. The earliest Guatemalan manuscript "The Annals of Cakchiquels" compiled by the nobels of Totonicapan in 1554 states that their ancestors were "sons of Abraham and Jacob" who migrated to America in 587 B.C. Legends of flying-machines and the existence of aerial-maps suggest people flying to ancient America like the Eskimos who claim their ancestors were ferried to Canada by huge birds.

If the primitive folk of America had remained completely isolated from Eurasia how could they have evolved languages, architecture, religion and astronomy similar to, sometimes surpassing the advanced cultures of contemporary Egypt and Babylon? Why do the Quiches have noses like the Jews, and Mayas slant eyes of the Chinese? Many authorities believe that the Old World inventions were independently developed in the New World, a logical progression of evolution; this theory ignores that Australia was cut off from civilization for many centuries, there the Aborigines apparently degenerated and invented only the boomerang, living more primitive than Adam. The striking resemblances between Amerindian and Eurasian cultures suggest diffusion of ideas by intercourse of peoples from east and west promoted by the lost continents of Lemuria and Atlantis. A more fascinating source was probably the world-wide civilization long ago inspired by spacemen.

The Okanogan Indians of British Columbia tell an interesting legend which evokes the destruction of Lemuria and Atlantis. Long ago in mid-ocean existed Samah-tumi-whoo-lah, meaning "White Man's Island", whose white giants were ruled by a tall white queen called Scomalt with the powers of those supernatural beings, the Tahmahknowis. After ages of peace the giants warred killing each other, arousing Scomalt to anger; the queen broke off that portion of the island peopled by the wicked giants and pushed it out to sea. As the island floated tossed by wind and wave, all the people died except one man and a woman; before the land sank they built a canoe and paddled away for many days and nights until they reached America, smaller than it is now, and finally wandered to Okanogan country. During their long sea-journey both were so burned by the sun and lashed by storms that their white skins became tanned to reddish-brown; that is how the Indians got their color. This naive tale may be a race-memory of survivors from Lemuria and Atlantis who fled to America. Ethnologists now doubt whether America was originally peopled only by Mongols crossing from Siberia to Alaska and eventually wandering thousands of miles down to Patagonia; adventurous immigrants would probably land all along the Atlantic and Pacific coasts, then move inland as happened again after Columbus.

Since no remains of anthropoid apes or primitive ape-like men have been found in America, anthropologists who support Darwin's theory believe that the continent therefore had no indigenous inhabitants; with equal validity it could be argued that as there were no apes in America the first Americans did not descend from monkey-like creatures but from colonists from other planets; admittedly zoologists do establish close similarities between the behavior of Man and monkeys, some men claim to have much in common with their noblest friend, the dog. What does that prove?

The Hopi Indians, east of the Grand Canyon in Colorado, believe their ancestors emigrated to Earth from Mars and Maldek before the latter planet was destroyed by its evil inhabitants. The Navajos and the Zunis venerate blond sky gods and believe in other worlds from which their tribes travelled to Earth. The Hopi are said to resemble the Essenes, they practise simple farming and preach a cosmic philosophy and seem to have an astonishing affinity with the Old Testament Jews. Dr. George Hunt Williamson, who has made a profound study of the Hopi, claims that during the Miocene age many migrants arrived on Earth from planets around Sirius; this may account for the special veneration accorded to Sirius by the Egyptians and the Chinese. South-western America, once part of Lemuria, in far ancient times was known as Telos, visited by teachers from Venus in ships of light.

The Indians believed that the whole universe thrilled with life; every stone, every star, was possessed by a spirit; every tree, every bird, every animal, had a soul and language of its own; the very wind was the breath of some supernatural being. Some spirits were good, others evil; the Indians tried to win their favor or protection and to avoid their malevolence. This ancient peoples of Tibet, China, Greece and primitive folk all over the Earth even today, the latest discoveries in sub-atomic physics now suggest that all creation is one single, sublime thought; men and matter are all manifestations of spirit. Such a recondite view of

61

the universe in a glorious Pantheism reveals that the Indians, far from being superstitious savages, cherished many of the findings of our modern science; their witchdoctors or shamans practised occult powers controlling nature, their ritual dances often evoked rain from a cloudless sky just as some Tibetan lamas could call down showers of hail-stones. Most tribes believed in reincarnation, many great chiefs told how they had actually chosen their own parents and the time of rebirth as in Tibet the Yogis claimed to have decided the condition of their own rebirth by the constellations spangling the sky. These wonderful concepts, quintessence of occult wisdom, surely emanated from some world-wide advanced civilization or were taught by spacemen from the stars.

Powerful spirits lived on the mountain-tops; the bravest Indians never climbed above the snow-line lest he angered the gods, the most valiant Greek dared not scale Mt. Olympus to meet Father Zeus, demons danced on the hills of Japan; in every country in the world were sacred mountains, abode of the gods, were they landing-places for spaceships?

In 1883 within full view of Mt. Shasta, one of the loftiest peaks in California, Frederick S. Oliver began to write down occult communications from Phylos the Thibetan, an Atlantean adept, who revealed that as recently as thirteen thousand years ago Arizona was covered by Miti, an inland sea, the wonderful scenery and the gorge of the Grand Canyon in Colorado were the results of an awful dance of the solid crust of the globe, which drained the waters into the Gulf of California leaving the sea-bed as the Arizona desert. Phylos claimed that in one of the walls of the cliff at the base of Mt. Shasta was the entrance to a marvellous temple where he met masters of the Lothinian Brotherhood, who taught him their wisdom-religion during his last incarnation about 1885. This remarkable revelation appears to be confirmed by Wisher S. Cerve, he states that at the foot of Mt. Shasta live a strange community who sometimes materialize unexpectedly dressed in pure white and in sandals with long curly hair and majestic appearance, occasionally odd-looking individuals tall and graceful with lofty foreheads emerge from the forests and trade gold nuggets for commodities in neighboring towns, they avoid being photographed by suddenly disappearing. The strangers are said to hold midnight ceremonies beaming bright lights high in the air illuming buildings of marble and onyx. Long before 1947

when Kenneth Arnold saw his famous flying saucers near Mt. Rainier further north, Professor Edgar Lucien Larkin, Director of Mt. Lowe Observatory in southern California, saw three gold-tinted domes rising above the tree-tops near Mt. Shasta; at night they were surrounded by great white lights. Local people described peculiar, silver-like vessels rising in the air and floating above the mountains; when motor-cars approached the area their electric-circuits mysteriously failed and the engines stopped, phenomena associated with UFOs today. On a stone set up on the outskirts of the forests are hieroglyphics under which is an inscription "Ceremony of Adoration of Gautama". Wisher S. Cerve states that the word "Gautama" means the "Continent of America", however "Gautama" was the sacred name of Buddha; the annals of the Chinese empire for A.D. 499 include the document "Frisong" describing the visit of the Chinese Buddhist priest, Hoei-Shin, to Central and South America in the fifth century, he is said to have encountered a king named Ichi in Mexico; it is believed that a Chinese monk, Fa Hsien, landed in Mexico in A.D. 412. The visits of Buddhist priests many centuries ago arouse speculation whether this mysterious sect are Buddhists, although their ceremonies do seem associated with spacemen. Mt. Shasta is alleged by some sensitives to be frequented by the Titan-Atlan race, survivors of Lemuria and Atlantis, inhabiting the subterranean civilization of Agharta, one of whose tunnels to our surface-world emerges amid the California mountains.

Many tribes believed in a supernatural being called the Changer, who transformed the world at the inspiration of the Great White Spirit, the Indian conception of God. The Modocs said that Kumush, Old Man of the Ancients, descended with his daughter to the beautiful underground world of spirits, then he travelled to the upper world and built a house for himself and his daughter in the middle sky, where they are said to live even today. The Puget Sound Indians told how men became so wicked warring on each other that Dokibatle, the Changer, caused a flood on Earth destroying all mankind except an old woman and a dog from whom were born the next race of people. An enchanted giant bear from the south menaced all creatures, the Changer then sent a spirit-man with magic powers who brought wonderful gifts, taught men agriculture and hunting and showed the girls how to make skirts from the inner bark of trees. The spirit man killed the bear and built a large house with only one door in which he locked all

62

the evil deeds and diseases in the world. For many years people lived in bliss; then a young daughter with eager curiosity opened the door and released all the evils to plague mankind. A fascinating tale like Pandora's box told by Indians! The Changer was so angry he created an aerial demon to swoop down and seize any woman straying from home, an intriguing parallel to those amorous celestials in the Sanskrit classics. A Puyallup myth described how two sisters fell asleep and woke up in starland. there they married starmen but were so unhappy they dug a deep hole and climbed down a rope back to Earth where the elder sister gave birth to a baby; later the Changer descended to Puget Sound and taught men to make fire, his footprints can still be seen on the shores of Chuckanut bay. The Quillayutes recalled a time when a wicked man stole the sun, people shot arrows up into the darkness and made an arrow-ladder from ground to sky; they seized the sun and left it fixed in the heavens. This story probably summarizes Indian memories of the same cosmic catastrophe blotting out the sun mentioned in Greek and Chinese legends. The Blackfeet Indians believed every star was once a human-being, a race-memory perhaps of spacemen; they told a popular myth about seven sisters in the skies, the next-to-youngest loved a mortal, she grew weary with grief and covered her face with a veil then vanished, so people now see in the heavens a cluster of only six stars called the Pleiades. The prophet, Job, sang of "the sweet influence of the Pleiades", the Greeks extolled them as the Seven Daughters of Atlas, the Chaldeans called them "Chimah", the "hinge" of the heavens. How did the Indians without telescopes (?) know of the disappearance of a star in this far distant constellation, an awareness shared by ancient peoples all over the world? The Indians fervently believed in the sky people who often descended to Earth; they pictured the lord of the sky as an old chief on a cloud, once when the sky was much nearer Earth he became so angry at the constant strife among men that he moved mountains and caused earthquakes. The Snohomish in the lands near modern Washington complained that the Creator had made the sky so low that tall people bumped their heads against it, others climbed trees and entered the sky world. Wise men from local tribes decided to push the sky back, the people assembled one day and pushed with long poles exerting all their strength; after prodigious effort and shouting they succeeded in pushing the sky to its present height, since then no one can climb into the sky world. The Queets

rememberd how two young girls on the prairie watching the stars were suddenly taken by two men up into skyland, the chief and all his tribe ascended a ladder of arrows from Earth to Heaven, they defeated the sky people and brought the girls back to Earth.

Many Indian stories mentioned supernatural creatures, notably the Thunderbird, an eagle with an extra head on its abdomen which was powerful enough to carry off whales in its talons, lightning flashed from its beak, the flapping of its wings roared thunder. This giant bird lived in a lofty mountain-cave and so terrified men with his noise that none dared approach. Ages ago when the land of the Quillayutes was lashed by storms and the sea roared, the people unable to hunt or fish were starving to death. The chief prayed to the Great Spirit. Soon all heard thunder and flashes of lightning. The Thunderbird descended with a giant whale which saved the tribe from starvation. This memory may signify a spaceship which landed with food to save the Indians' lives, similar aid from celestials is recorded in legends all over the world.

On the great plains the Dakotas worshipped a watchful sky father guarding the world, watching and directing men and animals; the spirits in the sky often descended to Earth in human form inspiring warriors, controlling storms and altering the path of migrating buffaloes. The Indians believed the spirits could only be propitiated by human pain, so inflicted on themselves fearful tortures during their ceremonial sun dances. In the spirit world one's ancestors lived in villages greater and more beautiful than those of Earth. Like the Irish, Germans, Japanese and peoples all over the world the Indians believed in fairies, hob-goblins, water-spirits, the "little folk", living in other realms and often materializing before men. The Iroquois of the eastern woodlands believed that a woman fell from the sky pregnant with twins; Tsentso was good, Taweskare evil, together they shaped the Earth; this myth agrees with legends from Greece and Scandinavia suggesting that Earth was colonized by men from the stars. The Arikara on the prairies thought men came from a previous world under the Earth, which recalls the tales of that great subterranean civilization Agharta said to be peopled by survivors from Atlantis. The great sky spirit, Nesaru, sent a flood to destroy the evil giants on Earth, he created men from seeds underground and sent the corn mother to lead them to the sunlit surface. The corn mother like the Greek goddess, Demeter, brought maize and taught the people agriculture, after she had

63

returned to the skies the Indians quarrelled, so the corn mother descended again with Nesaru himself, a wonderful man with beautiful long hair, together the celestials taught men about the stars, the gods in the sky, how to live in peace and cure disease. They evoke Osiris and Isis, who came from the skies to civilize Egypt. The Indians held maize or Indian corn in special veneration as a special gift from the Great Spirit. The Odjibwa-Algonquins called maize "Mon-da-min" or "spirits' grain" and told of the stalk in full tassel descending from the sky under the guise of a handsome youth. This symbolism may represent virility, but it could be a race-memory for space-teachers who are believed to have brought wheat to Earth from the planet, Venus. The poet, Henry Wadsworth Longfellow, in "Oneota", p. 83, relates that it was the practice of the Indian squaw when a field of corn had been planted, to choose the first dark night and to make a complete circuit of the area entirely naked trailing her robe behind her; her footsteps were believed to radiate a protective magic ensuring a full crop and drawing a charmed line which insects and worms would not cross. Our own farmers complaining of poor crops now know what to do, a walk round the field by their nude wife might do more good than Lady Godiva.

The Chippewas told of Betsune Yeneca, a magic boy from the stars, the Osages referred to the Mikake or star people. In the northern forests the Crees believed the sky father was aided by the trickster known as Wisagatcak or Manabozo, who taught men civilization or occasionally behaved like a demon causing wilful destruction. Henry Wadsworth Longfellow embellished a cycle of Algonkian legends about this fascinating celestial for his epic "Hiawatha", although the real Haio-hwa-tha was a distinguished Mohawk chief who sought in the fifteenth century before the white man, to unite all the tribes in an Indian United States. Longfellow portrayed his hero as an American-Prometheus and copied the meter of the Finnish "Kalevala". The scene of the poem "By the shores of Gitche Gumee, by the shining big sea water", was set among the Ojibways on the southern shore of Lake Superior. Hiawatha like Quetzalcoatl in Mexico taught agriculture and the arts of peace; he fought and slew a giant from the shining wigwam of the Manito of Wampum, a mighty magician suggesting a spaceman; and his mission complete soared toward the sunset in his magic canoe which moved with a melodious sound at the hero's command. The Nootkaus remember the visit of a god who came long ago in a copper canoe, an intriguing parallel with Vainamoinen, hero of the "kalevala" who sailed off in a copper boat to a celestial land in the skies; copper was universally regarded as a metal with occult properties and associated with the planet, Venus.

In her fascinating book "He Walked the Americas" L. Taylor Hanson quotes tribal legends telling of a white prophet, perhaps an Essene, an early follower of Jesus, who roamed through North and South America preaching divine truth, healing the sick and teaching all men the arts of peace. The Chippewas described him as bearded and pale of feature with grey-green eyes, copper colored hair, arrayed in long white robe wearing golden sandals; he wrought wonders in Georgia, Oklahoma, Mississippi, Dakotah, Wyoming and Mexico, where he was venerated as Quetzalcoatl. Some legends state this fair god arrived by ship from beyond the seas, a Pawnee tale says he suddenly appeared "like a creature from another planet, shining with a strange radiance, each hair of his head luminescent, his garments glowing and his sea-eyes flashing with lightning"; a description strangely evocative of those "angels" in the Bible and even of Orthon from Venus who met George Adamski. The ancient Pawnee medicine-men were great astronomers, they dominated the tribe by prognostications from the planets; like the Egyptians, Babylonians and Chinese the Indians held special reverence for the north star, associated with the gods, probably spacemen visiting Earth through the north polar vents in the Van Allan radiation-belts. To Venus, the morning star, the Pawnees every four years sacrificed a young maiden stripped nake, painted half-red and black. The fair victim tied to a scaffold was killed by young warriors with a rain of arrows, the people believed her blood blessed the tribe ensuring propitious fortune during the next four years. This veneration for Venus rather than for the moon is most significant and suggests some occult link with that lovely planet. The white prophet appeared in many parts of the American continent in an age when travel by conventional means was difficult, he may symbolize mariners from Minoan Crete or even the many spacemen who landed in America long ago.

The Blackfoot Indians tell a beautiful story of a maiden called Feather-woman who met by the river-side a fair young man who said he was the morning star and had descended from the sky in answer to her prayers that she loved him. He took a rich yellow plume from his hair and asked her to hold it in one hand and a juniper branch in the other, she closed her eyes and when she opened

64

them again she was standing in the sky country. Eventually the pair had a son but the girl become so homesick that she asked the spider man to let her down by a web, she returned like a falling star to the lodge of her people. Soon the girl longed to return to her husband in the skies, this was forbidden and she died of a broken heart; the son, Pois, (Scarface) after many adventures succeeded in reaching his father, Morning Star, in the sky country. A story in reverse was told by the Chippewayas. Algon, a hunter, while walking over the prairie discovered a circular pathway worn by many feet, although outside the perimeter no marks were visible. He hid in the long grass and hearing the sound of wondrous music growing louder and louder he beheld a white speck slowly expanding into an osier car in which were seated twelve beautiful maidens. They descended into the magic ring and danced round and round with such exquisite grace that Algon fell in love with the youngest girl, she eluded him and rushed to the car and all flew whence they came. Next day she returned, they married and had a son. The star maiden still thought of her own country, one day she made a basket of osiers, sang the magic song and returned with the child to the skies. Algon's grief was bitter, for years he mourned spending nearly all his time in the magic circle; at last he was overjoyed to see his wife and son descend and he willingly agreed to return with them to the star country. This story recalls that Apsara, Urvasi, who winged down to marry her earthly lover, Pururavas;

also that beautiful damsel from space who in A.D. 1070 married Edric the Wild after he had met her and her sisters dancing in a forest inn; both these brides left their husbands and returned to their celestial home; the same tale is told in Tibet and Scandinavia. Why should this romance of a celestial marrying an earthman be so popular world-wide? Can it be some race-memory of intercourse with extraterrestials in ages past.

The Navajos tell of a prophet who made a strange voyage in a hollow log with windows of crystal and guided by the gods.

The ancient civilizations of North America were probably devastated by the cataclysms destroying Lemuria and Atlantis; the shattered Eastern seaboard was left forlorn like the west coast of Europe. Some legends suggest that the red Indians may be descendants from survivors who had taken refuge in caverns deep underground from cosmic-ray bombardment. It is difficult to separate fact from fancy; archaeologists of genius have devoted their lives to unearthing ancient America; even their most brilliant researches cannot resurrect the civilizations which must surely have existed in the west as in the east during the remote past. Whatever the truth, the Atlantic was veiled in mystery for many milennia, very few ships crossed the ocean, on both sides once prosperous ports filled with silt sprawled in desolation. Such tremendous events in our world's history must surely have been watched by spacemen.

Chapter Nine
Space Gods of the
Aztecs and Mayans

"It is many days according to our writings since we were informed by our ancestors that neither I nor all those who inhabit this land are natives of it. We are strangers and came hither from far distant parts. We are equally aware that a lord whose vessels all were, brought our race to this country, then returned to his own land."

In A.D. 1519 Emperor Montezuma II welcomed Hernan Cortes and his conquistadores to Tenochtitlan with all the honor our own queen would accord to men from Mars; he explained that the Aztecs were only recent arrivals in Mexico, whither their ancestors had been led by a bearded white man of great wisdom, Quetzalcoatl, who ruled with beneficence then sailed toward the sunrise. The ill-fated Montezuma told how before the hero departed, he promised that his descendants would return to subdue the country and reduce the people to obedience. Quetzalcoatl himself would return and restore the Aztecs to their faith. In awe the emperor added:

"You tell us that you come from where the sun rises, the things you tell us of this great lord or king who sent you hither to us, we believe and take it for certain that he is our natural lord, especially as you tell us that he has known of us for many days. And therefore you may be certain that we shall obey you and accept you as lord in place of this great lord of whom you speak."

Montezuma surrounded by his brilliant court surrendered himself, his people and all his possessions to the bearded Spaniards, later to learn in disillusion before he died that these plundering white men were not gods but gangsters.

Fourteen years later in Peru Atahualpa venerated Don Francisco Pizarro as descendant of the divine Viracocha; before he was tortured, then strangled, the Inca saw his land sacked by the gold-crazed conquistadores.

How did a few hundred Spanish adventurers smash two great empires and drag their golden civilizations down to slavery, when the powerful Aztec and Inca priests could have stretched all the ruffians on those stone altars and torn out their bleeding hearts for the gods?

Long before the thirteenth century when the Aztecs wandered from Aztlan, north of the Colorado to settle among the Toltecs on the plateau of Mexico, the peoples of Central and South America treasured memories of a fair god who had taught their ancestors all the arts of civilization then left them warning that one day he would return in a one reed year bringing a time of tribulation. Those highly religious souls who willingly sacrificed themselves to the sun for eternal life probably anticipated the return of their savior with the same fervor that the Jews awaited their own Messiah. The Aztec priests divined that the god would be white-skinned with black beard and dressed in black, he would chasten the sinful land with deserved sorrow. In the one reed year corresponding to A.D. 1363 the nation waited in vain, the prophecy then centered on the following one reed year 1467 and finally all the omens prognosticated the fateful one reed year 1519. Aztec traditions prophesied that in the thirteenth

66

era white strangers would arrive from the east, dethrone the emperor and enforce a new religion; the Maya priest, Chilan Balam, in a strange prophecy declared that at the end of the thirteenth age the signal of god would appear on the heights and the cross would manifest brought by barbarians, bearded guests from the east; in Peru the dying Inca Huayna-Capak prophesied that during the reign of the thirteenth Inca (Atahualpa) white men would "come from the sun" and subjugate the Incas. All these prophecies came true!

Montezuma, elected to the Aztec throne in 1502, was renowned as soldier and priest; he had earned distinction in the imperial wars raising the empire to its glittering zenith overlording Central America; like Numa Pompilius of ancient Rome he communed with the gods and devoted much time to religious observance, honored even by the Spaniards, for the Codex Mendoza described him as "a learned astrologer, a philosopher and skilled in all the arts". This tragic hero-king haunted by a destiny he could not avert was aptly named, for "Montezuma" meant "sad or severe man", he was grave and reserved inspiring sanctity; the messengers announcing his election to the throne found their future monarch sweeping the steps of the war god's temple. After his accession Montezuma suddenly abandoned his former humility for estentation and extravagance evoking the Roman emperors and displayed an arrogance which alienated his allies and gravely weakened the empire. At the time of the conquest he was aged about forty; tall and graceful, dignified like a benign prince, his features were paler than his copper-colored countrymen; his white cotton cloak and sandals were studded with jewels, his head was crowned with plumes symbolizing the emperor's descent from the gods, the spacemen. For years strange portents alarmed the Aztecs. In 1510 the lagoon became convulsed without earthquake or storm, water flooded the streets of Tenochtitlan destroying many buildings; in 1511 the great temple of the sun suddenly burned with a fire which could not be put out, arousing speculation as to whether these erratic incidents were possibly caused by spaceships, for in subsequent years comets were seen which could have been UFOs. Like King Conn of royal Tara, Montezuma is said to have patrolled the roof of his palace every night scanning the skies fearful of hostile influences from the air; fears well-founded for the belief in aerial demons kidnapping people persists in Mexico to this day. Shortly before the Spaniards landed a strange light shone in the east.

"It spread broad at its base on the horizon, and rising in a pyramidal form tapered off as it approached the zenith. It resembled a vast sheet or flood of fire, emitting sparkles, or as an old writer expresses it, seemed thickly powdered with stars. At the same time low voices were heard in the air, and doleful wailings, as if to announce some strange, mysterious calamity."

This intriguing UFO evokes those curious lights which in times of crisis haunted the skies of ancient Rome.

The superstitious king sought counsel from his chief astrologer, Nezahualpilli, who shattered him by interpreting the omen as presaging the swift destruction of the empire.

The much-loved Franciscan friar, Bernardino de Sahagun, contemporary with the conquest, whose great work "Hostoria Universal de Nueva Espana" awaited three hundred years for publication, was told in 1518 the emperor fell into a trance; looking into a mirror on a bird's head he perceived "reeds like men approaching and mounted on deer". Montezuma had probably consulted the black mirror, said to have been brought to Central America by ancestors of the Quiches from ancient Egypt, also known to the Hindus, Tibetans and Chinese wherein the adept could behold past, present and future unfolded before his eyes. Soon messengers arrived from the coast describing white-skinned, bearded, long-haired strangers who landed from "hills moving in the sea", the galleons of Juan de Gujalva; they all sailed east but their leader promised that other men like himself would return the following year. Fray Diego Duran in his "Historia de las Indias de Nueva Espana" finished in 1581 tells of a shepherd in the province of Tezcoco calmly plowing his fields when a mighty eagle descended upon him and transported him to a dark cave high in the mountains; there a voice commanded him to go and warn Montezuma that his god was angry, the emperor's reign was coming to an end, he had been the cause of his own ruin.

The most extraordinary wonder of all, reported by the Abbe Clavigera in "Storia Antica del Messico" (Cesena, 1780), concerned the resurrection of Montezuma's sister, Papantzin, the day after her burial to warn the monarch of the approaching downfall of the empire. The funeral of the princess was attended by the emperor in person; her body was interred in the subterranean vaults, their entrance secured by a stone. Next morning Papantzin appeared in the garden to her young niece, friends who saw her swooned or fled,

67

eventually she persuaded her uncle, Nezahualpili, the chief astrologer, to conduct her to the emperor at once. Montezuma accused her of being an evil demon, who had taken the likeness of the princess, she soon convinced him and his noblemen, then told the assembled court an extraordinary story. At the moment of death the princess had found herself in a valley beside a great river of rushing waters.

"By the borders of this I saw a young man clothed in a long robe fastened with a diamond, and shining like the sun, his visage bright as a star. On his forehead was a sign in the figure of a cross. He had wings, the feathers of which gave forth the most wonderful and glowing reflections and colors. His eyes were as emeralds and his glance was modest. He was fair, of beautiful aspect and imposing presence."

The apparition took her by the hand and conducted her through the valley where she saw black people building a house.

"Turning toward the east for a space, I beheld on the waters of the river a vast number of ships manned by a great host of men dressed differently from ourselves. Their eyes were of a clear grey, their complexions ruddy, they carried banners and ensigns in their hands and wore helmets on their heads. They called themselves 'sons of the sun'."

The wondrous strangers enjoined the princess to return to her people and announce to them what she had seen, that it might profit them. That distinguished authority, Lewis Spence, comments that Papantzin's resurrection is "one of the best authenticated incidents in Mexican history" and he adds, "it is a singular fact that Papantzin was one of the first persons to embrace Christianity".

Although this tale evokes well-known stories alleging spacemen, it seems likely that the princess was a highly-developed psychic, perhaps a partaker of the sacred mushroom a potent hallucinogen with strange powers popular today in Mexico. She probably fell into a deep trance, mistaken for death; after burial in the vault the princess had the good fortune to recover consciousness and get out.

This warning confirmed the emperor's worst forebodings; all the heavenly signs prognosticated that within twelve months in the next reed year Quetzalcoatl would fulfil his promise of long ago and return, presaging dire calamities. Tradition suggested the fair god would come by sea but Montezuma and his expert astronomers, no doubt aware of the UFOs haunting their land, probably

expected him to descend from heaven. Montezuma, a highly-cultured philosopher-king, believed in previous world-ages and realized that soon their own civilization was destined to be destroyed; he and his priests took long and solemn counsel on how the god should be received. In their natural peril religious faith triumphed, when at last their god returned, all must welcome him with humble submission. Montezuma was no weakling, he had led the Aztecs with energy and enterprise in nine great battles and had raised the empire to unparalleled splendor; with overwhelming superiority he could have annihilated Cortes and all his conquistadores on the beaches as they were landing. Less superstitious members of the council opposed Montezuma's surrender and urged resistance to the invader. Mexico was a theocracy like ancient Egypt and Tibet, religion dominated life from birth to death; for centuries the Aztecs had awaited the return of Quetzalcoatl, the decision of the priest-king meant divine law. Christians believe in the second coming, how would Man today react if some wondrous personage suddenly appeared?

Montezuma's dilemma may confront us. What if spacemen this century land in our cities with a science eclipsing our own? Shall we receive them in peace or war? Like that ill-fated emperor of the Aztecs could we avert our destiny?

Hernan Cortes, a ruthless adventurer aged thirty-four from Estremadura, lured by those tales of fabulous treasure exciting Spain, stormed the New World with a fleet of eleven ships, the largest only one hundred tons, ten cannon, six hundred men and sixteen horses, to plunder a powerful empire, an exploit unparalleled in history. This extraordinary character in stature above middle height with pale complexion, large dark eyes, grave yet cheerful, well-proportioned, excelling in fencing and horsemanship, closely resembled Julius Caesar in temperament and martial enterprise; in his youth he failed as a lawyer so turned to arms to fulfil his restless ambitions; his notorious gallantry with women, scandalous even in that licentious age, hastened his departure for Cuba in 1506 where he eventually obtained command of the expedition to Mexico. Incensed at the cavalier conduct of Cortes, the governor Velasquez intended to give command to someone else; learning this Cortes sailed clandestinely before the orders for his dismissal could arrive. The young general vaunted the spirit of knight-errantry nearly a century before "Don Quixote" smiled Spain's chivalry away, cautious yet daring, generous but avaricious;

68

immoral though bigoted, Cortes showed greatness eclipsing the cruelty with which he is charged; he deliberately destroyed one empire to build another. Beloved by his men like Caesar he made powerful enemies, on return to Spain for a time he basked in the favor of Charles V enjoying honor and wealth, then fell into debt financing a disastrous expedition to Mexico. He died of dysentry near Seville in 1547, sixty-four; his bones were eventually deposited in a crystal coffin in the hospital of Jesus of Nazareth in Mexico City but a patriotic mob in 1823 scattered them to the four winds. A poetic revenge by the people he had conquered!

The conquistadores landed at San Juan, Ulloa, near the future Vera Cruz on April 21st 1519; eight months later after skirmishes, ambuscades and massacres on their bloody march through hostile country they reached the capital, Tenochtitlan. It was the good fortune of Cortes to have as interpreter, Marina, a spirited Indian slave, who soon became his mistress and gave him shrewd advice on native customs and tribal dissensions. The novel use of guns and horses new to Mexico won to the Spaniards many tribes rebelling against Montezuma but initially the superstitious Aztecs were paralyzed by their identification of the white men with their old gods. Cortes with his white skin and sable beard dramatically dressed in black, appeared to the Aztecs as the reincarnation of Quetzalcoatl, who had come from the East long ago, taught their ancestors the arts of civilization then departed promising one day to return; they were soon to suffer sorry disillusion. Montezuma's troubled soul soared beyond the harsh realities of deceit and violence around him; while he brooded over the miraculous return of the fair god and destined retribution the Aztec civilization was being destroyed, its people enslaved. Montezuma was probably aware of some landings by white men in North America since Columbus in 1492, just as we today marvel at rumors of spacemen; awed by omens and prophecies, perhaps deluded by destiny, the emperor felt he was acting out his fated role in a tragedy demanding his own death. The lust for gold, the brutality, the bloodshed, soon convinced Montezuma that Cortes though not a God had verily chastened his people with those dire tribulations warned by the prophets. Like the Quislings during the Hitler war Montezuma by his collaboration with the invaders outraged the whole nation; even then his unquestioned courage and leadership could have inspired the Aztecs to victory but in his heart he knew the fateful part he

was destined to play and submitted to Cortes. As the emperor attempted to appease the assembly with a pacifistic speech, the multitude incensed at this betrayal threw stones and wounded him in the head, a blow which did little harm. The Aztecs rose against the Spaniards, after savage fighting Cortes and his men fled from the City. Fray Diego Duran wrote that when the people stormed the palace to lynch Montezuma they found him dead with a chain about his feet and five dagger-wounds in his chest; murdered at the early age of forty-one presumably by the "white gods". W.H. Prescott in moving valedictory declared a century ago "Alas! the subject of this suspicious invocation lived to see his empire melt away like the winter's wreath; to see a strange race drop, as it were from the clouds on his land." We in our generation have seen the British empire melt away. Are we too destined to see "a strange race drop, as it were, from the clouds" on our own land?

Who was Quetzalcoatl, whose beneficence inspired the peoples of Mexico for hundreds probably thousands of years and whose emblem, the feathered serpent, dominated monuments and temples of Central America? The Italian Abbe Francisco Javier Clavigero described Quetzalcoatl as high-priest of Tula, center of Toltec culture.

"He was white in complexion, tall and corpulent, broad in forehead, with large eyes, long black hair, thick beard; a man of austere and exemplary life, clothed in long garments, gentle and prudent. He was expert in the art of melting metals and polishing precious stones which he taught the Tultecans."

Fray Juan de Torquemada, the 16th century Franciscan missionery, described him as fair and ruddy with long hair; like his twenty companions he was dressed in a long robe of black linen cut low at the neck with short sleeves, a dress worn by natives to this very day. The reign of Quetzalcoatl was the golden age of Mexico.

The origin of this fair god mystified the Aztecs and outraged the Spaniards startled at his close affinity with Christ; today his identification of this great culture hero varies from cosmic grandeur to folk-romance; the truth must be sought from his name Quetzalcoatl evoking that mellifluent language of Atlantis. The "quetzal" was a rare bird with green feathers, "coatl" a Nahua word for "snake", a combination of the Maya "co", "serpent" and Nahua word "atl" meaning "water", signifying "winged serpent". The Mayas called him "Kukulcan", the Quiches of Guatemala as "Gucumatz"; as "god of the air" he was known to

69

the Aztecs as "Ehecatl" and "Nanihehecatl" or "lord of the four winds"; his most intriguing title "Tlauizcalpentecutli", the "lord of light of dawn" identifies him with Venus. Legends state that Quetzalcoatl's mother was the virgin-coatlicue, his father the sun, resembling the divine birth of all saviors; one version alleges that his mother swallowed an emerald, the green jewel occultly associated with the planet, Venus. Traditions vaguely agree that Quetzalcoatl was a wise king who suddenly appeared from the east bringing the arts of civilization law, healing, the calendar and writing; also maize to the Nahuas, early inhabitants of the Mexican plateau. Like Buddha he taught men compassion and cosmic wisdom, the message of love and peace with a sublime reverence for transcending those bloodthirsty rites which degenerate priests were later to perpetuate in his name.

The Toltec myths state that Quetzalcoatl ruled men in wondrous peace and prosperity like the golden age of Saturn and those idyllic times mentioned in the Egyptian, Indian and Chinese classics. Envious of such good fortune Tezcatlipoca, god of the air worshipped by the invading Nahuas, plotted his downfall; their rivalry vaguely recalls the conflict between Osiris and Set, Saturn and Zeus. With a cunning suggestive of the Scandinavian Loki causing the death of Baldur, Tezcatlipoca disguised as a white-haired old man induced Quetzalcoatl, temporarily paralyzed, to drink a healing potion so efficacious that the hero recovered with sufficient virility to seduce his own sister, Quetzalpetlatl. In remorse at this fall from grace Quetzalcoatl decided he must return to the sun; after sad farewell to his sorrowful people he sailed eastward on a raft of serpents to the fabled land of Tlapallan, the country of bright colors. It intrigues us to wonder whether the raft of serpents was a spaceship whose force-field flashing electric discharges could perhaps be symbolized by serpents. This speculation is enhanced by another legend which tells how the god flung himself on a funeral pyre and from the flames ascended to the planet Venus evoking those translations to the skies of Hercules, Enoch, Elijah and Romulus. The Mexican "Codex Borgia" states that the evening star, Venus or Quetzalcoatl was represented by the Nahuas with the solar disc. Quetzalcoatl was occasionally regarded as the sun god but more often pictured as if emerging from the sun, his dwelling-place. Conventional interpretations may be wrong, perhaps the paintings depict a god alighting from a flying saucer? Fantastic though it

seems, this suggestion is surely more logical than the idea that Quetzalcoatl came from the sun itself, admittedly a belief which some early Christians associated with Christ. Temples to Quetzalcoatl were circular in shape, generally thought to signify the "yoni", the feminine sexual orifice honored in the old fertility-cults, however there is a growing suspicion that the ancient stone circles inspiring religious architecture actually represented spaceships. South America, particularly the Marcahuasi plateau, abounds with evidence of spacemen in ancient times; like Osiris, Jehovah, Saturn and Indra, Quetzalcoatl could have manifested in Mexico by spaceship.

Mythologists doubt the reality of Osiris, Indra, Zeus and Woden, they dismiss these gods as anthropomorphisms of natural forces humanized by the primitive peoples of antiquity; historians generally agree that one or more culture heroes called Quetzalcoatl really did suddenly appear to teach a brilliant civilization to Central and South America. Many rulers in Mexico and Peru like kings in Europe and Asia deliberately destroyed ancient records so that their people could not learn of the past, such vandalism obliged the priests to preserve their lore in hieroglyphics, whose esoteric concepts were incomprehensible to the uninitiated; the few writings which did exist were burned by the Spaniards as works of the devil until the Jesuits, Sahagun, Diaz, Torquemada and other scholars sought to preserve the native traditions. The identity and date of Quetzalcoatl challenge many distinguished authorities to offer widely divergent theories. Shortly after the conquest Alva de Ixtlilxochitl, an Aztec chronicler, compiled notable annals wherein he declared that Quetzalcoatl succeeded the defeated giants and lived during the third age, "El Sol de Viente", (the sun of the wind) contemporary with Lemuria, a view advanced by Dr. George Hunt Williamson and James Churchward, the latter suggests 32,000 B.C. Harold T. Wilkins and Marcel F. Homet believe he was an Atlantean "divine man" about 11,000 B.C.; Hyatt and Ruth Verrill identify Quetzalcoatl as Naram-Sin, who led an expedition from Babylon to South America before 2000 B.C. Miss Constance Irwin considers the fair god to have been a Phoenician perhaps 600 B.C. L. Taylor Hansen after twenty-four years research quotes several fascinating Amerindian legends and concludes that "Katezahl" was an Essene, perhaps a witness of the crucifixion of Jesus, who sailed to America in a Roman ship, approximating the Catholic belief that he was St. Thomas. Mexican archaeologists reject all these claims and estimate that Quetzalcoatl led the Mayas to Yucatan in A.D. 967. The Mayas know the great white stranger as "Kukulkan", the Peruvians as "Virachocha", the Columbians as "Bochica", the Quiches as "Gucumats", the Polynesians as "Wakee"; he was known under many names by the Indians of North America.

The most impressive study of Quetzalcoatl was probably made by a university professor, writing in German under the pseudonym of Pierre Honore "The Enigma of the PreColumbian White God" published in French by Plon, Paris, in 1962. Rene Fouere, dedicated editor of "Phenomenes Spataux", states in the September 1970 issue that this deeply researched work affirms that the legend of the white god in the Americas had historical foundation from the arrival on the American continent of Cretan mariners about 1500 B.C.

In Central America the Lemurian colonies flourished for thousands of years and preserved the sun culture of the motherland long after Mu was destroyed. William Niven, a mineralogist, in Mexico discovered evidence of highly civilized races there tens of thousands of years before the ice age; beneath a buried city over 200,000 years old he found traces of a second city and below that a third city of fantastic age; all three existed before the present high plateau was raised, they were probably destroyed by cataclysms obliterating civilization. Nearby Niven unearthed over 2,600 stone tablets more than 12,000 years old, whose symbols Churchward interpreted as from Mu, the motherland. Some races in Mexico traced their origin to an (Atlantis) Aztlan, according to Ixtlilxochitl the Olmecs during the third age came from the east in ships. The many affinities in religion, architecture, customs and language suggest intercourse between ancient Mexico and the Mediterranean lands. Lord Kingsborough, a wealthy eccentric early last century squandered a considerable fortune endeavoring to prove that Mexico was colonized by the lost tribes of Israel; he compiled nine volumes of Aztec and Maya codices supporting his theories, unfortunately his enthusiasm outran his means, unable to pay the cost of publication he ended his days amid all the degradation of a debtor's prison swarming with insects where he caught typhus and died.

Most archaeologists limit civilized Man in Mexico to only a few milennia and ignore the discoveries of Churchward and Niven; a few unorthodox experts influenced perhaps by the palaentologists unearthing human skulls elsewhere

millions of years old now seriously wonder whether those Aztec traditions of five suns, implying four previous civilizations which flourished then fell, were actually true. Myths are not fiction generally believed, they form oral history, race-memory of stupendous events remembered down many centuries, garbled in the telling, distorted by descendants, for whom the events had lost significance yet still containing a substance of truth. Already our new generation despite the experiences of their parents, the avalanche of books and television programs are sadly ignorant of the Hitler war, today few people in Britain care about their noblest queen, Boadicea, and no one positively knows what happened here thousands of years ago. These memories of times when the skies rained fire and Earth quaked, when cities perished and people drowned in floods, haunted the Mexican soul, promoted astronomy, perverted religion and finally induced submission to the Spaniards. Jacques Soustelle, the brilliant ethnologist, believes that our own fifth civilization is in some respects a degenerate age after those former periods of greatness. As in the old world so in the new the traces of Man are being found in a past whose remoteness would have astounded those scholars who believed history started with Abraham. Dr. Juan Aramento Carmacho has proof that Man in Mexico hunted camels and mastodons with implements of flint 30,000 years ago; from the deepest Pleistoncene strata are unearthed the bones of horses extinct long before the arrival of the Aztecs. Human artifacts have been dated by carbon-14 tests at 8000 B.C., civilization certainly flourished at 1500 B.C. The earliest culture of the Olmecs at La Venta, Vera Cruz, is dated about 800 B.C. contemporaneous with the Etruscans, who had an intriguing affinity with the peoples of ancient America. Some archaeologists date the Mayas as recently as A.D. 500, others suggest centuries earlier; when such learned experts fail to agree regarding the age of this brilliant civilization it is not surprising that they totally ignore evidence of visitors from space.

In the National museum in Mexico City are many Totonac or Zapotec figurines each wearing headgear resembling a helmet with a ring around their neck and a little box on their chest suggesting our familiar conception of spacemen; these tiny models are similar to the Homon Dogus, the clay figures or "haniwa" found in prehistoric tombs in Japan which could represent little men in space suits and helmets evoking Oannes who taught civilization to Babylon. Near Tres Zapotes in the

71

Vera Cruz jungle partly buried in soil amid giant ferns were found several enormous nomolithic heads of black basalt and stone altars in deep relief; one great nine-feet head weighed sixteen tons, the huge stone block had been transported over mountains and marshes from a quarry more than sixty miles away, a feat parallel to the transport of those blue Sarsen monoliths from South Wales to Stonehenge. How was the head moved this distance over difficult country and across a thirty-foot deep gorge in perfect condition in the alleged absence of the wheel or domestic animals? Archaeologists agree that like all the stone and pottery figures found in the area these great heads have broad foreheads, bold features, wide noses, thick drooping lips and appear amazingly negroid in character, quite unlike any native American race past or present; such heads are not found in Africa. The faces appear serene evoking the statues of Buddha, as though they belonged to transcendent beings not of this world, each wears a close-fitting helmet; these Olmec sculptures recall the famous Martian of the Tassili frescoes in the Sahara and that famous prehistoric painting discovered in a cave near Ferghana in Uzbekistan which the Russian newspaper "Pravda Vostoka" likened to "a man wearing an air-tight helmet with antennae and on his back some sort of contraption for flight". The Olmec priests must have had great reverence for these personages whom they worshipped as gods, perhaps the stones were transported by aerial craft or levitation, the fashioning of these sublime heads proves the sculptors were artists with lofty perception and sensibility of soul anxious to perpetuate in stone these men from the stars just as the Nahuas and Aztecs erected great statues to Quetzalcoatl. Some prehistorians believe these ancient statues to be representations of the sun god. Why would the peoples of Mexico portray the sun god like a spaceman unless they were accustomed to see wondrous beings from the skies?

Mexico City stands on the site of Tenochtitlan, the Aztec capital ravaged by Cortes and his gold-hungry conquistadores. The Aztecs believed that long ago their ancestors, the first men, emerged from seven caverns at Chicomoztoc, north of Mexico, a tradition shared by the red Indians, the Quiches and the Incas, suggesting refuge underground from cataclysm or aerial war. Traditions recall that the Aztecs, people of the crane, about A.D. 1160 were directed by their sun god, Huitzilopochtli, to leave their home Aztlan far north of the Colorado river and migrate southward to their promised land indicated by an island in a lake where they would see an eagle devouring a serpent. Six of the tribes bearing an image of their God came to the land of Anahuac and for decades followed the spirit of Huitzilopochtli manifesting as a white eagle which led them in confusion like Jehovah leading the children of Israel for forty years in the wilderness, a significant parallel, expecially if both the Aztec and Hebrew gods were spacemen; the "white eagle" leading the Aztecs may have been a spaceship? Finally about 1325 the descendants of the original wanderers arrived by the shores of Lake Tezcoco, where they saw an eagle perched on a cactus, its talons clutching a snake; the tribes halted and the priests scanned the heavens awaiting the god's command. Huitzilopochtli ordered the Aztecs to build here their city, Tenochtitlan, called Mexico by the Europeans after the war god, Mexitili, from which the Aztecs would expand to a prosperous empire and conquer the Earth. These symbols of the sun god, eagle and serpent, evoke the legend of the post-diluvian Babylonian king, Etana, associated with an eagle and serpent, who flew to the skies; the eagle and serpent symbolizing the sky god and wisdom feature prominently in world-wide religions. The long trek of the Aztecs during the thirteenth century led by priests inspired by signs from heaven is strangely similar to those familiar stories of the patriarchs in the Old Testament following the "power and glory of the Lord". It may be significant that today Mexico's national emblem is an eagle on a cactus grasping a serpent.

When Cortes and his forces, not four hundred men, marched from Cholula through beautiful savannahs, climbed the pass by the volcano, Popocatepetl, worshipped as a god, and descended into the pleasant valley of Mexico, they marvelled at the wonder of this new world. On 8th November, 1519 the conquistadores crossed the broad causeway to Tenochtitlan, in this "most romantic moment in all history" according to Torquemada, they gazed astounded at the grandeur and beauty of that spacious city surpassing the old capitals of Europe with all the wonder of Hannibal after crossing the bleak Alps looking down on that memorable view of Rome. Tenochtitlan at the time of the conquest was a busy metropolis with 300,000 inhabitants dwelling in 60,000 houses amid algoons, dykes and floating islands of flowers; this Venice of ancient Mexico enjoyed running drinking water from reservoirs, fountains played in the broad streets and vast market-place. The city like golden Babylon was adorned with palaces and "teocallis" or temples, shrines to the gods; the

72

public found pleasure in the aviary and zoo and the human menagerie of monstrosities kept as a circus, botanical gardens bloomed with exotic flowers and shrubs. Like Solomon, Montezuma had a harem with a thousand wives; perhaps this was why he bathed once a day, changed his dress four times every day and never wore the same clothes twice, giving the discarded garments to his attendants. This sylvan city evoking Atlantis was dominated by the great temple to Huitzilopochtli measuring 375 feet by 300 feet built in six platforms like the Babylonian temple of Marduk, 340 steps led to the upper platform bearing two lofty towers 56 feet in height crowned by statues of the gods. The sadistic streak marring these gay people found expression nearby in Tzampantli (pyramid of the skull) where the Spaniards counted no less than 136,000 skulls; all around were the monasteries of thousands of priests who performed their religious though bloody devotions with all the fanaticism of their Christian conquerors.

At Cuicuilco to the south of Tenochtitlan rises a pyramid half-buried in lava, the geologists confound the historians by dating the eruption as eight thousand years ago.

Thirty miles north of Mexico City sprawl the abandoned ruins of Teotihuacan, the city of the gods, built according to legend during the second age, Tlachitonatiuh, (Earth-sun) by a race of giants, the Quinamatzin, in the days of Atlantis. After the cataclysm Atlantean survivors in their Mexican colony were conquered by the Olmecs, who inhabited this great city under the beneficent rule of Quetzalcoatl. Madame Laurette Sejourne observed that "Far from implying any gross polytheistic belief, the term 'Teotihuacan' evokes the idea of human divinity and shows that the 'city of the gods' was the very place where the serpent learned miraculously to fly." That haunting phrase referring to serpents which learned to fly in this ancient "city of the gods" arouses wonder as to whether Teotihuacan like Lhasa was built by spacemen? The patient archaeologists scorn such tales of vast antiquity and conjure diverse theories dating the construction of Teotihuacan as 6000 B.C., 1500 B.C. or 600 B.C., proving the impossibility to establish reasonable chronology. Religious architecture honoring the sun god rivalled ancient Heliopolis on the Nile and bore witness to the fervor of the people comparable with the Christians building those great cathedrals in Europe. The imposing pyramid of the sun measures 760 feet by 720 feet at its base rising to a height of 220 feet, this huge edifice contains a

million cubic yards of stone and still reveals the masterly genius of its architects; a temple at the top housed a colossal statue of the god with a breastplate of gold. The pyramid of the moon is only slightly smaller; to the south stood the temple to Quetzalcoatl. In the year A.D. 856 Teotihuacan was destroyed by the Toltecs from Tula, once the most splendid capital in all America famous for its beautiful palaces, gem-encrusted walls, house of feathers and its pyramid-temples to Quetzalcoatl.

Sixty miles south-east of Mexico City stands Cholula, the Mecca of the Aztecs, of great antiquity, believed to have been founded by the Olmecs; Cortes found it a city of 150,000 inhabitants, a great commercial center whose people excelled in various mechanical arts, metal-working, cotton manufactures; they made a delicate pottery rivalling in beauty the wares of Florence. In honor of Quetzalcoatl arose the most colossal edifice in the continent, a "teocallis" or truncated pyramid measuring 1400 feet on each side covering 42 acres and more than 210 feet high, a stupendous structure of millions of bricks more than twice as big as the pyramid of Cheops.

In the graphic words of W.H. Prescott:

"On the summit stood a sumptuous temple in which was the image of the mystic deity 'god of the air' with ebon features unlike the fair complexion which he bore upon Earth, wearing a miter on his head waving with plumes of fire with a resplendant collar of gold round his neck, pendants of mosaic turquoise in his ears, a jewelled scepter in one hand and a shield curiously painted, the emblem of his rule over the winds in the other. The sanctity of the place, hallowed by hoary tradition, and the magnificence of the temple and its services, make it an object of veneration throughout the land, and pilgrims from the furthest corners of Anahuac came to offer up their devotions at the shrine of Quetzalcoatl."

Under the base was a labyrinth half a mile long evoking that great labyrinth in Egypt which aroused the wonder of Herodotus.

The Aztecs believed that Atonatiuh (water-sun), the first world-civilization, was destroyed by a deluge caused by the planet Maldek between Mars and Jupiter which exploded into the asteroids producing great floods on Earth. The "Codex Chimalpopoca" tells in Nahuatl of how the god Titlacahuan warned a man named Nata and his wife Nana to "hollow out a large cypress and enter it when in the month of Topoztli the water shall

73

approach the sky". Ancient paintings represented the heads of a man and woman with a boat floating on the waters at the foot of a mountain, a dove was also depicted. This Mexican Noah and his wife were giants, for a pre-conquest legend states:

"After the deluge which destroyed the primeval world seven giants survived. One of them, Xelhua, built the great pyramid of Cholula in order to reach heaven. But the gods destroyed the language of the builders."

This extraordinary edifice recalls Genesis, chapter XI.

"And they said Go to, let us build up a city and a tower, whose top may reach unto heaven. . .And the Lord came down to see the city and the tower. . .And the Lord said. . .Let us go down and confound their language. . .So the Lord scattered them forth from thence. . .Therefore is the name of it called Babel. . ."

Archaeologists are reluctant to credit this building with immense age but are nevertheless struck by its resemblance to the Tower of Babel, the pyramids of Egypt and mounds all over the prehistoric world used perhaps as observatories and for communication with the gods. The building of this immense pyramid demanded immense labor, mathematical skill and engineering techniques which would tax our experts even today. Why were the resources of the whole nation conscripted for this pyramid? What religious conception inspired its erection? Were the builders prompted by the "gods", the spacemen?

Cortes had little time to admire Cholula's architecture. Marina, his mistress, learned that the Cholulans planned massacre. Cortes summoned the entire population into the square, closed all exits, then at his signal the Spaniards raked them with gunfire while the cavalry trampled people down. Friar Bartolome de las Casas said the total slain numbered 30,000. Cortes ordered a hundred chiefs to be impaled or roasted at the stake. During the massacre this tough Spanish general is said to have recited an old romance describing Nero rejoicing at the burning of Rome.

In south-west Mexico near Oaxaca stand the forlorn but spectacular ruins of Monte Alban shrouded in mystery, the remains of five distinct epochs, a challenge to archaeologists, surprised to find no trace of early Man. The pyramids and temple-courts, once crowded with worshippers watching the white-robed priests tear out with their bare hands the hearts of the finest youths in the country, seem to have been suddenly planted there as from another planet. This valley once fertile with trees was deliberately desolated, the landscape redesigned; the Olmec builders tore the top off a mountain, uprooted the forests and levelled the plateau with terraces covering thousands of acres, they used the rubble to fill small canyons and holes: The Olmecs brought massive blocks of stone from many miles away to build their great city with splendid temples and tombs, a feat of engineering unsurpassed even today. Hyatt Verrill denies that this colossal enterprise involving the removal of hundreds of thousands of tons of rock levelling hundreds of acres and the erection of huge, impressive buildings, could have been achieved by slave-labor without steel tools, explosives and wheeled-vehicles; even so such a task with crude implements must have taken many centuries. Life-size rock drawings of dancers with flat noses and thick lips distinctly negroid and various ceramics suggest the builders were Olmecs who, according to Ixtilxochitl, the native historian, succeeded the giants and flourished during the reign of Quetzalcoatl. The plateau evokes Baalbek in Lebanon which may have been a landing-platform for spaceships; it is tempting to speculate that the cyclopean structures at Monte Alban were inspired by spacemen. Many murals show cripples and deformed humans leading to wonder as to whether Monte Alban was shrine of a healing-god, an ancient Lourdes. The colossal architecture is almost surpassed by treasures found in the later Zapotec tombs. Surely only a most gifted people, heirs to milennia of culture, could have carved cloak-pins from jade and jet, fashioned ornaments of copper, glittering jewellery, necklaces of pearls and gold, and have wrought an immense gold breastplate of superb magnificence. Here was practised lost wax-casting, hundreds perhaps thousands of years before this technique became discovered in Europe by Benvenuto Cellini (1500-1571). What marvellous tool cut obsidian and jade with a delicate precision most difficult today? The ruins of Monte Alban constitute a most baffling enigma, some of the architecture evokes early Babylon but who initiated this grandiose plan no one really knows. Perhaps we must view it in the stupendous age of the giants and space gods?

The Mayas flourished in south-east Mexico, Yucatan, Guatemala and Honduras; venerated as the scientists of ancient America, these mysterious people still baffle us today; a hieroglyph at Quiriga records a date about four hundred million years

74

ago, its accuracy said by Mr. J. Eric S. Thompson, the noted Maya scholar, to be "unquestioned"; colonists from other planets could have settled in Yucatan long ago like the Hopi Indians who believe their ancestors came from Maldek and its moon, Malona.

The "Codex Tro-Cortesianus" mentions that Central America was torn by many convulsions, lands in the interior which once supported 25,000,000 people now sprawl desolate; the Mayas believed in five ages of Man during hundreds of millions of years. The almost complete absence of records makes dating most difficult; a remarkable system called glottochronology analyzes the separation of related languages and concludes that the Maya language, Huaxtec, separated from Man 3,600 years ago and Plencano-Chal from Quiche 2,600 years ago, suggesting considerable antiquity. Last century Dr. Augustus Le Plongeon, who lived and excavated in Yucatan, believed that more than eleven thousand years ago the ancient Mayas had spread their civilization over the whole world inspiring the Hindus, Chinese and Egyptians. James Churchward claimed the Mayas originated from the drowned continent of Mu, while Ignatius Donnelly linked the Mayas with the proto-Phoenicians via Atlantis. Religious and cultural affinities with Babylon certainly do suggest some commerce with the ancient Middle East. The brilliant French scholar, Abbe Charles Etienne Brasseur de Courbourg in 1864 translated the Mayan "Troano-Codex" and stated that Votan, the great culture-hero of Yucatan, visited king Solomon at the time of the building of the temple and revealed to him the wonders of the lands in the west. The Bible states that Solomon's temple was built by "angels" (spacemen?). Votan is sometimes identified with the Scandinavian Woden. Extraterrestrials appear to have been active on Earth about 1000 B.C. Votan may have been a spaceman? The Mexican Nagal was probably the Chaldean war-god, Nergal; the Aztec civilization greatly resembled the theocracy of Egypt.

The zero date from which Mayan chronology begins goes back to the fourth millenium B.C.; one carbon-14 reading for pottery is 1300 B.C., another 965 B.C. Generally archaeologists date the Mayan empire from A.D. 104–987 when the Mexicans invaded. Then its prosperity waned until final extinction by the Spanish conquest. The collapse of the "empire of the snake" has been attributed to revolt against priestly domination, foreign invasion, calamitous hurricanes then pestilence; the abondonment of great cities to the jungle may have been due to impoverishment of the soil and the drying-up of local water-supplies which forced the inhabitants to move elsewhere, since for all their genius the Mayas lacked a scientific agriculture able to feed their high population. Experts still debate the Mayas, the origin of this gifted people and the cause of their sad decline, so evident in their stunted descendants today. The Mayas like the Etruscans and the Khmers shone in splendor then burned out, their inspiration exhausted, only their mighty works remain evoking our wonder.

The Mayas worshipped Kukulkan, sometimes identified with the leader of the Itza invaders who seized Chichen Itza in A.D. 987 introducing the culture of the Toltecs; his name meaning "feathered serpent" suggests he was actually Quetzalcoatl; like the Aztecs the Mayas were renowned for their fine buildings which probably attracted spacemen. At Palenque near the mountains of northern Chiapus, temples and pyramids rise in desolate grandeur resembling the sacred buildings of Teotihuacan. In the Temple of Inscriptions the Mexican archaeologist, Alberto Ruz, in 1949 noticed a trap-door revealing a stairway leading down about seventy-five feet to an underground vaulted room; in 1952 he finally crawled into a long narrow chamber decorated with large stucco sculptures of sumptuously robed priests. The vault was dominated by a huge sarchophagus covered with a carved stone slab 12 feet by 6 feet weighing five tons. Archaeologists claim that the fifty-four Maya hieroglyphics include dates corresponding to A.D. 603 and A.D. 623 surrounding the figure of a young man with large nose and mongoloid features leaning backward and sitting on an "earth-monster"; however G. Tarade and A. Millou in "Clypeus", 4-5, 1966 interpret the remarkable drawing as representing "a cosmonaut piloting a vimana." Removal of the inner lid revealed the crumbling skeleton of a man about 5 feet 8 inches tall, 6 inches taller than the average Maya, his teeth painted red were not mutilated in the fashion of the Maya nobility. A magnificent mask of jade, more precious to the Mayas than gold, in two hundred fragments covered his face, reminiscent of those golden masks protecting the faces of the Achaean dead found by Heinrich Schliemann in the tomb at Mycenae. Noting that his morphology is totally different from that of the Indians, Pierre Honore thinks the dead man was the white god, Kukulcan, himself. G. Tarade and A. Millou suggest that the demi-god could have been the last extraterrestrial educated

75

among the ancient Mayas, a fantastic conclusion not wholly beyond credulity since many stories of the gods descending to Earth in vimanas are mentioned in the Sanskrit classics. In startling revelation G. Tarade and A. Millou wonder if the Mayan hieroglyphics conceal some galactic message and speculate daringly:

"These hieroglyphics certainly concern the conditions of the pilotage of the ship. The person whom we see on the sculpture and whom we call 'the pilot' wears a helmet and looks toward the prow of the ship; his hands are occupied and seem to maneuver levers; his head leans on a support, an inhalator penetrates his nose. The bird reposing on the prow of the ship is a parrot which in the Mayan conception is the symbolism for the sun god. Still on the prow we find three 'receivers' which accumulate energy and other 'capturers' forming three series; three on the right, three in the front and three on the left. The motor is subdivided into four parts, the ship's propulsion-system is housed behind the pilot. The thrust is clearly visible and manifests in the form of the flame at the rear end of the vimana. It appears subdivided into two interblending contrary forces, one of solar origin (touches the tail of the bird), the other of terrestrial or magnetic origin, basically and freely they are symbolized thus by two masks."

Scholars who believe the Palenque tomb contained the remains of a Maya chief about 7th century A.D. would scorn these suggestions in "Clypeus" that the skeleton was of a spaceman ten thousand years ago; James Churchward would probably have agreed, he dated the youngest ruins in Yucatan as at least 15,000 years old. The T (Tau) and the astronomical cross of Egypt, a circle enclosing a cross, are traced in several sculptures at Palenque; one standing figure, his right hand with index and middle finger pointing to heaven, adopts the precise position of a Christian bishop giving his blessing, the one in which Jesus is often represented while at the Last Supper. Le Plongeon found on the walls of Uxmal, the thrice-built city, an inscription which read "This edifice is a memorial consecrating the destruction of Mu, the lands of the west, whence came our sacred mysteries." In Honduras at an altitude of 2000 feet lie the ruins of Copan covering seventy-five acres with an enormous plaza likened to the Roman Circus Maximus; near the temple is an artificial lake similar to the lakes in the precincts of Karnak,

Nagkon-Wat and Santa Cruz del Quiche with great religious significance. The greatest city of the Mayas, Tikal in Guatemala long uninhabited, has many pyramid-temples towering above palaces and squares, one massive structure rises to 229 feet, all abandoned to the jungle.

The holy city of Chichen Itza dedicated to Kukulkan is dated by archaeologists as roughly A.D. 600-900; James Churchward alleged it was built during the Can and Peu Dynasties about 16,000 B.C., a claim supported by Harold T. Wilkins who considered a carving on a temple pillar represented a tall, fair refugee from Atlantis. Le Plongeon interpreted a codex as relating the tragedy of prince Coh, youngest son of the last king Can; he was murdered by his brother, Aoc. Queen Moo, a Mayan princess, after the tragic death of her brother-husband, when Atlantis sank fled to Egypt and initiated the Egyptian civilization. Chichen Itza was famous for its sacred well down which were cast beautiful virgins, willing sacrifices to the gods; the gold and jade trinkets found there were surpassed only by the treasures in the tomb of Tutankhamun. The Mayas apparently had their own "Helen of Troy"! About A.D. 1185 young Chab-Zil Chac was ruler of Chichen Itza; he stole the bride of Ah Ulil, head-chief of Izamal during the wedding festivities and because of this Humac-Coel, chief of Mayapain supported by Mexicans stormed Chichen Itza which like Troy disappeared from history.

The Aztecs and Mayas recorded their wisdom in a curious picture-writing suggesting flowing galactic symbols on parchment, paintings and stone glyphs; these magic scrolls excited the Spaniards as works of the devil. The first archbishop of Mexico, Don Juan de Zumeriago as Ximenes destroyed all the Arabic documents in Granada twenty years earlier, collected all the national archives from the great Aztec library at Tezcuco and burned them all; priests and soldiers wantonly destroyed every native manuscript they could find. Bishop Diego de Landa with fanatic zeal made bonfires of all the paper-books he could lay hands on and burned many thousands of priceless records, suddenly he repented and endeavored to preserve the old traditions but such wilful vandalism had destroyed almost all the records of this great civilization; only three Aztec manuscripts survived, the "Codex Paris", "Codex Dresden" and "Codex Madrid"; also the "Books of Chilam Balam" written by a priest. A companion of Cortes Bernal Diaz del Castillo in his "Historia Verdadera de la Conquesta de Nueva Espana" fortunately gave a brilliant eyewitness

76

account of the invasion with comprehensive details of the customs and religion of the Aztecs. The Mayas themselves jealously hid their secret lore from the invaders, most of our knowledge of these fascinating people comes from the chronicles of Spanish friars. The Mayan hieroglyphics still baffle scholars. The Soviet linguist, Yuri Knorozov following clues from de Landa's "Relacion de las Cosas de Yucatan" claims to have unravelled the Maya language; a Siberian computer produced exasperating translations but to date no reliable interpretation of these fascinating glyphs is resolved.

Our knowledge of Maya mythology is mainly derived from the "Popol Vuh" (the collection of written leaves), bible of the Quiches, a collation of traditions assembled by a native Christian in Guatemala in the seventeenth century, copied in Quiche and translated into Spanish by a monk, Ximenes. The "Popol Vuh" describes the creation of the world and the frustrations of the gods creating Man. The first men were made from mud but dissolved in water, next the gods created beings from wood with no souls or intelligence then destroyed them in torrents of resinous rain. A fantastic imposter appeared called Vukub-Cakix, whose giant sons challenged the gods. They were finally destroyed by the heavenly twins, Hunapu and Ixbalanque. The hero-brothers descended to the underworld and after desperate ordeals defeated the subterraneans in a game of ball, pok-a-tok, similar to basket-ball, said to have been invented by the Olmecs, the rubber people. Finally the gods from a paste of yellow and white maize created four men, ancestors of the Quiches, who possessed superhuman wisdom and could see to the uttermost part of Earth. The gods could not permit men to be their equal; they obscured men's vision and to complete their confusion created women. The "creation" story in the "Popul Vuh" has intriguing affinity with Genesis, even to gods similar to Jehovah and the Elohim. Vukub-Cakix and his giant offspring evoke Uranus and the Titans, the first four wise men recall the golden age of Saturn, the wonderful world-wide civilization of the space gods. How did the most revered teachings of the Old Testament, those glittering legends of the Greeks, come to inspire the ancient Mayas in the jungles of Guatemala? Did Central America once share a world-wide culture with Israel and Greece?

The idealism of Quetzalcoatl preaching universal love and beauty, the worship of a beneficent heavenly father honored by gifts and flowers was acclaimed by the Toltecs and Nahuas, the early Aztecs followed the old religion until 1428 when the emperor Itzcoatl (obsidian snake) defeated the Tepaneca, rulers of Azcapatzalco until then masters of the island on which the city of Mexico-Tenochtitlan was built. Suddenly the whole pattern of Aztec life was changed by a Hitler-like character, Tlacaelel, chief-counsellor to three successive kings. Tlacaelel resolved to inspire Aztec grandeur by completely re-writing history and instilling martial concepts of blood and conquest; with all the propaganda of a Dr. Goebbels perverting the Nazis, he burned all the old codices and instigated new rites promoting worship of their god, Huitzilopochtli, identified with the sun and preached that the Aztecs were deity chosen people destined to conquer all nations on Earth. Tlacaelel and the Aztec priests taught a mystico-martial philosophy designed to prevent the death of the fifth sun, ominously recalling the satanic myth of the Nordic superman proclaimed by the Nazis.

The Aztecs like many ancient peoples believed in world-ages, each destined to crash in universal destruction. Race-memory still recalled that last cataclysm of flood and fire. The "Codex Chimalpopoca" relates:

"The sky drew near to Earth and in the space of a day all was drowned. The mountains themselves were covered by water. It is said that the rocks we can see today rolled about over all the land dragged by waves of boiling lava and that there suddenly arose mountains the color of fire."

Such catastrophe confirmed by geologists today shattered the world-wide civilization of prehistory. Mexican traditions tell of earthquakes, tidal waves, flaming volcanoes, cities swept into the sea, millions of people and animals destroyed and a few frantic survivors fleeing to caves underground waiting for months in darkness praying for the sun to return. Humanity remembered four cataclysms, four world ages, four suns apparently destroyed leaving Earth to freeze in darksome night; when at last the fifth sun appeared, people crawled from their shelters and gazed on a desolate world, then set about the slow and painful task of rebuilding civilization. The Aztecs like many of our modern thinkers believed in eternal recurrence. What has been will be again, the future lies in the past! Tlacaelel formulated the concept that the sun and the universe were sustained by the mystic qualities of blood, this miraculous substance which kept men alive held powers to preserve the life of the sun; the offering of human blood would keep the

77

fifth sun alive and sustain the lives of all the peoples on Earth. The Aztecs began to wage ritual wars to secure prisoners for sacrifice to Huitzilopochtli, the sun god, and so extended their sway across Central America. Men who died in the wars were transformed into exquisite birds accompanying the sun across the heavens, women dying in childbirth with a child in their womb also became attendants of the sun.

Many wise Aztecs questioned this bloody doctrine just as many Germans questioned Hitler and opposed the sacrifices. Before the ideological conflict could bring reform the philosophers were silenced by the Spaniards.

When the temple of Huitzilopochtli was "consecrated" in 1486 during four days sacrifice 80,400 men in turn from dawn to dusk were stretched over the sacrificial stone and their hearts torn out with a flint knife by a priest and offered to the god, a death far more merciful than hanging. In Mexico-Tenochtitlan alone there were five thousand priests who performed the twenty thousand human sacrifices a year. Wars were conducted not to win territory or plunder but mainly to capture prisoners for sacrifice to the gods, for without this daily offering of bloody hearts the world would end! The Mayas in Yucatan to a lesser degree followed the same bloody ritual. Later the priests decided that if Tlaloc, the rain god, were not propitiated with blood, the whole land would become parched with drought, a menacing problem for an agricultural people. The Mayas abandoned many fine cities probably due to impoverishment of soil.

It is thought that before the last great cataclysm Earth revolved around the sun in 360 days, perhaps the collision of some cosmic body hurtled our planet further into space or retarded its solar revolution; afterward the survivors were startled to find the year had lengthened to 365 days. These five extra days were an annual reminder to the Aztecs of the catastrophes past and the catastrophe to come; their superstitious souls still thought these days unlucky. During the last five "empty days" of each year fires were extinguished, sexual intercourse ceased, business stood still, no one worked, all waited anxiously wondering if the world would end. On the fifth day the priests would propitiate the gods with sacrifice, evil would be averted, the sun would shine, an annual triumph for official religion. An the end of each 52-year cycle there were special rejoicings celebrated with stupendous sacrifices.

The Aztecs and Mayas continued the world-wide sun worship by all the peoples of prehistory originally taught by the sky gods or spacemen, who ruled the earliest civilization; when the extraterrestrials departed worship of the sun god lost its pure esoteric meaning and its ritual became mingled with the fertility cult of the earth mother. The androgynous supreme deity manifested in many forms, chiefly as the creative gods, Tonecatecutli, (male) and Tonicuatly (female) who made the heavens, Earth and Man, Chicamacatl, the earth goddess (Demeter), Tlazaltecatl (Persephone), Xochiquetzal (Venus), Huitzilopochtli (Ares), Tezcatlipoca (Jupiter) who waged fantastic conflict with Quetzalcoatl (god of the air), also Tlaloc, god of the rain. Mexico was a theocracy ruled by a priest-king; people were devoutly religious in following their peculiar beliefs, convinced that nothing ever happened by chance, life from birth to death was ruled by the gods, everyone believed in astrology and implacable destiny to be averted only by supreme self-sacrifice to the divine will as interpreted by the infallible priesthood who dominated every aspect of daily life. The Mexicans called the father of their trinity Yzona, the son Bocib and the holy ghost Evach, received from their ancestors. Like the Catholics the Aztecs believed in a future life in heaven, purgatory or hell, the Jesuit priests were shocked by the startling similarities between Christian and Aztec rites; both religions worshipped a heavenly father with the symbol of a cross; Aztec priests baptised babies with holy water and functioned at marriages, they administered confession and absolution. Monks and nuns lived in humility and mortified the flesh by fasting and penance. The Jesuits who could not admit that much Christian ritual was borrowed from the same original sun worship damned the Mexican religion as blasphemy inspired by the devil. The Inquisition therefore persecuted all followers of the old gods in the name of their own god of love, since fundamentally to the simple natives Christianity seemed about the same as the teachings of Quetzalcoatl. They were superficially converted, although even today the old pagan superstitions still haunt the Mexican soul.

The holocausts of human sacrifice in ancient Mexico seem to us bestial and devilish appeasing satanic demons with blood, yet the Aztecs accepted them as essential for Man's survival. Comparisons between peoples with different cultures, indoctrinated with different beliefs, are sadly difficult, as we discover in our strife-torn world today, but perhaps it may be salutary to

78

consider what an Aztec might think of us. This century scores of millions of men and women have been killed in wars, men are being killed somewhere fighting at this very moment, millions more may be killed before the century ends. Why have they died? For freedom, prosperity, peace? The sorry world gives silent answer. The Nazis murdered seven million Jews with a scientific ferocity no Aztecs could match. For what? In Britain today thirteen people were killed on the roads. Sacrificed for speed? To save time which might have been wasted. Why? The Inquisition and the witch-hunters in western Europe burned hundreds of thousands of men and women, wars of Religion killed millions of Christians. Why? The young Aztec warrior sang with joy as he lay on the sacrificial stone, the beautiful virgin cast herself into the sacred well in ecstasy. They did not ask why. Their deaths would ensure that next dawn the sun would rise again; they were dying for more than Mexico, they were dying for Man all over the world. The Aztecs welcomed death as entrance to new life and would have deplored those Christians, who preaching of heaven seem so reluctant to leave Earth. Everyday for centuries Aztecs died, their bloody hearts were offered to the sun, next day the sun did rise again, so the people applauded the knowing priests. Now the sacrifices are no more, the sun still rises. Was the Aztec religion wrong? For nearly two thousand years Christians have killed each other and slaughter still. What of our own religion? Perhaps in five hundred years time our descendants may judge us as we judge the Aztecs. Is our civilization really more humane?

Today the Tzotzils, descendants of the ancient Mayas, who believe in the immortality of the soul and reincarnation, perpetuate the old beliefs; each November 2nd they celebrate the day of death in total mourning. The chief divinities of the Tzotzils are the sun and moon, without the sun the world becomes chaos, dark and frightening; they are scared of the night and never begin a journey before dawn. Christianity has still not obliterated the ancient religion; the Tzotzils regard the crucifixion of Christ as a human sacrifice; in 1868 the Chamulas of Chiapra choose a boy of ten or eleven called Diego Gomez Chechels and led him to a place named Tzezal Hemel, there they nailed his hands and feet on a cross. The Tzotzils imagined that a Christ of their own would bring to the Indians all the power and wealth the white Christ had brought to the white men. Still the natives live in abject poverty. A problem for our theologians? In the evening of November 24th, 1967 Mr.

Brian Stross, anthropologist from Berkeley, California, who was studying the customs of the Tzeltal Indians of Tenejapa in Chiapas, Mexico, was astonished to see "what appeared to be a bright star moving rapidly across the sky; it had a powerful light that dimmed a little every once in a while, and was going in the opposite direction from the path that the sun takes (i.e. from west to east)." He learned from people in Tenejapa that the brilliant light probably signified an Ikal, a three feet tall, hairy, black humanoid which was believed to be a humanoid from another world often flying with some rocket propulsion attached to its back. Mr. Gordon Creighton, a Fellow of the Royal Anthropological Institute, and a world-renowned authority on UFO phenomena, who has lived in Mexico, comments that among the Tzotzils, neighbors of the Tzeltals, the Ikal is the commonest form of the god of death who flies through the air and steal women, reminiscent perhaps of the "Erl Konig" feared in mediaeval Germany. During the last twenty years numerous incidents have been reported concerning luminous spheres from which black dwarf-like creatures have emerged and attacked people often with a paralyzing dazzling light. These humanoids may not be creatures from outer space but unknown denizens of Earth. The Aztecs believed that "the night so favorable to ghosts filled itself with fantastic monsters, dwarfish women with flowing hair, death's-heads that ran after travellers, footless, headless creatures that moaned and rolled upon the ground", certain presagers of misfortune. Did Ikals menace the Aztecs, Mayas and Incas? Little people are said to have inhabited forgotten cities amid the Amazon jungles, some probably lived in Mexico.

The Aztecs and Mayas had a profound conception of time, the ancient astronomers apparently sought to calculate the date and hour of the creation of the present universe, its long duration, its cessation and beginning again; they believed in eternal recurrence, the same things happening over and over again, a most profound concept distilled from milennia of thought. The succession of world-ages impelled astronomers to study the courses of the stars acquiring data for the prediction of the next cataclysm; their astronomical figures carved in strange glyphs on the stela at Quirigua record a date of ninety million years ago and another four hundred million, "accompanying glyphs record that the starting point of those calculations was thousands of millions more years in the past." These immense

79

figures are eclipsed by the fantastic Assyrian cuneiform text found at Kunjujik near Nineveh recording a mathematical series whose end product would be 195,955,200,000,000; the Mayan and Assyrian concepts contrast with the ancient Greeks who thought of the number 10,000 as a large uncountable aggregation. The Mayas measured time in "tuns", years of 18 months, each 20 days, or 360 days, plus five "empty days" ascending in multiples of periods to an "alautun", about sixty million years. The Maya calendar was a work of supreme mathematical skill covering the 52 years period with 18,980 different combinations of day-names, numbers, and months, the great "stone of the sun", known as the Aztec Calendar Stone dedicated in 1479 stood thirteen feet high and weighed two tons, it correlated the dates of previous world-ages, details of transits of Venus, planetary cycles and great lunar-solar periods. The philosophical implications compounded in these extraordinary complex calendars reveal a wisdom accumulated through many millennia contrasting with the crude beliefs of the mediaeval Church which swore the sun moved around the Earth. The Mayas calculated the year as 365.242198 days compared with our modern calculation of 365.242129 days, a difference of only six seconds in one year, proving that the precision of their celestial observations equalled our own. The ancient Mexicans knew that five years of Venus are the same as eight solar years, they observed the heliacal risings of the planet for centuries and calculated the time which elapsed from one transit of Venus to another; making due corrections for planetary variations they achieved a fantastic accuracy with an error equivalent to one day in 6000 years. The Greek and Roman astronomers believed Venus to be two stars, Lucifer and Hesperus; the Mayas like the Assyrians knew it as one. The domes of the Mayan observatories were better orientated than one erected in Paris in the seventeenth century. Like peoples all over the ancient world the Aztecs and Mayas knew that the Pleiades apparently had one star fewer than several thousand years ago; they were aware like those writers of the "Talmud" that some cataclysm involving the Pleiades had ushered in a terrible cold on Earth. At the dawn of the winter solstice the Aztec priests assembled on the mountain of Uixachtecatl near Tenochtitlan and watched the Pleiades mount toward their zenith fearing this constellation would suddenly stop, causing the end of the world. At the timely a moment a prisoner would be sacrificed by the priests, the Pleiades

would continue their course, mankind was saved.

Tenochtitlan mirrored a highly cultured civilization where nobels, merchants and common people lived in a complex social and political system dominated by the priests subject to their elected emperor. The capital was renowned for its music-schools, paintings and particularly for its feather-work, beautiful mosaics from the gorgeous plumage of tropical birds, pottery equal to the finest wares of Florence, cotton garments and Mexican carvings in wood, bone and stone, which attained a most delicate artistry. In the British museum is a life-size human skull carved from a solid piece of crystal, a supreme masterpiece of Aztec art. The Mexicans had paper and writing as early as 1000 B.C. long before Homer wrote his Iliad. The mellifluent harmonious language, Nahuatl, was exquisitely suited for the expression of all shades of meaning from abstract terms, poetical metaphor to factual descriptions of the physical world, evidence of long evolution. Wanton destruction robbed posterity of almost all the native literature but sufficient remains to reveal that inspired poetry and verse which so delighted those sophisticated scholars.

Mexico's jewellers and goldsmiths astounded the Spaniards with their wonderful workmanship. Montezuma greeted Cortes with fabulous presents of gold and silver, necklaces of emeralds, earrings of jade, and later gave the conquistadores all the treasures filling a sealed room. After Montezuma's death the Aztec uprising forced Cortes to flee from the city; during the "sad night" of 30th June, 1520 amid a torrential storm he buried the treasure at Popotlan under an old cedar beside a marsh. A year later after reconquering the capital, Cortes was dismayed to find the treasure gone. In fury Cortes tortured the last emperor, Cuauhtemoc, burning his royal feet in a brazier, but only drew from him the secret that the treasure had been thrown into a lake whence no one could recover it.

Among the presents given by Montezuma to Cortes were two flat discs of pure gold, each about ten inches in diameter, one a quarter of an inch thick, the other much thinner; these were said to be levitation-discs attuned to their owner's personal vibrations, a secret of anti-gravity from lost Atlantis or perhaps from spacemen. While there is no evidence that anti-gravitational force was used for public transport or warfare such a power possibly utilized by the priests does seem to be the only means for manipulating those huge blocks of stone to fit so accurately into the great pyramids. Montezuma is said to have been warned

80

of the approach of Cortes and his men by signals heliographed with obsidian mirrors. Although wheeled toys have been found in ancient Mexico, it is odd that the Aztecs did not use wheeled vehicles, even if they had no horses; their roads approached in excellence the wonderful road-system of the Incas. It is intriguing to speculate whether the Aztec emperors and priests had some method of locomotion not revealed, surely such brilliant intellectuals like the Mayas would not trudge across their empire like tramps?

The most important result of the conquest of Mexico was probably the introduction to Europe of vegetables such as cultivated maize, beans, cocoa, potatoes, tomatoes, pineapples, domesticated birds and hundreds of drugs, which improved living standards more than all the looted gold inflating the economy. During the last thousand years in Europe hardly any wild plant has been domesticated; the cultivation in Mexico of such a vast range of plants surely proves that Man in the Americas must have immense antiquity.

In the jungles of Guatemala the noted archaeologist, S.K. Lothrop, discovered enormous stone globes arranged in geometrical formation particularly obvious when viewed from the air like those intriguing sculptures on the plateau of Marcahuasi in the lofty Andes which are now believed to have had significance for visiting spacemen. The natives of Cerquin in neighboring Honduras tell of Comizaguel, a woman skilled in magic, who long ago descended from the skies to teach their ancestors civilization; she had three sons fathered by the "gods". Years later Comizaguel ordered her "bed" to be brought out of her house; amid flashes of lightning and rumbles of thunder she vanished. A few years ago in San Salvador was found a strange clay dish adorned with a picture of men in curious machines leaving a trail of smoke resembling some form of aircraft.

In 1593 on the morning of October 25th there suddenly appeared on the Plaza Mayor in Mexico City a soldier wearing the uniform of a regiment then stationed at Manila in the Philippines. Dazed at finding himself in Mexico the man had no idea how he came to be there, however he did reveal that His Excellency Don Gomez Periz Dasmarinas, governor of the Philippines, was dead. The military authorities puzzled as to how the soldier could have travelled 9,000 miles without even soiling his uniform jailed him for desertion. Eventually news arrived from Manila that the governor had been murdered on the very day the mysterious soldier appeared in Mexico. The Inquisition suspecting

witchcraft had the soldier shipped back to Manila; the most intensive investigation of eyewitnesses proved beyond doubt that he was in Manila on the night of October 24th, there was equally no doubt that the morning after he was in Mexico City. This well-attested incident was recorded in the chronicles of the Order of San Agustin and the Order of Santo Domingo; it was featured in the book "Sucesos de las Islas Filipinas" by Dr. Antonio de Morga, high justice of the criminal court of the Royal Audiencia of New Spain, and also in "Las Calles de Mexico" by Dr. Luis Gonzales Obregon.

Early in May, 1968 a well-known Buenos Aires attorney, Dr. Gerardo Vidal, with his wife, Senora Raffo de Vidal, motoring near Chascomus became suddenly enveloped in a dense fog. When they came to their senses they found themselves 4000 miles away in Mexico 48 hours later! Both felt strangely unwell, the surface of their car had curious marks as though burned by a blow-torch, their watches had stopped. Similar teleportations are now believed to have been caused by spacemen.

The fantastic translation of the soldier from Manila to Mexico in 1593 suggests that extraterrestrials were active in Central America during the sixteenth century, a fact well-known to Montezuma and his astronomers who so anxiously scanned the skies from their pyramid-observatories like the Chaldean astrologers on those lofty ziggurats of Babylon.

Montezuma was honored by his own people as a great soldier, victor in nine battles, his courage was unquestioned; the emperor was well-versed in the Aztec wisdom and advised by the most expert astronomers. He was aware not only of the ancient traditions but must have surely seen the UFOs haunting Mexican skies. The spectacular triumph of a few Spaniards was due to easy victories over a demoralized nation believing them to be gods; the decimation of thousands of Aztecs by smallpox brought from Cuba, and the uprisings of subject-races against Mexican rule. All the chroniclers agree that the initial success of the invasion, which could have been smashed, was ensured by Montezuma's superstitious conviction that Cortes was Quetzalcoatl returned to chasten Mexico with that tribulation he had threatened long ago.

Today we too await the return of the white gods. Whether they will come in peace or war no one knows.

May we welcome the spacemen with more success than ill-starred Montezuma!

81

Chapter Ten
Space Gods of South America

The brilliant realm of the Incas still basks in the sun, the vast green forests of the Amazon shroud the fabulous cities alluring explorers to their death, cyclopean ruins perched forlorn from a far-forgotten past drown dizzy crags touching the sky, mountain-tracks mark airfields inviting the stars, down deep canyons cryptic petroglyphs tell mysteries of lost peoples long ago. Golden El Dorado, white gods, giants, dwarfs, warrior-women, humanoids, fearsome creatures of the night; surely the secret of the spacemen lurks in those fascinating ancient lands of South America so haunted today.

Near Lake Titicaca in Bolivia stand the immense remains of Tiahuanaco, perhaps the oldest city on Earth, certainly the world's loftiest port for its quays and docks now dizzily perch high in the Andes about 12,300 feet above sea-level, suitable only for spaceships. The age of this remarkable city is not known; local Indians say that Tiahuanaco was built before there were stars in the sky, a somewhat unscientific assessment but hardly more wild than the guesses made by professed experts today. The Incas had no idea and aptly called the deserted ruins "Tiahuanaco", "the place of the dead". The Aymaras told the Spanish chronicler, Cieza de Leon, one of the earliest European tourists in 1549, that the city was built by bearded white men and "raised in a night". The Peruvians acknowledge the extensive city to be of far older date than the pretended advent of the Incas. W.H. Prescott records a fascinating comparison with ancient Mexico:

"Another legend speaks of certain white and bearded men who, advancing from the shores of Lake Titicaca, established an ascendancy over the natives and imparted to them the blessings of civilization. It may remind us of the tradition existing among the Aztecs in respect to Quetzalcoatl, the good deity, who with a similar garb and aspect came up the great plateau from the east on a like benevolent mission to the natives. The analogy is the more remarkable as there is no trace of any communication with, or even knowledge of, each other to be found in the two nations."

Hans Schindler Bellamy, the noted advocate for Hans Hoerbiger's cosmic ice theory wrote in "Built before the Flood" that Tiahuanaco must be at least 250,000 years old, a claim not quite so outrageous when considered with the assertion by Berossus that ten kings (divine dynasties) ruled Babylon 432,000 years before the flood or the allegation by Simplicius that the Egyptians had kept astronomical observations for the last 630,000 years; admittedly astonishing dates yet only yesterday in human chronology for Dr. L.S.B. Leakey has found fossilized jaw fragments of men twenty million years old. Consideration of the brilliant analysis of the Tiahuanaco calendar elucidated by Peter Allen obliged H.S. Bellamy to reduce his estimate; in "The Calendar of Tiahuanaco" written jointly with Mr. Allen he declared "Thus while we cannot establish any 'age' for the Tiahuanaco of the calendar, and, hence, for the calendar of Tiahuanaco itself—there can nevertheless be no doubt that its age must be many

82

decades of milennia." Colonel James Churchward claimed to have seen marked on a most ancient Tibetan map the site of Tiahuanaco, unfortunately not reproduced, which allegedly proved the port to have been founded by Carians from Mu at least 16,000 years ago long before the Andes were raised, a date supported by that great expert, Dr. Arturo Posnanski, from La Paz. Churchward confidently interpreted the great monolith at Tiahuanaco as recounting in Cara-Maya symbols fascinating details of "Mu, the empire of the sun" with diverting comments on prince Coh and queen Moo of Mayax. H.S. Bellamy and Peter Allen interpret the same symbols as an astronomical calendar, Alexander Kazantsev as a calendar for Venus. When great experts disagree, humbler mortals marvel!

To appease those critics most anxious for truth when none is possible, it must be admitted that archaeologists blandly ignoring astronomy, geology and Tibetan maps refuse to date the building of Tiahuanaco earlier than 500 B.C. Whatever its actual age, judging by the UFOs haunting the Andes today, in its long history enigmatic Tiahuanaco must surely have attracted the "gods", the spacemen.

Hans Hoerbiger, the Austrian cosmologist, (1860-1931), theorized that space must be permeated with hydrogen and water-vapor; the universe materialized the conflict between cosmic fire and ice symbolizing the eternal struggle between good and evil. This controversial theory postulates that the space around the sun is filled with ice-particles; the inner planets, Mercury and Venus, are covered with ice, a belief which would have vastly amused Adamski's Venusian friend, Orthon, who pictured his home as a tropical paradise; it would certainly outrage the Russians claiming Venus to sizzle at 700 degrees C., although they still hope to land there. Earth has apparently had several moons; in Tertiary times, date unknown, the predecessor of our present Luna spiralled close to Earth attracting the world's waters into a girdle-tide obliging the population to flee from the flooded coastal plains and climb higher and higher up the mountains establishing lofty asylums in "Andinia", Mexico, Abyssinia, Tibet, New Guinea and elsewhere. The first period of culture in the Andinian asylum was overwhelmed by a flood catastrophe caused by a precessional wobble of Earth's axis, the old temple and cyclopean buildings became buried in mud. Survivors of this cataclysm from many races returned to the Andes, by tradition the area

became called "Tsahua-ntin-Suyu", the "common gathering place of all nations", the name later appropriated by the Incas for their golden empire of Peru. For many milennia sea-level remained about twelve thousand feet higher than today, proved by highly elevated shore-lines and fossils of sea-creatures still discernible along hundreds of miles of the Andes. The Tertiary moon circled Earth at an average distance of only 20,000 miles, its gravitational attraction therefore increased the stature of all living organisms producing giant men, animals and plants. In the Andean Altiplano besides the huge bones of giants are also found the bones of the toxodon, a feline animal which became extinct in Tertiary times. The human remains do not belong to a homogenous people but include American, Nordic, Mongoloid and Negro types suggesting that international survival teams of scientists, artists and technicians from many countries took refuge here from approaching calamity, just as if today another world-catastrophe threatened, experts from all nations would assemble on high mountains to plan the survival of the human race for the new world. The waters of Lake Titicaca are salty, the region now abounds with salt deserts once the bottom of ancient seas. The giants in this second classical period basked in a tropical climate, probably that golden age extolled in legends world-wide; from their seaport at Tiahwanaco they traded with peoples all over Earth accounting perhaps for the common old stone age culture in many parts of the world. These "sons of the sun", who built grandiose Tiahuanaco, were great engineers, mathematicians and astronomers, the discovery of most ancient lenses implies the use of telescopes, their particular veneration of Venus suggests visitors from that lovely planet.

The megalithic ruins of Tiahuanaco stand now about twelve miles from Lake Titicaca which as the ancient docks prove, once washed the great walls of the city. All the buildings still show impressive grandeur in size and conception. The fortress of Akapana an immense truncated pyramid, rears 170 feet in height from a base about 650 by 600 feet. The temple of the sun, the Kalasasaya, measures about 440 by 390 feet and the palace of the sarcophagi 220 by 180 feet; the ruins of the Tuncu-Punku or place of the ten doors form an artificial mound about 50 feet in height and 200 feet square, such cyclopean structures would present problems for our own technicians today. Many huge stone slabs measure 36 by 7 feet and weigh 200 tons, the nearest quarries may have been

83

thirty, even ninety miles away. How could these immense monoliths be conveyed such distance over the Andean sea? Not on native balsa rafts! Did the giants levitate them by anti-gravity or utilize some aerial transport by spaceship? In 1961 the transport of a 200 ton block in Russia for a statue of Karl Marx was found to be barely within the means of modern technology. The stones, hard andesite, almost impervious to weather erosion, blunt our finest steel tools. No implements are found. How did the builders shape and groove those slabs to an accuracy of one-fiftieth of an inch? Mortar was not used, the walls were solid yet their foundations elastic, apparently resilient to earthquakes. When Pizarro's conquistadores scaled the dizzy heights and entered this city of the dead their superstitions were soon dispelled by the sight of monoliths riveted with huge silver bolts which in riotous destruction the looters extracted. Spanish chroniclers stated that some of these bolts of silver weighed three tons. Such wonderful architecture eloquently reveals the lofty minds of those giants who conceived and fashioned Tiahuanaco. "Portrait heads of the great men unearthed there show high foreheads, open faces, bold profiles, energetic chins", powerful personalities still impressive from the solid rock challenging time; like the Sphinx they stare beyond our tiny world out to the stars.

The most fascinating edifice in Tiahuanaco is the "gateway of the sun", entrance to the sun temple, cut out of one solid slab of greenish-grey andesite, an igneous rock of great hardness, the sun door stands about 10 feet high by 12½ feet wide and 1½ feet thick weighing about ten tons. This massive portal is encrusted with complicated groups totalling 1107 symbols comprising winged figures, heads of humans, condors, pumas and the now extinct toxodons. After a life-long study Dr. Arturo Posnansky concluded these signs represented a calendar, further analyzed by the German scholar, Edward Kiss in 1937. H.S. Bellamy and Peter Allen find this calendar in many respects superior to our own; it shows the four seasons, solstices and equinoxes but apparently divides the year into ten months of twenty-four days plus two months of twenty-five days making a year totalling 290 days each of 30.2 hours which suggests that when the calendar was devised Earth was rotating more slowly than today; the year was therefore 8758 hours, about the same duration as at present. A decade earlier in 1927 Hoerbiger had calculated that in Tertiary times the year consisted of 298 days, each 29.4 hours, a total of 8761

hours, reasonable agreement with the sun calendar at Tiahuanaco, which apparently supported his theory. As the Tertiary moon approached Earth's revolution accelerated, so shortening the day which before the satellite's disintegration had decreased to its present twenty-four hours, thereby increasing the number of days to 365 per year.

In 1962 Alexander Kazantsev, the Russian scientist, observed in "Komsomolskaia Pravda" that if according to the American astronomer, Cooper, Venus does rotate on its axis once in about 9 Earth-days, its orbit around the sun in 224 Earth-days constitutes 24-plus-a-fraction Venus-days. What if the twelve "faces" on the Tiahuanaco sun door signified years not months? Ten Venus-years, each twenty-four Venus-days plus two Venus-years each twenty-five Venus-days total 290 Venus-days in a cycle of twelve Venus-years; such agreement with the calendar at Tiahuanaco must surely transcend coincidence. Kazantsev speculated that the Tiahuanaco calendar showed the Venus-day equals 9 Earth-days and 7 hours, a fact soon to be confirmed when Russian cosmonauts would circumnavigate Venus. How could the Venus calendar have become known in those far ancient times? Whence came those legendary white strangers, sons of the sun, with blue eyes and beards? Reluctant to draw conclusions Kazantsev thought many answers might be secreted in the signs on this sun door. The symbols include winged humans evoking angels in the Bible and those winged sculptures in Babylon, could they too have represented spacemen?

Tiahuanaco flourished in splendor, suddenly its glory was shattered by volcanic eruptions and floods, shortly afterward the Tertiary moon crashed down on Earth amid titanic storms, cosmic bombardment and earthquakes, survivors in the Andes cowered in a long darkness, when at last the sun reappeared all were shocked to find that the sea freed from the moon's gravity had fallen several thousand feet exposing the mountains and leaving Tiahuanaco stranded in lofty mid-air. The atmosphere had become rarified and chill, people fled down to the plains. Near Bogota in Columbia prehistoric elephants like those mammoths in Siberia perished in the rarified air and freezing cold; their bones still litter the mountainous field of the giants. For thousands of years without any moon Atlantis flowered in the Atlantic, the site of Tiahuanaco was deserted. About 11,500 B.C. wandering Luna approached the Earth causing disastrous tides so people congregated again at lofty Tiahuanaco to build a second asylum but

84

Luna became caught in Earth's gravity before the refuge was ready; the cataclysm engulfed Atlanteans, most Andeans perished leaving their descendants to degenerate into the primitive Indians of today.

Hoerbiger's theory is ridiculed by astonomers and archaeologists whose own conclusions are not always inspiring; however this cosmic revelation does account for the destruction of those great civilizations of the antediluvian world and for the extraordinary elevation of Tiahuanaco.

The degenerate Indians still living in the Tiahuanaco region believe they are not ordinary men but belong to a different genus; their language and physiognomy are quite different from their Aymara neighbors; they claim to have lived in the highlands before the age of darkness and remember when the sun reappeared; all have a superstitious reverence for those benign, giant statues in Tiahuanaco. These Indians call themselves Urus, meaning men of light and claim magical powers. Such a magic must work backward for it is rumored that the Uru men are completely enslaved by their womenfolk, Amazons practising Voodoo witchcraft. The Urus of Tiahuanaco closely resemble that degenerate Dropa tribe on the mountains between China and Tibet who believe their ancestors were marooned there in ships from the skies. Professor Josef Shklovsky affirms that there exists a fantastic correspondence between the measurements made with the use of electromagnetic waves and the hieroglyphs of the gateway of the sun. These strange sculptures have not ceased to occupy researchers since American scientists believe they may represent ionic motors perhaps inherited from a vanished race most highly civilized. Did spacemen visit Tiahuanaco?

At Nazca about three hundred miles north of Tiahuanaco the plateau twelve hundred feet above sea-level flanked by the lofty peaks of the Andes is almost completely covered with a multitude of fantastic markings apparently made by removing the dark brown pebbles to expose the yellowish gravel underneath. At ground level the tracings seem somewhat confused, from the air they resolve into an astonishing pattern of bewildering geometrical figures, spirals, stars, cosmic symbols, beasts, birds and straight lines varying from half a kilometer to eight kilometers in length. Maria Reiche who has made a special study of this vast network is amazed at the technical skill and engineering knowledge required, apparently far beyond the Nazca culture known to us; radio-carbon readings suggest A.D. 500 but the

strange figures may have been traced there thousands of years earlier. Delineation of these cryptic patterns must have been a task approaching in complexity the erection of Stonehenge, they possibly had similar significance, perhaps the symbols traced a gigantic calendar, astronomical chart or folk-magic sign conjuring fertility, explanations inviting contradiction. It is difficult to explain why even gifted mathematicians would go to such tremendous toil and trouble to trace ingenious patterns across miles of plateau, almost incomprehensible seen from the ground but startlingly significant viewed from the air, unless the designers knew that beings existed in the air for whom the lines had meaning. Such markings would hardly have been traced with immense effort merely to amuse a solitary spaceman, those ancient people would only undertake this extraordinary complex of figures to attract a race of extraterrestrials whose friendship they treasured. It may be fatuous to suggest that those famous Martian canals were primarily designed to advertise to neighboring planets the existence of intelligent life on Mars yet some superficial comparison might be made with these lines at Nazca. Most significant of all perhaps, could the ancients have designed such patterns unless they viewed them from the air? Like those princes of old India wenching and warring with celestial cars, did the priests of lost Peru fly vimanas too? Why was the sun god of the Nascan people depicted flanked by the heads of jaguars, symbolizing gods from the air? Do these patterns not suggest signals to space?

High in the Andes not far from Nazca on the plateau of Marcahuasi Dr. Daniel Ruzo in 1952 discovered a most remarkable assembly of giant sculptures representing human beings, animals and birds, notably a great lion and several condors, symbols of the sun god. Many of the figures are only prominent when viewed from a certain angle, particularly in the sunlight, two altars twelve feet high suggest that the prehistoric builders must have been giants, perhaps those giant gods who, according to the Hunaca Indian legends, dwelt in the high places. Many carvings depict camels, lions, elephants, penguins, which as far as is known never existed in South America. Daniel Ruzo proved that they had been made by giants twelve feet tall. The fantastic shapes have suffered erosion through possibly hundreds of thousands of years, even such vast age cannot obliterate the serenity of those noble faces like the statues on Easter Island, which radiate an aura of transcendent wisdom akin to the Sphinx translating the soul to some far-gone era

85

beyond our understanding when Earth was visited by celestials, the gods. Why such monoliths should be grouped thirteen thousand feet high in the Andes far from human habitation baffles our comprehension until we discover from aerial photographs that among these statues exist other figures visible only from the air. Cosmonauts in our own space-capsules marvel at the extraordinary visibility of terrestrial objects seen from space, these strange figures incomprehensible to us may have had meaningful significance as beacons for spacemen.

Dolmens, stone circles and burial mounds on hill-tops often appear to be in direct alignment with prehistoric monuments standing on mountains miles away marking old straight tracks called "leys". Tracings on ordnance-maps disclose that sometimes ten or more leys converge on a single center, often the site of an important prehistoric landmark, pagan temple now christianized into a cathedral-town. Photographs taken near these ley-centers may become befogged by surprising radiation, it is believed that crystals inserted in the original stones emit ultra-violet light suggesting that the hill-tops might have been power-points for a vast electronic complex long ago. Every country honors hills and mountains sacred to the gods, whither the celestials would summon their prophets to whom they gave commandments, laws and divine guidance, bases for popular religion; the priests of antiquity mastered a psycho-electrical science not known to us and taught people to pray to heaven, sending forth mental and spiritual vibrations to be monitored by spacemen. Today many sensitives, notably disciples of the Reverend Doctor George King, president of the Aetherius Society, ascend certain mountains to breathe in the prana and magnetic energies producing an aura of power with cosmic beneficence, which destroys evil vibrations polluting Earth. Sightings of UFOs are often deployed in straight lines suggesting the flight-path of spaceships, phenomenon which its discoverer Aimé Michel called "orthoteny" from the Greek "orthoteneis" meaning "stretched in a straight line". Critics like the redoubtable Dr. Donald Menzel, professor of astrophysics at Harvard, attack orthoteny, admittedly its statistical analysis is open to challenge, nevertheless it seems surely intriguing that so many of these orthotenic lines of UFOs when plotted on maps are found to coincide with leys, the tracks of stone age peoples. The Machiguenga Indians of eastern Peru speak of the "people of the heavens who came (to Earth) on a

shining road in the sky"; the Quecha Indians of South America recall the "Illa Siva" or "light rings" evoking the Egyptian "Eye of Horus", and the "Rampa Livrac" or "litters of electric energies" that were seen in the days of "Lord Inca", the magical "flying boats" enchanting the red Indians. The lofty plateau at Nazca and Marcahuasi marked with those strange lines and sculptures may once have been centers for some ancient electrical civilization communing through radionics with supermen in the stars.

American traditions agree that during these great cataclysms when fire and flood ravaged Earth, people took shelter underground just as our own descendants must do some day. The Andes are said to be pierced with immense tunnels built by an ancient race of white men; a subterranean highway runs north-westward from Cuzco to Lima for 380 miles then turns due south to modern Bolivia 900 miles away, the southern end is lost in the deadly Atacama salt desert of northern Chile. Madame H.P. Blavatsky about 1853 visited the port of Arica, once in Peru now in Chile, there her curiosity was quickened by the appearance of an enormous solitary rock almost vertical, in the rays of the setting sun she discerned on the volcanic surface strange hieroglyphics. In the magnificent golden temple of the sun at Cuzco, old capital of Peru, at a certain hour of the day the sunbeams focussed through an aperture on to the inner wall revealing similar hieroglyphics at other times not visible. The same signs were also seen on the royal tomb of the Incas, inside this chamber cunningly contrived slabs distinguished only by these hieroglyphics turn on pivots giving entrance to the tunnel. Not far from Arica near the Payquina river stand three Andean peaks forming a curious triangle, in one of these peaks is the entrance to the corridor leading northward. Any attempt to blast a way into the tunnel would cause the burial of the tomb and all its treasures. A Peruvian told Madame Blavatsky a fascinating story that when the Inca Atahuallpa was imprisoned by Pizarro, his wife offered for his liberation a roomful of gold from floor to ceiling as far as he could reach. She kept her word, then the conquistador learning the Incas had an inexhaustible mine of treasures in a mile-long tunnel vowed to murder Atahuallpa unless she revealed the secret. The chief priest looking at a consecrated "black mirror" similar to the "mirror" in which Montezuma had seen Cortes, witnessed the future murder of Atahuallpa. The outraged queen ordered the entrance of the tunnel to be concealed under huge masses of rock, after

86

her husband's murder she killed herself. Despite many attempts by various governments neither tunnel nor treasure has been found. Mysterious tunnels, labyrinths and catacombs attributed to white Atlanteans are said to exist under Mongolia, India, Guatemala and South America leading to the subterranean civilization of Agharta, believed by some students to be the source of the flying saucers. Such fantasy confounds our understanding. Greek legends suggest that after interplanetary war the Titans and Cyclops, a most ancient stellar race, retreated underground. The ancients possessed wonderful powers mastering planetary engineering unknown to us, the tunnels were built long before Atlantis and were illumined with "cold" lights shining forever, perhaps the builders were Earth's first rulers, those supermen from space.

The Incas told the conquistador, Juan Alvarez Maldonado, that their ancestors originated from the great empire in the east which may have preceded Lemuria and Atlantis; legends marvelled at mysterious cities lost amid impenetrable jungle, still illuminated by perpetually shining white lights. In unknown country on the Rio Sinkibenia on July 10th, 1957 the noted anthropologist, Dr. George Hunt Williamson, discovered the fabled "Rocks of the Writings", not the rock carvings of primitive man but erudite hieroglyphics of a most ancient advanced race; they covered an area of cliff in a strip 85 feet in length and 8 feet in breadth. The figure of a young man with a magnificent helmet looking toward the west recalls those massive statues of strangers apparently wearing space-helmets erected by the Olmecs in Yucatan. The Machiguenga Indians tell of the days when their forefathers communicated with celestials in the sky, they belonged to the legendary Amazonian empire, El Gran Paititi. Dr. Williamson's expedition discovered high in the Andes the lost city, Pomatana, with about twelve hundred stone houses. In a cave nearby were found nearly two hundred burials, every skull had been deformed by a headband apparently in childhood and later scientifically trepanned, nearly all the skulls had an opening in the forehead artificially produced. The name "Pomatana" was derived from the Quechua "puman-huatama" meaning "hitching place of the lion", the lion or jaguar was believed to symbolize an extraterrestrial. Paititi was known as land of the jaguar king, who probably had affinity with the famous tiger god worshipped by the Chavins in the ancient Andean civilization of the Chavins at Cajamarca. Nearby arose a high

peak, site of an "intihuatana", "hitching place of the sun", a sun altar, where solar priests performed experiments. Stone carvings in a Peruvian temple of the wind in the Casma valley depict dancers with six fingers on each hand. Dr. G.H. Williamson and his companions examined many aerial photographs from the archives of Peru's Air Ministry; he states "Here we found fantastic evidence that the ancients of South America were in contact with a superior race from the stars". Pomatana is said to have flourished before the last cataclysm when earthlings had contact with the celestials mentioned in the legends of many countries, which all agree that after world-wide devastation communication with other planets was cut off, the spacemen became worshipped as gods. Earth's frantic survivors supplicated the gods to aid them as during the former golden age so they built spiral temples, cosmic symbols, perhaps resembling spaceships. Since direct flight to the stars was no longer possible, people had their skulls trepanned to open up psychic centers known as the third eye to facilitate telepathic communication with the spacemen. That intriguing and controversial Tibetan lama, Lobsang Rampa, states that in the days when the gods walked upon Earth all men and women could use the third eye which enabled them to perceive people's auras and perform transcendent adventures on astral planes; Lobsang describes the operation on his forehead to open his own third eye, a technique unknown to the west inherited by eastern initiates from far antiquity. The ancient pre-Inca Huari-Huanca culture fashioned golden skulls from pure gold, painted skulls on pottery and trepanning showed these ancients were greatly concerned with Man's telepathic abilities. The Chimus as Chan Chan had their skulls trepanned by pre-Incan surgeons, gold and silver plates covered the apertures, the patient evidently survived many years after operations requiring incredible skill. In the caves of Pomatana were said to be axes of copper and long copper rods, perhaps those legendary vril-rods of the Atlanteans, nearby were subterranean tunnels no Quechua would enter.

About 25,000 years ago the Amazon valley area was submerged under a vast land-locked sea. Colonel James Churchward claimed to have seen in a Tibetan monastery a most ancient map which showed most of Brazil as an immense lake connected to the Pacific and Atlantic by canals. During thousands of years Carians from Mu colonized the west coast of Peru then moved to the mountains marking their trails with cosmic

87

petroglyphs, many adventurers crossed the Amazonian sea on to Atlantis, then to the Mediterranean where they developed the prehistoric civilization of the Aegean and the Middle East. Generations later this migration was reversed, fair-skinned Atlanteans, ancestors of the Quechuas expanded their brilliant empire from Europe to South America, there they built fine cities, worshipped the sun and fostered a culture inspired by spacemen. Indian legends agree with traditions of Atlantis and annals of the ancient east that long ago shining gods descended from the stars to rule Earth in a golden age of peace and wonder described in the Sanskrit classics. It is believed that as long ago as 80,000 B.C. extraterrestrials had bases on Earth at the bottom of oceans and underground from which UFOs are said to appear even today. The Manacricas, a native tribe in Brazil cherish legends concerning "macumbeiros", flying wizards in circular luminous machines.

In a frightful catastrophe many milennia ago titanic floods and fires destroyed world civilization plunging the few survivors cowering in caves back to savagery. A lowering of the level of the Atlantic ocean drained the Amazonian sea and exposed the Andes, on the resultant swamps drying under the tropical sun spread a dense impenetrable jungle isolating any ancient cities not destroyed from the new civilized centers evolving on the coast. Communications with the planets almost ceased; a few extraterrestrials still remained to guide humanity, occasionally men were aided by solitary space visitors whom they met in secret areas, forbidden to popular gaze being segregated as sacred to the gods.

Dr. Alberto Perego believes that South Americans migrated beyond Egypt to Babylon, their word for "priests" was "sume", so they called themselves "Sumerians" and created a brilliant civilization inspired by Oannes and other extraterrestrials appearing from the sea. Oannes like other spacemen from Japan to Mexico wore goggles, breathing-tubes and antennae, similar to our own cosmonauts landing on the moon. Men everywhere welcomed the celestials as gods; as natives in Africa copied the white men of Victorian times so people in far antiquity copied the dress and manners of these wondermen from the stars; we no doubt would perpetuate memory of the spacemen on tape and film for marvelling posterity, the ancients remembered them in adoration by carving their likenesses in stone, statues of benign and noble beings with giant eyes, probably the goggles they wore. Some people stuck

feathers in their hair to represent electrical radiation from the heads of the gods or wore a circlet of gold on their brows signifying a helmet, others donned horns to imitate antennae. Today in Africa bushmen, like the red Indians, deck their heads with plumes to copy those great birds bringing the mysterious strangers from the skies whither they would return. How will any troglodites peering from their moon-craters copy our own lunarnauts landing there? Will their priests compound a theology praising some generous "Jehovah" from Texas opposed by a diabolical "Satan" from Sibera? Will the lunar temple, the house of the lord, look like Apollo 15? Will the hymns of the moon-people mimic the celestial music of the Earthmen, the latest "top twenty" tunes from their transistors serenading the universe? Such questions may not be quite so frivolous as they seem, intuitive minds may discern therein some basis of our own religion and rituals remembering our own space visitors of long ago. Many celestials married earthwomen, settled here and begat divine dynasties and for thousands of years communicated with their home-planets; gradually interest waned. After the decline of Babylon and Egypt the spacemen abandoned the Middle East, except perhaps in A.D. 610 when the growing wickedness of the Arabs prompted the "angel" Gabriel to land near Mecca and inspire Mahomet to regenerate his people in a spiritual resurgence of world significance. "Angels" later conducted Mahomet on a trip of wonder around the "seven heavens". George Adamski claimed to have met a Venusian and travelled to the planets; his cosmic teachings may yet prove to be the message our sorry world so sorely needs. Throughout the centuries the spacemen have continued to visit South America which humanoids haunt today.

A thousand years before Columbus Irish traditions told of a wonderful continent in the west. About A.D. 540 St. Brendan of Clonfert, born in County Kerry and thoroughly conversant with such marvellous tales, sailed with a few companions south-westward into the Atlantic searching for the "land promised to the saints". The adventurers swept by the current eventually reached a pleasant land and came to a large river. Seven years later St. Brendan returned; he told of the many wonders they had seen and founded a college for three thousand monks at Clonfert, possibly with treasures he brought back. Later generations believed the Fortunate Isles discovered by St. Brendan may have been the Azores, the

88

Bahamas or even Virginia; in 1492 before Columbus set sail the cartographer Behaim mapped these elusive islands close to the equator near South America. In popular imagination the Fortunate Isles become confused with Hy-Brazil or Royal Brazil, that romantic lost world of gold extolled in Irish legend, sought by idealists and treasure-hunters with all the enthusiasm that we today lavish on some shining new planet. The old Irish "breas-ail" meant "very good" or "blessed". In the eighth century the Irish Saint Virgile not only taught about the antipodes but actually went to Rome to prove to pope Zachary that the Irish had been accustomed to communicate with a transatlantic world. Today in the Argentine there is an Indian tribe speaking Erse, not really surprising since if Babylonians and Phoenicians voyaged to South America, surely some rumbustious Irishmen could sail there too. Did the Irish "breas-ail" give name to that "blessed" land of Brazil, perhaps it could be more appropriately called "Tir-nan-Og", that Celtic land of youth?

Since the days of the conquistadores legends persist concerning an ancient Amazonian empire, El Gran Paititi, with a mysterious white race ruled by a tiger-king hoarding fabulous treasures. In the Middle Ages Marco Polo ventured to golden Cathay, land of silk, other travellers sought Prester John, fabled emperor of Abyssinia, today the last secrets of Earth alluring adventurers are those lost cities of the Atlanteans with ever-burning lamps buried in the jungles of Brazil, bases perhaps for spacemen. It is difficult to believe in our age of satellites with television-eyes and aircraft photographing every square inch that any part of Earth still holds secrets yet we probably know less about the Matto Grosso than the mountains on the moon. Dense foliage makes aerial reconnaissance difficult, expeditions hacking jungle-trails are menaced by poisonous giant insects, man-eating ants, monstrous snakes, bone-crushing anacondas, savage jaguars; devil-trees trap unwary travellers in their tendrils, rivers abound with cannibal piranhas stripping flesh to the bone, the foetid moisture-dripping forests breed malaria and deadly tropical diseases; the greatest threat is starvation for by grim paradox in this wild profusion little edible grows. Vast tracts remain unexplored. Sir Arthur Conan Doyle in his fascinating romance "The Lost World" described a lofty plateau isolated since prehistoric times where huge dinosaurs battled with tooth and claw amid steaming swamps, fiction which strange animal-tracks may possibly make fact. The

deadliest menace are hostile Indians whose poisonous darts massacre any white men braving this green hell. Stories of the atrocities committed by Europeans in their greed for gold and rubber, their enslavement and extinction of natives along the Amazon have understandably inflamed many Indians against the white man; heroic missionaries have ventured into the deep forests but the message of the cross fails to convince tribes whose ancestors worshipped the true solar cross thousands of years before Christianity. The Amazon region reveals signs of a most ancient civilization, certain rocks are inscribed with cosmic symbols of world-wide sun-worship, cliffs are carved with hieroglyphics resembling ancient Egyptian, Semitic, Sumerian, Celtic and Irish signs, even old Phoenician; bewildering yet significant inscriptions prove intercourse with Europe and the Middle East long ago. After the death of Alexander the Great in 323 B.C. his great fleet is believed to have sailed eastward from the Persian Gulf never to be heard of again. From India the Greeks are believed to have wandered via the East Indies and Polynesian islands eventually landing in Peru, where Indians copied their characteristic Grecian helmets. A Roman weapon is said to have been found in old Peru. A fascinating link between ancient Greece and South America exists in the name "Amazon" itself. Greek legend tells of the beautiful Hippolyta, queen of the Amazons, a warrior-race of women defeated by Hercules, who took her girdle. Amazons were so-called because they cut off their right breasts that they might more effectually use bows and arrows; originating in Scythia around the Black sea they fought under their queen Penthesilea for the Trojans; she was unchivalrously slain by Achilles. Matriarchies flourished in the ancient world. Diodorus Siculus mentions that thousands of years ago the Amazons led by queen Myrina dwelled in Libya and defeated the Atlanteans; later they were swept up in those great migrations of prehistory and many found themselves in South America where their descendants waged war with the ninth Inca, Huari Capac, and subsequently baffled the conquistadores.

Long before the arrival of the Spaniards the Indians told of a Chibcha king who once a year smeared himself from head to foot with honey then gold-dust and bathed in the sacred lake in which worshippers cast gold and jewels to honor the gods. This legend of the "Gilded One", "El Dorado", fascinated the conquistadores who identified the mystic lake as the long and deep

89

Guatavita in Bogota, where the Indians threw their offerings of gold and silver and platinum to deprive the Spaniards; the conquistadores partially drained the lake and salvaged a few treasures, but most of the fabulous wealth was lost in the mud. The real El Dorado was believed to be near the Orinoco in north-west Amazonia. In 1536 the sole survivor of a gold-hunting expedition staggered from the jungle and later told of golden Manoa on an island in a salt lake in Guiana; in a description not unlike Plato's Atlantis he told of a city with glittering houses, statues and trees of gold on sands of gold dust; Sir Walter Raleigh in 1595 made his disastrous expedition to Guiana searching in vain for the golden city of Manoa, a failure contributing to his execution twenty-three years later. This gilded utopia intrigued the philosophers like our science-fiction today. Voltaire in 1758 described how Candide after sorry adventures found himself and his servant in El Dorado where they were welcomed by twenty beautiful young virgins who conducted them to the bath. Candide was hospitably received by the king and escorted around the magnificent city, wonderful though the treasures were, he was more impressed by the fact that these happy people had no parliament, prisons or priests.

Whether El Dorado actually existed or not, there is most impressive evidence that before the conquest the people of south America had skilled goldsmiths with an artistry unsurpassed. the Golden museum at Bogota displays most exquisite bracelets, jewellery, necklaces, statuettes, comparable to those golden treasures of Mycenae; the ancient pre-Columbians knew how to smelt, beat and refine gold, they could make leaf so fine it could be rolled without breaking, their metallurgists used different colors in various alloys and made metals hard or soft necessitating temperatures of 2000 degrees C., these old smiths worked in silver, also platinum not discovered in Europe by Watson until 1750. Antonio Julian, historian of the province of Santa Maria in 1787, related that wise men assured him that the Tayrona Indians knew a certain grass of the Sierra Nevada which had the property to soften gold. On his first expedition to Columbia Pedro Heredra obtained golden objects worth nearly $4,500,000 also a single gold idol weighing one hundred and twenty-four pounds. The Chibchas hid more treasure than the Spaniards found and in fury the conquistadores almost exterminated them. The inhabitants of El Dorado evidently possessed a high culture with great artistry and technology creating

exquisite golden treasures and perhaps many wonders of which we are unaware. How did the ancient South Americans acquire such knowledge? Was the "Gilded One" a native king or a spaceman? Did those golden houses of Manoa really exist or had the delirious Spaniard seen spaceships anticipating those gleaming UFOs haunting the same land today?

Many expeditions have searched for El Dorado, throughout the centuries the Spaniards have sought elusive Manoa in vain. Colonel Percy H. Fawcett with his son, Jack, set out in 1925 to discover dead Atlantean cities in the Matto Grosso among the territory of the Jivara headhunters. He was convinced from earlier quests that he had information which would definitely lead him to cities of most ancient times. An Indian once told Colonel Fawcett he had seen strange, fixed lights which never go out, shining from abandoned old buildings deep in the forest. Perpetual lamps with cold illumination from a preparation of oily gold were known to some of the ancients; such a lamp was found burning in the tomb of Tullia, Cicero's daughter, 1500 years after her burial, other lamps were found in Athens, Edessa and Antioch. St. Augustine was not impressed, for he sternly denounced such pagan lamps as works of the devil "who deceives us in a thousand ways". The saint must have forgotten his scripture, for in Exodus XXVII, v. 20 the "Lord" ordered Moses "And thou shalt command the children of Israel that they bring thee pure oil olive beaten for the light to cause the lamp to burn always", a directive repeated to Moses was an extraterrestrial, it is surely likely that he would impart such scientific knowledge to initiates in South America too. The reported existence of ever-burning lamps by natives unaware of their significance clearly suggest their installation by some superior civilization, perhaps by spacemen.

Colonel P.H. Fawcett wrote to his other son, Brian:

"I have heard from Indians about 'collections of stone houses' and clothed Indians who worship the sun and guard the approaches to their cities with savage determination. Records in the archives of missions and governments also talk of clothed white Indians occasionally sighted but never contacted, of lost cities in the Brazilian forests on a scale greater still than those of the Inca empire. My own investigations lead me to believe that two of the ancient city sites I propose to investigate are inhabited by the

90

remnants of the same race that built them, now degenerated into a state of savagery due to their complete isolation but still having traces of their original culture.

"I expect the ruins to be monolithic in character, more ancient than the oldest of Egyptian discoveries. Judging by inscriptions found in many parts of Brazil, the inhabitants used an alphabetical writing allied to many ancient European and Asian scripts. There are rumors, too, of a strange source of light in the buildings, a phenomenon that filled with terror the Indians who claim to have seen it."

It is generally believed that Colonel Fawcett, his son Jack, and their companion, Raleigh Rimmel, were killed by hostile Indians in the Matto Grosso during July 1925, although persistent rumors alleged they were taken into the interior as prisoners; bones alleged to be theirs have not been identified.

A Brazilian of German name wrote to Brian Fawcett that:

". . .his father and brother were advanced souls who were worshipped as gods by Indians and who were actually alive in a subterranean city called Matalir-Araracauga in the Roncador region of Matto Grosso. There were several underground cities in Brazil where dwelt the great spiritual avatars who ruled the world's events, and from these secret places issued flying saucers to make global reconnaissance-flights."

Skeptics may scoff at such phantasy. Students of UFOs past and present recall so many strange, significant phenomena. While we mourn the disappearance of Colonel Percy H. Fawcett and his two companions, still we wonder? Fascinating tales of humanoids and hostile spacecraft suggest that descendants of the old space gods may be returning to those mountains and forests of South America.

91

Chapter Eleven
Incas, Sons of the Sun

It may be profoundly significant for our own century that as the history and conquest of Mexico closely depended on Quetzalcoatl identified with Venus, so the history and conquest of Peru were associated with Viracocha, linked with the sun; their doctrine and deeds identical, these two teachers probably came from the same advanced civilization, perhaps another planet. Peruvian mythology exalted Viracocha as creator, lord of the sun, moon and stars, especially Venus; from stone he created giants and deposited them among primitive mankind confirming Greek legends of the Uranids, that giant stellar race from space; later he drowned all men in an immense deluge saving only one man and woman, the flood remembered all over the world. Viracocha, whose name meant "sea-foam" descended to Earth and created fresh men out of clay; legend states the god arose from the waters of Lake Titicaca in the Andes like Oannes who appeared from the sea to teach the first people of Sumer, suggesting that this fair god civilizing ancient Peru was possibly a spaceman.

Legends agree that Viracocha resembled Quetzalcoatl being a tall, impressive man with a beard, skilled in all the arts and crafts. Some declare his companions were men, others say the heavenly father in the sun sent down his son and daughter to teach mankind. The most famous chronicler of Peru, Garcilaso de la Vega, El Inca, grandson of the ill-fated Atahuallpa, related in his "Comentarios Reales" that Viracocha landed from the sun during the stone age; he told of a statue showing the culture hero holding by a chain a great unknown animal with lion's claws; he and his disciples were said to have walked on the sea without ships or boats, suggestive perhaps of spacemen, Some traditions teach that Viracocha built Tiahuanaco, other legends assert that he entered its most ancient ruins about 20,000 B.C. Peruvian memories of Viracocha closely parallel Aztec traditions of Quetzalcoatl although history records no communication between the two countries. The peoples of Columbia remember the pale god as Bochicha, other South Americans as Tama, Sume or Kon-Tiki Viracocha; in long white mantle or in a black robe with golden sandals he traversed the continent with an ease of a spaceman. At Caba Clos in Peru the prophet aroused the enmity of bigoted priests who bade the warriors attack him; like some biblical patriarch he raised his hands to the sky and called in a strange language, suddenly from the heavens whirled a curtain of flame, which circled around him, the arrows were repelled by this forcefield to pierce the hearts of those who sent them. In Cocha the healer again assaulted by soldiers prayed to the sky, a fire-flame darted down whirling in wonderful colors between him and his enemies; they turned to flee then stopped in terror at the second fire-circle behind them. In a flash all dissolved to dust; the stranger stood unsinged. Today the site is called Place of the Lightnings. Hyatt Verrill explaining affinities between the Sumerian and Peruvian civilizations claims that king Sargon of Agada reached Lake Titicaca and erected monuments on the island of the sun, he was also known as Viracocha. Before departing westward Kon-Tiki-Viracocha and his companions

92

noted for their long ears promised to return; they are said to have sailed to Easter Island inspiring Thor Heyderdahl's expedition on balsa raft from Peru across the Pacific proving that the ancestors of the Polynesians could have come from South America. Through the ages there were probably several Viracochas, sons of the sun.

The Peruvians originally acknowledged an infinite, immemorial and eternal god sustaining the universe, known as Pachacamac, sometimes personified as Viracocha; he was depicted as a giant condor god carrying the sun across the heavens and battling with the jaguar god of darkness. A most ancient legend states that the first inhabitants of Peru were born from bronze, gold and silver eggs which came from heaven, suggesting in ages past the landing of extraterrestrials, colonists from the stars, variants of this celestial egg theme are depicted in the famous Tassili frescoes, also in traditions from China to Greece.

The most fascinating account of the religion of Peru is given by Agustin de Zarate, a treasury official, seconded to Los Reyes (Lima) in 1548 to make an overdue audit of the royal accounts; his masterly work "The Discovery and Conquest of Peru" compiled from the stories of eye-witnesses and his own researches make it the most authoritative study on the exploits of Pizarro and the culture of Peru. Zarate states that the South American Indians believed that their ancestors forewarned of a great flood took refuge in great caves near the mountain-tops which they had prepared in advance with all the necessities of life and filled up the smallest openings so the waters could not enter. Long afterward when the waters retreated, dogs which the survivors had sent out returned muddy so the people ventured forth into a changed world. The Peruvians worshipped the sun and moon as actual divinities, particularly the sun, giver of light and life, father of the royal dynasty and founder of the empire. The Incas erected magnificent temples to the sun, lavishly emblazoned with gold, where priests with croziers and bishops' mitres exacted penance, prayed and fasted, gave communion and heard confessions, performing the sacred rituals with devout reverence. Virgins of the sun dedicated to the deity entered convents for a life of prayer such as tending the sacred fire and other holy service, they lived in perpetual chastity and continence, any who erred was buried alive, although if she swore on oath that the sun, presumably a celestial, was the father of her child, she was spared. Prayers were directed to a holy trinity and to the son of

god, who died and rose again, Inti, the sun god. So similar to the Christian faith was the religion of the Incas, that one worthy friar dared to write a book entreating that they should not be considered as infidels, the sole result was to bring him before the Inquisition, who had him convicted of heresy and burned at the stake. As with the sun worship of the Aztecs, so the astonishing resemblance of the religion and rites of the Incas to Christianity outraged the Catholic fathers as counterfeit by the devil; even today they refuse to believe they are fundamentally the same. The Incas believed in the resurrection of the flesh, the nobility were embalmed and interred in vaults with their costliest treasure and one or more of their wives, who often actually quarrelled for the privilege of accompanying their husband in death. When the Spaniards looted the gold and silver vessels, the Peruvians begged them not to disturb their ancestor's bones for fear of spoiling the deceased's restoration to life on the day of resurrection.

Inca theology reverenced the sky, worship of the sun and moon was expanded to include the morning and evening stars (Venus), thunder, lightning and the rainbow, the heavenly bodies and celestial phenomena. American traditions recall a cataclysm in far antiquity before the capture of Luna, our present moon, when Venus changed her color, shape and course, some cosmic intruder knocked Earth spinning into space spoiling its benevolent climate, lengthening the solar year and destroying the brilliant world-wide civilization. Such calamity should have aroused fear of this silver planet yet the Peruvians personified Venus as Chasca, a radiant youth with long and curling locks, as astonishing evocation of Orthon, the Venusian, allegedly met by Geroge Adamski. The Aztecs associated Venus with Quetzalcoatl, the Incas with Viracocha, probably agreeing with ancient peoples everywhere that the teachers of Earth's golden age winged down from Venus; admittedly modern science doubts such belief, the American Mariner 2 suggested a surface temperature of 700 degrees C. but scientists of John Hopkins university are not wholly convinced and speculate on the presence of water-vapor with oceans surpassing Earth's own seas. Some sensitives swear that extraterrestrials materialize from an etherean Venus, a phenomenon which may not have baffled the Incas as much as it confounds us. Con the thunder god, was elevated with the creator and the sun in the sacred trinity. ("The Devil stole all he could!" exclaimed the chronicler Herrera with righteous indignation in his great work

93

"Historia general de las Indias"). In the Coriconcha at Cuzco a great image of the thunder god was represented in human form wearing a headdress which concealed his face, symbolic of clouds; he had his own temple with sacred lands. It is intriguing to equate Con with Indra, Zeus and Thor brandishing thunderbolts; the veiling of the god's face suggests Jehovah on whose countenance not even the prophets dared look, like Con Jehovah was accompanied by thunders and lightnings with a temple of his own; the early Jews associated Jehovah with the pre-Christian trinity; all these gods may have represented spacemen. Magnificent chapels at Cuzco were dedicated to lightning and the rainbow, personified as living beings, reminiscent of the Etruscans and the Greeks; Iris, goddess of the rainbow, was messenger of the gods; the rainbow symbolized a bridge, communication between men on Earth and those wondrous celestials in the sky. People all over the ancient world personalized thunder, lightning and the rainbow, a most startling conception, unless such phenomena actually manifested with beings in human form, that is, spacemen. The ancient civilization of the Chavins at Cajamarca high in the Andes was noted for its great tiger god, which in some mysterious fashion haunted the cosmology of the Peruvians about 1000 B.C. significantly contemporary with Solomon, whose famous temple according to tradition was built by "angels" possible extraterrestrials. Through the ages cats have been reputed to possess occult powers, there may be some affinity between the tiger god of Peru and Bast the cat goddess of Egypt. Why did those long-forgotten Chavins isolated in the lofty mountains erect a single stone of white granite carved in low relief to represent a human figure with feline fangs, why did so many motives on sculptures and pottery feature jaguars? Viracocha was also known as the tiger or jaguar god; this culture hero may have come from Atlantis or Babylon, like Quetzalcoatl he could have originated from space. It is perhaps straining credulity to suggest that Kuti-Kunda, the condor god carrying the sun, represented a spaceman yet the conception of a god like a bird associated with the sun does evoke Horus in his "Eye of Ra" who now appears to have been a space king. Mama-Cocha, the fish god, was sometimes described like a whale, the same description could conceivably suit those UFOs plunging into the Pacific then as they are said to do today.

The Incas worshipped consecrated objects termed "huacas", unusual things found in nature, especially stones fallen from the sky, just like the Mahommedans still venerate the "kaaba", the black meteorite at Mecca. The Peruvians worshipped a host of inferior deities, elementals presiding over the winds, the air and mountains, nymphs in the rivers and dwarfs deep in the Earth, beliefs shared with the Tibetans, Chinese and Greeks. The Incas lived in a universe teeming with invisible entities hovering in the air mysteriously influencing the destinies of men, all strikingly similar to those sylphs so vividly described by Montfaucon de Villars in seventeenth-century France. Such supernatural beliefs scoffed at in our scientific age are slowly becoming respectable again, for students of UFOs now speculate that many strange entities plaguing us today may be denizens of other dimensions. It is fascinating to learn that the Incas held a notion shared by philosophers in India and Greece that everything on Earth had its archetype or idea, its mother, as they emphatically styled it, which they held sacred, as, in some sort, its spiritual essence. This belief that all physical objects are concretions of spiritual archetypes existing in a fifth dimension is cherished by many advanced psychics today; it is certainly astonishing to discover that such esoteric wisdom links initiates in old Peru with philosophers in ancient Greece and ultra-modern thinkers today.

Legend recalls that the first Inca, Manco-Capac, and his wife, Mama-Ocllo, suddenly appeared at dawn on the sacred Lake Titicaca in the Andes like Viracocha ages earlier and announced to the marvelling people that they were the children of the sun sent down by the sun god to teach men civilization. Even today at Capacobana opposite the island of the sun thousands of Indians during the month of August go in pilgrimage to the famous sanctuary where once landed the first extraterrestrials who colonized South America. Reports today persist in describing unknown flying saucers seen to dive and vanish without trace in the waters of Lake Titicaca as though the spacemen enter some subterranean base there. A most ancient tradition suggest that the original Manco-Capac was a white, blue-eyed Atlantean from Hy-Brazil who civilized the barbaric ancestors of the Peruvians. One astonishing tale alleges that in the twelfth-century an English sailor, young and handsome, was shipwrecked on the Pacific shore, though how he reached there is not revealed. The castaway waded ashore to be welcomed by a prince who called him "Ingasman-Capac", (handsome Englishman). Later he became known as Inca

94

Manco-Capac, founder of a dynasty of thirteen Incas ruling like dogs for about four hundred years until ill-fated Atahuallpa was ignominiously garrotted by Pizarro.

The title "Inca" meant "of the sun" relating to "Inti", the sun god, significantly very similar to "Inda" (pronounced Engar) the Sumerian sun god. The erudite Harold T. Wilkins interprets an old chronicle in archaic Dutch, the "Oera Linda Boek" as mentioning a white Frisian mariner, Inka, who in the second milennium B.C. with his argonauts of Finns and Magyars sailed from Heligoland over the western ocean never to be heard of again. Apparently there is evidence that in a remote age white Frisians actually reached Chile and possibly Peru. Such a claim though surprising can hardly be dismissed, today adventurers sail alone around the world, surely thousands of years ago some daring voyagers must have ventured westward eventually to land somewhere in the vast Americas. The Incas expanded their empire of Tshuantinsuyu across the whole of Peru and Bolivia also most of Chile giving their name to the Quechua and Aymara Indians living there.

The Inca, son of the sun, was renowned as divine, he was god come down to Earth, the people, the land, the treasures, all were his; from the most powerful general to the meanest slave, all belonged to him without question in complete dictatorship. This domination though real in practice was not supreme, actual administration was by a cabinet controlling an oligarchy of nobles directing an enormous civil service in a welfare state where every man, woman and child were numbered and under surveillance, a most remarkable yet effective blend of theocracy, monarchy, socialism and communism which flourished because from birth to death everyone was completely conditioned to accept it. No Peruvian thought of rebelling, who could dissent from the son of god. Even the most bigoted Spanish chronicler generously agreed that no Inca misused his powers, though a despot he was paternal, benevolent, a tribute they would hardly accord to their own kings. The Incas were said to be tall, fair-skinned with delicate features, aquiline noses and red or brown hair, a description often applied to Atlanteans; analysis of tissues from the mummies of Incas showed that the first inhabitants of Peru belonged to blood-group A unknown in Latin America until the arrival of the Europeans. The Inca married his sister to ensure a divine descendant from the holy family like the pharaohs of Egypt, although he dispersed his kingly powers by fertilizing hundreds of favored concubines.

The nobility had several wives, the peasants only one. Every man must marry at twenty-four, each woman at eighteen, all unmarried of both sexes over these ages were lined up in the village square and the local mayor forced each man to select his mate there and then. After eight days trial-marriage an ill-favored or bad-tempered wife could be sent back home, seeing there was a penalty for remaining single the rejected woman had to mend her ways and work for better luck next time. Surely a solution to suit today's marital market! Widows were in great demand and seldom remained widows for long; they preferred to marry young bachelors, while widowers chose innocent virgins, widowers never married widows, marriage customs showing more than shrewd common sense. Not surprisingly perhaps divorce was easy but adultery severely punished unless with one of the local geisha girls, who were highly respectably. The peasants lived like serfs cultivating their allotted land or working in the gold and silver mines. Peru did not export precious metals, they accumulated for centuries giving the country greater stocks of gold than all the rest of the world. The civil service was extraordinarily efficient and honest making the people commendably content. Mancio Sierra writing from Cuzco in September 15th, 1589 stated that the Spaniards never found a liar, a thief or sluggard in the entire empire, a claim which no social historian could make for any country today. As a man was born, so he died; however industrious he could never own property or advance his social position. The nobles paid attendance on the Inca whose life was ruled by elaborate ritual; he ate from gold or silver plates held by his chosen women and at least four times a day changed his sumptuous clothes which he never wore twice. When the Inca died his body was mummified and seated on a throne, a life-size statue of gold was served daily with food as though he lived, as indeed he did in other realms, for Incas were gods. Members of the royal family, nobles, civil servants, and priests were exempt from taxation which was all paid by the people as in contemporary Europe.

Like most dictators before and since, the Incas believed it their divine mission to impose their rule upon all their neighbors; at first they tried bribery and propaganda, when such blandishments failed, they used force. The campaigns of the Incas equalled the blitz-kriegs of our own bloody century. The regular army reinforced by trained reserves totalled two hundred thousand men

95

organized into battalions and companies, like the Romans the Peruvians fought with long, metal-tipped spears, swords and deadly slings, the lack of cavalry was compensated by the magnificent road-system giving the army swift mobility. By A.D. 1500 the vast Inca empire extended for 350,000 square miles from Argentine to Columbia, the Pacific to the Amazon with a population totalling perhaps ten million. The first step after conquest was to introduce worship of the sun, otherwise local laws and customs were tolerated; all officials had to learn Quechua, the Latin of South America. The martial Incas easily crushed their native enemies and might have beaten Pizarro had he not held hostage Atahuallpa treacherously captured, however their individual style of fighting and their ritual tactics dependant on the full moon could not prevail against ruthless Spaniards deploying cavalry and armed with guns, whose thunder and lightning convinced most Peruvians that the white invaders must be the old gods returned from the skies. Mounds of animal bones prove that the horse once roamed America but all were destroyed in cataclysms flooding the continent. The Incas regarded the Spanish horsemen like things from outer space; they thought the rider and the animal were one single monster; in one battle Pizarro and his men hotly pressed faced defeat, suddenly a cavalier fell from his horse; the Incas astounded at this startling division of the monster into two halted in confusion thus allowing the Spaniards to escape. This ludicrous accident possibly saved Pizarro's life causing the eventual conquest of Peru.

The renowned Incan Road ran more than four thousand miles from Quito in Ecuador to Tucuman in Central Chile; the highway twenty-five feet broad scaled lofty mountains, swaying suspension-bridges of osier-cables spanned canyons, tunnels penetrated cliffs, hundreds of miles of pavements crossed deserts and swamps, even shallow lakes, part of the road was surfaced with asphalt, branchroads crossed the Andes to jungles on the eastern side. Every twenty miles were rest-houses, stations for imperial runners, signals by day and flares at night transmitted messages from one end of the road to the other in about four hours. Fish, fruit and game from the coast were taken three hundred miles to the capital within twenty-four hours, quicker than some railway deliveries today. Transport was by man-power or llamas, sometimes in caravans of a thousand. Some ancient Americans knew of the wheel; the Aztecs had wheeled toys, stone-wheels are said to have

been found in Tiahuanaco. People must have seen felled trees rolling down slopes giving at least one man ideas of locomotion. Theocracies discourage change; Egypt and Tibet remained static for thousands of years, in Europe the Church stifled progress for centuries, the sterile social system of Peru froze people's minds in a rigid thought-pattern, invention must emanate only from the divine Inca, the greatest reactionary of all.

The Incas deliberately destroyed the records of earlier cultures in their own land and in territories they conquered to obliterate tradition and to "brain-wash" the population into believing only the official propaganda, a wilful destruction of historical annals perpetrated by dictators ancient and modern. The unique system of recording data was by quipus, knots of various sizes in strings of different colors, which to the quipu interpreter were as informative as the punched cards to our own computer operators; unfortunately since the death of the last quipu reader decades ago all that remain of all the detailed records of the Peruvian civil service are bundles of gaily-colored strings. A moral perhaps for those bureaucrats so assiduously documenting us all today. A rudimentary form of writing once existed but was not developed. The expressive Quechua language preserved a few legends and a passionate drama called "Ollantay", which tells how the chieftain, Ollanta, falls madly in love with the Inca's daughter, Curi-Coyllu (Joyful Star), he is slighted by the Inca so he leads a rebellion to victory. Curi-Coyllu gives birth to a daughter, Yma Sumac (How Beautiful) and is imprisoned in the gloomy convent of Virgins. Ollanta is defeated then pardoned by the new Inca who at the plea of Yma Sumac frees her mother, thus restoring the princess to her lover, both blessed by the Inca—and their daughter, How Beautiful. Could Shakespeare with bundles of colored strings knot together a play as entralling as "Ollantay" staged today with a cast of hundreds to tunes from the Itahuanaco "top-twenty"? Peruvian singers in their popular songs could often range through four octaves with a brilliance astounding to Eruopean ears; dancing swayed to those exotic South American rhythms still thrilling ballroom dancers all over the world.

Peru had a powerful and well-developed aesthetic tradition mainly expressed in stonework and pottery, and had complex methods of weaving beautifully colored wools and cottons. The Spaniards were dazzled most of all by their wonderful metalwork; the Peruvians not only

96

wrought jewellery and ornaments with enchanting artistry but knew how to plate copper with silver and gold, a technique since lost. The Incas did not consider gold to have any special intrinsic value except for its obvious evocation of the sun, that happy land had no gold currency, few imports, fewer exports, no balance of payments problems; much of the gold originated from mines and pannings in rivers, but most was probably exacted as tribute from subject peoples; almost all the treasure accumulated in temples and palaces. During the first twenty-five years after the conquest more than one thousand million dollars of gold was looted and sent to Spain. For more than two centuries many thousands of gold and silver bars and countless marvellous gold-ware were carried by mule-trains down the Andes to Lima then shipped to Spain; such plunder of a defenceless country was a disgrace to Christendom; the lordly galleons attracted Elizabethan sea-dogs, pirates and buccaneers, who ensured the booty was more fairly shared. Much more important than those shiploads of gold which inflated Europe's economy was the introduction of potatoes, pepper, cotton, cocoa, tomatoes and an astounding profusion of exotic fruits and flowers to improve Europe's diet. The cultivation of these plants from wild varieties proves many milennia of farming and is irrefutable evidence of the immense antiquity of pre-Inca peoples.

Unlike the Mayas the Incas were not noted astronomers, although in the absence of written records evaluation of their attainments is difficult; they checked their 360-day calendar plus the five "lost days" by the moon and the Pleiades, the priests paid special veneration to Venus but somewhat irrationally shouted at the moon during eclipses. Hyatt Verrill toyed with the speculation that the pre-Inca initiates could materialize ionized bridges of light over which they cross inaccessible canyons; when the Inca Yupanqui besieged the Chimus in their fortress at Paramanya he threatened to shut off the sun unless they surrendered, the Chimus presumably thought this possible and surrendered at once. The transportation over long distances of immense stones weighing hundreds of tons is nowadays usually attributed to utilization of sonic forces to produce levitation. An Italian priest in Peru has lately advanced a unique alternative method. There may now be reason to believe that the Incas used a kind of decomposing substance which could soften stones into a malleable clay, easily portable; on arrival at the desired site the plasma was kneaded to the required shape, after a time the mass petrified into hard, smooth stone. The secret of this novel method is said to have been known to the builders of the Pyramids, perhaps also to the Britons who built Stonehenge. The softening of huge stones into malleable, portable plasma by some wonder-solvent, fantastic as it may seem, is nevertheless more probable than their levitation by anti-gravity or manipulation by thousands of slaves. Some archaeologists believe that the Incas did not use stone-masons' cutting-tools but applied a radio-active paste which dissolved the granite to the shape desired; it is significant that conventional stone implements can make no impression on the massive monoliths, some different technique for those wonderful carvings must have been used.

All the old chroniclers agree that the cyclopean cities in the Andes were built ages before the Incas who did not rule in Peru until about A.D. 1200, more than a century after the Norman conquest of Britain; the complete absence of written records baffles conservative archaeologists who somewhat illogically allege that for thousands of years the Peruvians apparently lived in the fresh air like their llamas then seven hundred years ago suddenly had the urge and the technique to build those wonderful cities. The natives themselves, who are not misled by foreign scholars, proudly believe that Cuzco 11,000 feet high in an Andes valley was built where the legendary Manco Capac rested after his wanderings, there his golden staff given him by the sun god vanished when he threw it to the ground, an intriguing comparison with the staff or vril-rod of Moses. Cuzco was laid out in the symbolic form of the condor, the fortress of Sacsahuaman forming the head, the Rodadera and the Andenes representing the neck while the body was the city proper with the Kori-Pata for the tail and the surroundings both simulating the spread wings. The city was enclosed by immense walls with some stones weighing each thirty tons. Cieza de Leon marvelled that the city with more than two hundred thousand inhabitants surpassed all the Spaniards had yet seen in the new world. Scores of palaces and nearly four hundred temples and religious houses glowed with burnished plates of gold, "the tears of the sun god"; through all the buildings and exquisite gardens flowed running-water conducted through pipes from reservoirs. The fabulous temple of the sun astounded the Spaniards dazzled by marvels. W.H. Prescott in a memorable description wrote:

"The interior of the temple was the most worthy of admiration. It was literally a mine

97

of gold. On the western wall was emblazoned a representation of the deity, consisting of a human countenance looking forth from amidst innumerable rays of light which emanated from it in every direction in the same manner as the sun is often personified with us. The figure was engraved on a massive plate of gold of enormous dimensions, thickly powdered with emeralds and precious stones."

The ancient Peruvians must surely have had some special reason for planning their wonderful capital high in the mountains to resemble a giant bird and to fashion their fabulous golden sun disk with the face of a god. Was Cuzco itself like those fascinating monuments at Nazca and Marcahuasi designed to attract the gods, the spacemen?

The cyclopean fortress of Sacsahuaman frowning down on Cuzco fills the mind of every traveller with astonishment and admiration. The wonder of Cieza de Leon in the sixteenth-century is echoed by sophisticated scholars today. Hyatt Verrill marvelled:

"...titanic stones were hewn, fitted and erected countless centuries before Columbus set sail from Palos, centuries before the birth of Christ, I stood late one afternoon awaiting the sunset. The spot whereon I stood was the apex of a single cut stone, a monolith of flint-hard andesite over twenty feet in height and weighing, perhaps, two hundred tons, yet but one of hundreds, that, fitted together without mortar or cement, formed a sheer smooth wall with scarcely a visible crevice between the stones."

Three immense parapets combined to form a wall sixty feet high with only three doors built on a mountain-top artificially levelled covering several hundred acres like Monte Alban in old Mexico; the Spaniards who first saw it were astounded. Many of the megalithic buildings suggestive of giants astonishingly have passages apparently designed for dwarfs, probably that race of "little people" said to have been the builders of the fabulous Zimbabwe in Africa. Twenty-four miles north-west of Cuzco surmounting an acropolis of rock rises the great fortress of Ollantay some of whose massive stones weigh three hundred tons, chiselled and fitted together so that the thinnest blade could not penetrate the cracks. The most remarkable fort in Peru was probably Machu Picchu more than ten thousand feet high in the Andes overhanging a three thousand feet high precipice. This remote citadel not visited by the Spaniards built long before the Incas is attributed to some ancient Andean civilization. Sacsahuaman, Ollantay, Machu Piccu and other great fortresses so high in the mountains intrigue us today as never before. How were these immense blocks of stone transported to such dizzy heights, fashioned and fitted with such fantastic accuracy? Why were these forts built amid the clouds? What enemy did they resist? These cyclopean defences recall those vitrified forts on mountain-tops all over the world, associated in legend with those wars between the gods and giants. Is it too fantastic to suggest that these mountain citadels of Peru were built by some ancient race as protection against spacemen?

Eusebius Newcombergus the Jesuit, in his 5th book of Natural History, says that near the port of Lima as the people were working a gold mine, they found a ship on which were many characters very different from ours. Had this vessel been tossed ashore in some cataclysm and buried thousands of years ago en route to lost Lemuria?

Early in the sixteenth century Huayna-Capac extended the Incan empire over most of South America; at the height of his power he felt prophetically disturbed by rumors of white men, probably the first expedition under Pizarro and Almagro, which reached the Rio de San Juan a hundred leagues south of Panama. Huayna-Capac realized from the accounts he received that the white men with their skill and wonder-weapons represented a civilization with powers eclipsing his own, soon they would land in Peru. Supernatural prodigies appeared in the heavens, comets (UFOs?) flashed through the air, the moon was girdled with rings of many colors, thunderbolts shattered one of the royal palaces, earthquakes shook the land. Huayna-Capac summoned his counsellors as he was dying and announced the imminent conquest of the empire by a race of white and bearded strangers; mindful of those legends of the god, Viracocha, who had vowed one day to return, the Inca commanded his subjects not to resist the will of heaven but to fulfil their destiny in submission to the white gods.

When his son and heir was born, the Inca had celebrated his birth by the manufacture of a golden chain seven hundred feet in length and the links nearly as thick as a man's wrist, so heavy that six hundred Indian chieftains could scarcely lift it, the boy's name, "Huascar" meant "cable". In Quito the victorious Inca married its princess, a beautiful girl who died of grief; he became very fond of their son, Atahuallpa. Before his death Huayna-Capac made a most disastrous decision, flouting that wise

98

statesmanship for which he was so renowned, he divided his empire between Huascar who was given Peru and Atahuallpa bequeathed Quito. For nearly five years the two princes ruled their domains in uneasy peace and friendship, the ambitious Atahuallpa aspired to the throne of the Incas uniting all the empire under one rule; he provoked civil war with his peace-loving elder brother and routed Huascar's army on the plain before Cuzco taking him prisoner. Atahuallpa invited the Inca nobles and the whole of the royal family to Cuzco, treacherously murdered all the men and ordered all the women of the blood royal to be put to death with the most refined and lingering tortures in the presence of the impotent Huascar, an act like Greek tragedy exacting a destined retribution. The chronicler, Gonzalo Fernandez de Oviedo, doubted this slaughter and wrote that the prolific Huayna-Capac left a hundred sons and daughters, most of whom were still alive. Atahuallpa's treachery brought short-lived triumph; he was now the thirteenth Inca of Peru, a country torn and bleeding, ripe for conquest.

A few months later on November 16th, 1532 Don Francisco Pizarro, the sixty-year old conquistador, who had so long lived under the shadow of the great Cortes, with a small company totalling only 178 men, 67 horses, three arquebuses, three small cannon and a few crossbows confronted proud Atahuallpa with 6,000 picked troops at Cajamarca. Completely outnumbered the Spaniards faced appalling danger, flight was suicide, attack most desperate. Pizarro remembered the strategem of Cortes in similar straits at Cholula; he cordially invited Atahuallpa to dinner, Fray Vincente de Valverde, a Dominican friar, vainly attempted to convert the Inca to Christianity then turned to Pizarro said "I absolve you". Pizarro at once gave the fatal signal. He waved a white scarf in the air. Cannon and musket-fire raked the Inca army who trusting to Pizarro's good faith were massed without weapons in the square below. In a few bloody hours the Peruvians were massacred, Atahuallpa taken prisoner and resistance crushed.

A comet (UFO?) was seen in the air, Atahuallpa gazed at it in foreboding for some minutes and remarked that a similar sign had appeared in the skies before the death of his father, Huayna-Capac. Like Montezuma, whom he never knew, Atahuallpa foresaw his doom, he felt he was playing out his destined part, as prophesied long ago the white "gods" had returned bringing to his country tribulation and to its ruler death. The Inca made forlorn attempts to ransom himself with fabulous treasure but could not placate the avaricious Spaniards, who brought him to mock trial and sentenced him to be burned at the stake. When Atahuallpa was bound to his funeral pyre Valverde promised that if at the last moment the Inca embraced Christianity, the Church in her mercy would change the mode of execution to garrotting, the punishment reserved in Spain for criminals. On August 29th, 1533 Atahuallpa abjured his ancient religion, accepted Christianity and within the hour was choked to death. The chronicler, Xerez, wrote that Atahuallpa "paid the penalty of his errors and cruelties for he was the greatest butcher, as all agreed, that the world ever saw". The ancient land of the Incas plundered and raped was destined for more suffering from the Spaniards and their hideous Inquisition.

Since those golden empires of the Andes the spacemen must have watched this fabulous South America, their compassionate eyes marvelled at the rise and fall of the Incas. What portents do they see menacing those strife-torn dictatorships today?

99

Chapter Twelve
Lost Civilizations

Mysterious America haunts Man more than ever in our space age, behind the modern glamor today we sense that muted wonder of the ancients and feel those silent, shrouded lands of the sunset slumbered under some secret spell cast by the gods long ago. From the Arctic to the Amazon colossal mounds with buried treasures, strange sculptures crowning mountain-tops, unknown writings carved on cliffs, challenge us with some civilization lost in dim prehistory. Legends of white gods from the stars confirm those classic tales of Titans, that stellar race of supermen who once ruled Earth in a golden age shattered by wars and cataclysms drowning continents and smashing to desolation the culture of the west. Lemuria and Atlantis still trouble our dreams, fitful memories bedazzle our minds with marvels beyond belief; imagination resurrects those mighty kings, bejewelled queens, the fabled splendors of fair cities; suddenly the glories fade leaving us all forlorn. Mindful of our tragic times we wonder if those plaintive ruins foretell our own fate. What has been shall be again, the future lives in the past!

The whole universe throbs with life. Astronomers agree that our own galaxy, the Milky Way, must have myriads of planets, at least a million with beings wise and foolish like ourselves. Speculation on life in space has hitherto been theoretical, however in December, 1970 NASA stated that for the first time Man possessed irrefutable proof of extraterrestrial life. Dr. Cyril Ponnamperuma, head of a research-team, analyzing a meteorite which fell on September 28th, 1969 at Murchison in Australia, announced the discovery of amino-acids and hydrocarbons, constituents of complicated organic cells. The meteorite may originate from the belt of asteroids, possibly debris of a planet destroyed ages ago. Radio-astronomers all over the the world now listen for intelligent signals from space and are devising ingenious techniques for communicating with any extraterrestrials they may contact.

Today as our cosmonauts begin their conquest of space a new dimension of consciousness challenges the old terrestrial concepts of religion and science. The purpose of life is to people the universe. Time is only relative, many stars may have had planets whose highly civilized peoples visited Earth then a virgin world many million years ago. When the Bible states God created Man in his image what precisely does it mean? What can be the image of God, the Absolute, creating and sustaining the vast universe with a parallel universe of anit-matter and many universes of finer dimensions beyond our perception? If by God the writers of Genesis meant a wondrous being from the stars then primitive Man might have got the impression that their celestial teacher had created Man in human form just like himself.

The old evolutionists were ignorant of atomic radiation, viruses and cataclysms which may cause sudden mutation of species. The solar system in its trajectory through space toward Sagittarius encounters different potentials of cosmic radiation causing violent changes in terrestrial magnetism with startling effects on all life-forms. There have probably been many appearances of Man. Cybernetics proves that the millions of cells make our brain a fabulous computer, scientists admit we use only about 4% of our potential powers. Perhaps we function in a lowly stage of evolution; in the far past as in the distant future species of Man may have developed 15% even 50% of their latent genius attaining wisdom and powers like gods to transform our Earth in those marvellous civilizations we now suspect when Man really did commune with his cosmic brothers from the stars.

The Hindus, Mayas, Greeks, Irish and other ancient peoples recall four world ages preceding our own when civilization was destroyed then slowly rebuilt. Egyptian priests told Herodotus that eleven thousand years before the axis of the Earth became displaced, "the sun had removed from his proper course four times and had risen where he now setteth and set where he now riseth." Apollodorus in Epitome 11, 10-3, states that Atreus took Mycenae from the usurper, Thyestes, when the sun went backward and set in the east as promised by Zeus. This reversal of the sun's course in the sky noted in legends all over Earth is poetically described by Ovid in "Tristis" ii, 391, and "Ars Amatori", i, 32, Hyginus, Fab. 88 and 258, Seneca "Thyestes" 776, and Martial, iii, 45, confirming that cataclysms in ancient times were known to the Greeks and Romans, now agreed by our own geologists. Scientists still question Atlantis but all accept that in our Earth's long history lands have become seas and seas now lands; islands arise from the ocean depths and others sink today, ten milennia hence the world-map may look quite different. Some scholars now suggest that displacement of Earth's axis and the ice ages may have been caused by immense nuclear bombs, calcined rocks in Ireland, Czechoslovakia and California seem evidence of some great cataclysm.

Man's existence here on Earth is far older than historians dare imagine. Palaentologists in Kenya unearth human skulls twenty million years old, even these are transcended by Mayan records in Yucatan of ninety million and four hundred million years confounding belief, were it not for those intriguing metallic objects sometimes found embedded in deep coal-seams, presumably lost amid those giant forests of the Carboniferous age so long ago. The noted psychic, Edgar Cayce, gave revelations of Atlantis ten and a half million years since making the reign of those divine dynasties in Babylon 432,000 years before the flood seem only yesterday. Vast ages must have elapsed for the primeval world-language to evolve into the thousands of tongues spoken today; countless

milennia of culture were needed to mature the theology of the Sanskrit Vedas and the sublime wisdom of the Bhagavad Gita. Ethnologists now believe that Homo Sapiens of Paleolithic times 34,000 years ago had attained high mental powers. Alexander Marshack of Harvard university states this ancient Man had compiled a complicated lunar calendar and used a system of writing, the strange signs on bones and stones from the ice age may record intelligible data we cannot decipher. Soviet archaeologists excavating the grave of two boys who were buried near Vladimir north of Moscow about 25,000 B.C. claim to have found remnants of shirts, leather trousers, fur-lined boots and headgear similar to the clothing worn by local inhabitants today. Plato in his "Critias" describes the admirable civilization of Athens 12,000 years ago. Pythagoras told of ships' anchors found on mountain-tops, evidence of men sailing seas now dry land. The antiquity of Man is much greater than scholars admit.

The Greeks like the Sumerians, Egyptians, Hindus, Japanese and Mayas believed in a golden age when Earth was ruled by the gods then heroes and superhuman kings. Aeschylus, Sophocles, Euripides and Aristophanes honored the gods in their great plays like wondrous beings surveilling mankind and frequently resolved their plots by a "Deus ex machina" (god from the machine), the sudden appearance of Apollo or Athena to pronounce divine judgment. Classical scholars somewhat baffled usually construed "machine" in this context as meaning the "visible universe" but it is tempting to interpret "god from the machine" literally as an extraterrestrial descending from a spaceship, especially as there is reason to suppose from the experiences of Ezekiel and Daniel in Babylon, Aethalides and Epimenides in Greece, Romulus and Numa Pompilius in Rome and the emperor Jimmu in Japan that in the sixth and seventh centuries B.C. spacemen actually were manifesting on Earth. Pindar, the greatest lyric poet of Greece, born about 522 B.C. only three years younger than Aeschylus, shared popular belief in the gods; in his "Epinicie" celebrating the victories gained in the Nemean Games, he wrote in his Sixth Ode:

"There is one race of men, one race of gods, both have breath of life from a single mother."

This belief in the gods reverently supported by Plato permeated Greek thought; Apollodorus, an Athenian historian, wrote:

"Sky was the first who ruled over the

101

whole world."

The Greek word "ouranos" meaning "sky" could have referred to Uranus, the planet known to the ancients, but it probably signified the god, Uranus, symbolizing a most ancient race of Titans like the giant Asuras of India or the sorcerers and wizards of Central America. The Uranids may represent some galactic race from an advanced planet when our world was young millions of years ago long before Adam. The "Genesis Rabbre", a midrash or commentary on the Book of Genesis compiled in the fifth century in Palestine states:

"In the beginning God created numerous worlds destroying one after the other as they failed to satisfy Him. All were inhabited by Man a thousand generations of whom He cut off having no record of them."

Far from being unique the main traditions of the Old Testament were reflected in the myths of Greece and epics of Ugarit in Canaan expressing a common East Mediterranean culture influenced by the Sumerian "Gilgamesh Epic", the Egyptian "The Book of the Dead" and the wonderful "Ramayana" and "Mahabharata" of fabulous India. The Jews never lived in isolation as the Bible suggests. Israel traded with Greece and Italy, the Phoenicians ventured to Britain; Dr. Cyrus H. Gordon, the most eminent professor of Mediterranean studies at Brandes universtiy, U.S.A., has deciphered inscriptions found in a mound in Tennessee in 1885 and concludes that the Hebrews landed in America many centuries before Columbus, not really surprising since the Babylonians apparently reached South America about 2000 B.C. A spaceman gliding over Mt. Olympus was revered as Zeus, crossing the Syrian coast he was called Baal (rider of the clouds), when his "power and glory" touched down on Mt. Sinai the Israelites worshipped him as Jehovah, over the Himalayas in sunny Bengal he was welcomed as Indra, while in Japan the emperor honored him as "Mikoto, son of the sun". The different names denoted the same extraterrestrials, as the centuries elapsed, generic names for spacemen like our world-wide "G.I. Joe".

A recent revelation of spacemen in ancient times is so startling that by some strange block in our conditioned minds its colossal importance is completely ignored. The 1970 edition of the New English Bible, Genesis, Chapter 6, verses 1/2 states:

"When mankind began to increase and to spread all over the earth and daughters of men were born to them, the sons of the gods saw that the daughters of men were beautiful so

that took to themselves such women as they chose."

Sons of the gods! A footnote to the New English Bible text states that the probable Hebrew reading is "In those days and also afterward" suggesting that the sons of the gods consorted with earthwomen for centuries all over the world.

The cataclysmic importance of the New English Bible rendering of Genesis, Chapter 6, verses 1/2 "sons of the gods" compared with the earlier translation in the Authorized Version of James I as "sons of god", a vague, theological connotation confounding learned commentators, wondrously transforms our whole conception of antiquity and has pregnant implications for our UFO-haunted Earth today. "The Book of Enoch" regards the "son of man" as a supernatural being in a "power and glory", later Daniel appropriated him as the "Messiah" with immense significance for Judaism and Christianity: today we may consider the "Messiah" meant a spaceman descending like the ancient gods to save mankind.

The Dead Sea Scrolls confirm the presence of spacemen before the flood. Lamech, a sixth generation in descent from Adam, accused his wife, Bathenosh, of having consorted with a son of heaven; she bore Noah, who like Enoch walked with God. The Lord, a spaceman, would naturally warn Noah, possibly son of a spaceman, of the coming flood and advise him to build an ark to save his wife and family thus to perpetuate the race. The Greeks state that Zeus destroyed mankind in a great flood when Propetheus advised his son, Deucalion, to build a boat for himself and his wife, Pyrrha. Similar flood legends of the angry gods drowning the sinful world in floods survived by culture heroes divinely forewarned are told in the epics of India, Babylon and Mexico and by peoples all over Earth.

Lest our thesis of spacemen in antiquity be dismissed as capitalist propaganda confounding true Marxist ideology it is encouraging to know that our views find welcome support across the Iron Curtain. Professor Virghinsky in "Znanie-Sila" (Knowledge is Power) describes how the ancient Scythians around the Black sea were convinced that the gods had thrown from the sky down to the first men on Earth tools and equipment, the plow, the axe, the cup, basic utensils for the advent of civilization together with the sacred fire. Vladimir V. Rubtzov in "Na Sushe i na More" (On Land and at Sea) tells of the wonderful civilization of Shamballah and the immortals winging down in vimanas. In the same journal Vyacheslav Zaitsev

102

writes a much-quoted essay revealing to the western world the discovery by Chinese archaeologists of odd-looking stone discs in the Bayan-Karan-Ula mountains on the border of China and Tibet apparently recording the crash of a spaceship there about 12,000 years ago, whose small, gaunt, yellow-faced crew mated with local women becoming ancestors of the Dropa tribe; later this brilliant Russian persuasively suggests that the spires and domes of temples and churches copy the "house of the lord", a spaceship. The noted Soviet scientist Alexander Kazantsev insists that highly-advanced creatures from Mars have visited Earth many times until the present day. M. Agrest in the "Literaturnaya Gazeta" believes that Sodom and Gomorrah were destroyed by nuclear bombs and that the cyclopean terrace at Baalbek in Lebanon might have been a launching-site; he theorizes that those intriguing tektites in the Libyan desert were fused by the blast of spaceships taking-off. The redoubtable Josef Schklovsky, member of the Sternberg Astronomical Institute of Moscow, a noted exponent of extraterrestrials, in collaboration with Carl Sagan of Harvard, suggests that the Sumerians were taught civilization by Oannes and other akpallus "semi-demons" from space.

Space-archaeology interests the Rumanians. The "Drum Nou" (New Way) on July 29th, 1969 published a fascinating article "Astronauti Ai Unor Civilizati Disparute" which we hesitantly read as reviewing the evidence for spacemen in prehistoric times. Extracts are translated from Alexander Gorbovsky's fascinating book "Zagadki Drevenishi Istorii" (Enigmas of Ancient History) which reveals that objects discovered in the tomb of the third century Chinese general Tsao Chu contained 85% aluminium, a metal obtained by electrolysis, a technique considered unknown in that era. Gorbovsky refers to the contradiction that though the Mayas never used wheeled vehicles archaeologists have unearthed a toy which had wheels, evidently from a civilization so ancient that after the horse in America became extinct the use of wheels was forgotten. The "Drum Nou" discusses the vast astronomical knowledge of the Egyptians, the "flying chariot" of the Hindu hero, Rama, explaining its propulsion by a "special linear" fire obtained from the disintegration of mercury, a nuclear-reactor described in the "Samarangana Sutra". Tribute is paid to the Soviet savants, A.P. Kazantsev and G.V. Sciatski, their discoveries of drawings of apparent spacemen at Ferghana in the U.S.S.R. are compared with similar drawings found in Australia, the Sahara and Japan. NASA is quoted as admitting that the intriguing Jomon Dogu statuettes exactly resemble the American cosmonauts in helmets and spacesuits. The Rumanian writer concluded by wondering whether extraterrestrials had visited us in the past and whether there had existed on Earth ancient civilizations destroyed by cataclysms, recent interpretations by scientists would throw new light on many old theories concerning Man's life on Earth. Such conclusions regarding spacemen in prehistory by the Rumanians and Russians are welcomed by all students in the west.

The controversial Italian writer, Renato Vesco, suggests that spacemen from a dying planet with an attenuated atmosphere, have an oxygen deficiency in their blood giving them that blueish tinge noted in cardiac patients. Traditions among all peoples associate blue blood with royalty implying that the earliest kings of Earth really had blue blood because they originated from space.

Far from the haunts of men today on mountain-tops or dusty plain, even deep in the jungle, stand immense stones, some carved with cosmic symbols, relics of a remote past. Alien and forlorn these erratics trouble our consicousness arousing fleeting recognition of ancient wonder only to vanish like a dream. Sensitives touching these solitary rocks feel their fingers suddenly thrilled by some potent force, photographs are often befogged by an aura of strange vibrations beyond our science. In populated areas alignments from hilltops, beacons and stone circles crisscross the landscape in magnetic lines often coincident with prehistoric tracks and apparently followed by UFOs sighted today. Where these leys converge were usually sites of pagan worship now cathedral towns, power-points of cosmic force fixed by some forgotten race in far antiquity. Initiates of the Aetherius Society with their founder, Dr. George King, inspired by cosmic masters ascend once sacred mountains and by occult techniques re-activate dormant energies projecting beneficent vibrations to destroy malevolent rays menacing mankind. From Britain to Tibet, China to Peru, a vast grid of magnetic force still persisting from an unimaginable past covers the entire Earth, invisible evidence of some electronic, world-wide civilization lost in pre-history.

Many milennia of cataclysms, wars and human folly have destroyed the monuments of ancient Man yet a few solitary works remain to challenge memory. The cyclopean ruins of Tiahuanaco, megaliths in Mexico, burial-mounds in America,

103

earth-zodiacs in Britain, tunnels under Africa, caves in India, tombs in Japan, rock-paintings in Australia, the Pyramid, the Sphinx, all stand in majestic grandeur conjuring a marvellous panorama of Earth ruled by Titans, sons of the gods.

The Japanese, whose Mikado claims descent from Amaterasu, the sun goddess, believe the space people visited Japan. In August 1969 a summer festival was held at Sapporo, capital of Hokkaido, the northernmost island, a Dogu suit and figurines of spacemen in helmets with large goggle eyes and spacemasks aroused the enthusiasm of all the visitors, conscious of their cosmic past.

Fragments of knowledge from the old civilizations were preserved by initiates in many lands. Astrology even in its present fanciful form echoes some universal science which measured the radiations from the stars and their influence on the mind of Man now suspected by psychiatrists. The Kabbala, Hermetic writings and the books of magic studied by the alchemists associated metallurgy with theosophy, metals were said to possess elemental spirits, no such a bizarre conception since all matter is ultimately reducible to electric potentials. The alchemists distilled and re-distilled a metal over and over again and eventually from the soul of the subtle distillate achieved transformations like our nuclear reactions. Thousands of years ago the Chinese isolated hormones and by acupuncture wrought cures baffling our western medicine like the strange powers of witch-doctors today; the use of herbs and drugs suggests a pharmacopia milennia old. The famous maps copied by the Turkish admiral, Piri Reis, in 1513 and 1528 show mountains in an Antarctica free of ice, two broad gulfs in Queen Maud Lans and reveal that Greenland consists of three islands, lately confirmed by our oceanographers; the original maps were apparently drawn before the ice age 10,000 B.C. from surveys taken high in the air. The siting of the Great Pyramid in the exact center of the world's land-mass implies an aerial survey of our Earth long ago. Intriguing links between West and East surely prove some common culture. The Incas like the ancient Egyptians were ruled by a priest-king, they shared similar religion and theocracy, utilized identical metallurgical and agricultural techniques, they mummified their dead. That notorious curse laid by the Egyptian priests against tomb-robbers suggests some radio-active poison persisting for centuries like the alleged cold light. A cult of the dead was practised by Neanderthal Man more than two million years ago, evidence of a sublime

theology. Mayan astronomers rivalled in skill the Magi of Babylon, their precise observations impress us as much by their incredible accuracy as by the science required. Stonehenge built four thousand years ago was an observatory of immense complexity for studying eclipses of the sun and moon, the erection of its great trilithons poses problems still unsolved. The Druids, the Etruscans and people all over Earth anxiously scanned the skies for centuries with a vigilance like our own world-wide radar-watch. Did the ancients fear invaders from space, the return of the sky gods?

From this far age no intelligible records are recognized, all documents have long since perished by cataclysms, wars, vandalism and in the destruction of the great libraries at Alexandria, Pergamum and Tenochtitlan; a few weather-eroded petroglyphs all over the world still baffle comprehension. Future generations will store information on magnetic-tape or miniaturized into micro-dots. Suppose the savants of that psycho-civilization bequeathed their data in electric-circuits or time-capsules as legends suggest? Psychics claim that arch-types, noumena of terrestrial phenomena, exist in a fifth-dimension, matrices in thought of objects on Earth, occultists tell of akashic records reflecting everything that has ever happened, psychiatrists suspect a universal mind from which sensitives receive memories of the past, a gifted seer may obtain accurate information by methods unknown to science. Edgar Cayce in Reading 378-16 revealed that a record of Atlantis from its beginnings to final destruction will be found in an underground chamber between the paws of the Sphinx.

Legends from all over the world strain our belief by telling of gods and heroes winging down from space like our own cosmonauts. Rama flew across India in a palatial flying-car, Padma Sambhava visited Tibet on a winged horse, the gods of China rode fiery dragons, those august deities honored Japan in a heavenly rocking-boat, Jehovah astounded the Israelites in his "power-and-glory", Horus sped through Egyptian skies in a solar boat, Shamash touched down near Babylon from a winged disk, Athena alighted gracefully in Greece with winged sandals, Odin roared over Scandinavia in an aerial car, Cuchulain dazzled the Celts with his enchanted chariot, Quetzalcoatl sailed on a raft of serpents, the Eskimos marvelled at great white birds, the red Indians told of great spirits on thunderbirds, the Hawaiians remembered flying cherubs, African tribes treasured white teachers descending from huge birds, many of these celestial

104

visitants came in peace, others blasted Earth with lightnings and thunderbolts, weapons evoking our nuclear bombs. Our wonder is quickened by a remarkably translation from an old Sanskrit text by Maharshi Bharaduraja of Mysore called "Aeronautics, A Manuscript from the Prehistoric Past", which confounds us by describing vimanas flying to the planets with techniques like radar and aerial photography, even detailing the diet of their pilots. "Teotihuacan" in the ancient Nahuatl language of Mexico is said to mean "The place where men flew like gods".

The flying machines were all destroyed ages ago and their secret lost but surprising evidence still remains to bewilder us. Frescoes in the Jugoslave monastery of Visoki Decani depict astronauts flying craft apparently propelled by rockets; the phoenix, the mythical bird which perishes in a flame to be reborn, could conceivably be some memory of a missile-launch. The slab of a tomb at Palenque in Mexico bears a stylized drawing of a young man apparently piloting a spaceship. A clay vase in San Salvador is decorated with palm-trees over which fly men in a strange machine emitting flames and smoke. In the state bank at Bogota is a gold trinket only 33 mm long, once thought to represent a curious bird or fish, experts on re-examination now discern an aerial craft showing the captain's cabin, its triangular wings and tail give a startling likeness to the Concorde.

The Explorer satellites discovered around our Earth vast bands of most powerful radiation known as the Van Allen Belts with a broad neutral corridor near the north and south poles. UFOs obviously traversing this sector approach in the west and account for those frequent visitations of the gods recorded by the red Indians, Aztecs and Incas, also the spacemen haunting America today. Many psychics confirm the prophecies of Nostradamus that wars and cataclysms will ravage our Earth before this century ends, much of America will sink and Atlantis will arise from the sea. Already earthquakes are causing increasing destruction in California and Peru. On Good Friday, 1966 when a great tremor destroyed Anchorage in Alaska our Earth rang like a bell and most of the American eastern sea-board arose two inches then fell. Seismologists fear that quakes along the notorious San Andreas fault zone may shatter the continent like Lemuria and Atlantis. Before final destruction the white gods of Montezuma will land again.

America's fate may depend once more on those spacemen in the ancient west.

105

Bibliography

The author wishes to express his gratitude and sincere acknowledgements to the authors and publishers of the literary works enumerated below and to all authorities inadvertently omitted.

1 Sandrelli, Antonio.
 "Qualcosa viaggia piu in fretta della luce"
 Clypeus 22. April 1969, Torino.
2 Asimov, Isaac.
 "Vers les hyper-vitesses"
 Le Nouveau Planete, No. 12. Nov. 1969
3 Barker, Gray.
 "They knew too much about Flying Saucers"
 University Books, New York.
4 Williamson, Dr. G.H.
 "The Saucers Speak"
 Neville Spearman Ltd., London.
5 Vallee, Jacques.
 "Anatomy of a Phenomenon"
 Neville Spearman Ltd., London.
6 Holmes, Capt. David C.
 "The Search for Life on other Worlds"
 Bantam, New York.
7 Shklovski, Josef. and Sagan, Carl.
 "Intelligent Life in the Universe"
 Holden Day, New York.
8 Bergier, Jacques.
 "Les Extraterrestres"
 Planete, 23, J/A 1965.
9 Calder, Nigel.
 "Violent Universe"
 B.B.C. Publications.
10 Barbadoro, Giancarlo.
 "Un Mistero Celeste"
 Laforghiana, L/A, Anno IV-4, Torino.
11 "Sunday Mirror".
 August 23, 1970. London.
12 Edwards, Frank.
 "Flying Saucers—Serious Business"
 Mayflower Dell, London.
13 Leslie, Desmond and Adamski, George.
 "Flying Saucers have landed"
 Neville Spearman Ltd., London.
14 Caporlingua, Massimo.
 "Per la pace sulla Terra, intervento degli untraterrestri"
 "Il Tempo", 3 Agosto 1970.

15 Shuttlewood, Arthur.
 "The Warminster Mystery"
 Neville Spearman Ltd., London.
16 Williamson, Dr. G.H.
 "Road in the Sky"
 Neville Spearman Ltd., London.
17 Drake, W. Raymond.
 "Gods or Spacemen?"
 Amherst Press, Wisconsin, U.S.A.
18 Swedenborg, Emmanuel.
 "Heaven and its Wonders and Hell"
 Swedenborg Society, London.
19 Hebwynd, J.D. and Rytov, V.A.
 "The Living Universe"
 Neville Spearman Ltd., London.
20 Fort, Charles.
 "The Book of the Damned"
 Holt & Co., New York.
21 Vallee, Jacques.
 "Challenge to Science"
 Neville Spearman Ltd., London.
22 Leighton, Robert B.
 "The Surface of Mars"
 "Scientific American", May 1970
23 Fort, Charles.
 "New Lands"
 Holt & Co. New York.
24 Sade, Marquis de.
 "Quartet"
 (Trs. Margaret Crosland) Panther, London.
25 Fort, Charles.
 "Lo!"
 Henry Holt & Co. New York.
26. Adamski, George.
 "Inside the Spaceships"
 Neville Spearman Ltd., London.
27 Allingham, Cedric.
 "Flying Saucer from Mars"
 Frederick Muller, London, 1954.
28 Gilman, Peter.
 "Do the Cherubim come from Mars?"

106

Flying Saucer Review, S/O 1967.
29 King, Dr. George.
  "The Nine Freedoms"
  The Aetherius Society, Los Angeles.
30 Dickhoff, Robert E.
  "Homecoming of the Martians"
  Health Research, Makelumna Hill, California.
31 Adamski, George
  "Flying Saucers Farewell"
  Abelard Schuman, New York.
32 Menger, Howard.
  "From Outer Space to You"
  Saucerian Books, Clarksburg, West Virginia.
33 Shklovski, Josef and Sagan, Carl.
  "Intelligent Life in the Universe"
  Holden Day Inc. New York.
34 Williamson, Dr. G.H.
  "The Saucers Speak"
  Neville Spearman Ltd., London.
35 Palmer, Ray.
  "Flying Saucers", June 1970.
  Amherst, Wisconsin, U.S.A.
36 Yogi Ramacharaka.
  "Gnani Yoga"
  L. Fowler & Co. Ltd., London.
37 Gardner, Martin.
  "The Ambidextrous Universe"
  Pelican, London.
38 Vallee, Jacques.
  "Anatomy of a Phenomenon"
  Neville Spearman Ltd., London, 1966.
39 Budge, Sir Wallis E.A.
  "The Book of the Dead, Papyrus of Ani"
  British Museum, London, 1 1895.
40 Centro Unico Nazionale.
  "Notizario-UFO", No. 1, G/F 1970,
  C.U.N., Casella Postale No, 796, 40100, Bologna.
41 Blavatsky, Mdm. H.P.
  "The Secret Doctrine"
  Theosophist Press, Pasadena, California.
42 Perego, Dr. Alberto.
  "Interplanetarischer Verkehr in Erdgeschehen"
  UFO Nachrichten, Nr 8, August 1963, Wiesbaden.
43 Williamson, G.H.
  "Other Tongues, Other Flesh"
  Amherst Press, Wisconsin, U.S.A.
44 Shklovsky, Josef and Sagan, Carl.
  "Intelligent Life in the Universe"
  Holden Day, Inc. New York.
45 Wendt, Herbert.
  "Before the Deluge"
  (Trs. R & C Winston) Gollancz, London, 1968.
46 Silcock, Bryan.
  "Fossil find dates first animal"
  "The Sunday Times", 14th May 1967.
47 "Einstein, a-t-il mis la physique sur une fausse piste?"
  Planete, M/J 1967, 42 Rue de Berri, Paris 8.
48 Shklovsky, Josef.
  "Did an Exploding Star kill the Dinosaurs?"
  "Sputnik", February 1968, Moscow.
49 Heezen, Dr. Bruce.
  "Nature"
  London, April 1967.
50 Davy, John.
  "Did flipping Earth kill the dinosaurs?"
  "The Observer", London, 25th June 1967.
51 Piccardi, Giorgio.
  "Alla ricerca di un metodo"
  Pianeta, No. 1, M/A 1964, Firenze.
52 Blavatsky, Mdm. H.P.
  "The Secret Doctrine",
  Theosophical Publishing Co., Pasadena, California.
53 Plato.
  "Timaeus", (Trans. Rev. R.G. Bury)
  Heinemann, London.
54 Dutt, Romesh.
  "The Ramayana and the Mahabharata"
  Dent, London, 1961.
55 Drake, W. Raymond.
  "Spacemen in the Ancient East"
  Neville Spearman Ltd., London, 1968.
56 Eydoux, Henri Paul.
  "The Buried Past"
  Weidenfeldt & Nicholson, London.
57 Churchward, James.
  "The Children of Mu"
  Neville Spearman Ltd., London, 1959.
58 Roy, Protop Chandra.
  "Bhisma Parva, (Drona Parva)"
  Bharata Press, Bombay, 1888.
59 Tacitus.
  "Annals"
  Dent, Everyman, London.
60 Dio Cassius.
  "Roman History"
  Loeb Classics, Heinemann, London.
61 Saurat, Denis.
  "Atlantis and the Giants"
  Faber & Faber Ltd., London.
62 Gresti, Gaspare.
  "Gondwana, il continente perduto"
  "Domenica di Sera", 5 Agosto, 1962.
63 Davy, John.
  "New Image of the Earth"
  "The Observer", London, March 22, 1964.
64 Silcock, Bryan.
  "The Secret at the Bottom of the Sea"
  "The Sunday Times", London, November 19th 1967.
65 Silcock, Bryan.
  "Testing the Expanding Earth Theory"
  "The Sunday Times", London April 16th 1967.
66 Bellamy, H.S.
  "Moon, Myths and Man"
  Faber & Faber, London.
67 Ingalese, Richard.
  "The History and Power of Mind"
  Fowler & Co. Ltd., London.
68 Blavatsky, Mdm. H.P.
  "The Secret Doctrine"
  Theosophical Publishing Co. Pasadena.
69 Philippe, Robert.
  "Ulysse, est-il alle en Bretagne?"
  Planete, No 22, M/J, 1965, Paris.
70 Blavatsky, Mdm. H.P.
  "The Secret Doctrine"
  Theosophical Publishing Co., Pasadena.
71 Fort, Charles.
  "The Books of Charles Fort"

107

Henry Holt & Co., New York.
72 Edwards, Frank.
   "Stranger than Science"
   Pan, London, 1963.
73 Besant, Annie & Leadbeater, C.W.A.
   "Man, Where, Whence and Whither"
   Theosophical Society, London.
74 Pinotti, Roberto.
   "Siamo Extraterrestri"
   Clypeus, Turin, Anno 111 No 4/5, Ottobre 1967.
75 Carter, Lin.
   "Thongor at the End of Time"
   Bantam, New York.
76 Plato.
   "Selected Passages" (Trs. R.W. Livingstone)
   Oxford University Press, 1960.
77 Scott-Elliott, W.
   "The Story of the Lost Atlantis and the Lost
   Lemuria"
   The Theosophical Publishing Co.
78 Yogi Ramacharaka.
   "Gnani Yoga"
   Fowler & Co., London.
79 Blavatsky, Mdm. H.P.
   "The Secret Doctrine"
   Theosophical Publishing Co., Pasadena.
80 Cerve, Wisher S.
   "Lemuria"
   AMORC, San Jose, California.
81 Wilcox, Elizabeth G.
   "Mu, Den sjunkna Kontinenten"
   Parthenon, Halsingborg, Sweden, 1964.
82 Churchward, James.
   "The Children of Mu"
   Neville Spearman Ltd., London, 1959.
83 King, Dr. George.
   "The Nine Freedoms"
   The Aetherius Society, California. 1963.
84 Williamson, G.H.
   "The Secret Places of the Lion"
   Neville Spearman Ltd., London, 1958.
85 Churchward, James.
   "The Sacred Symbols of Mu"
   Neville Spearman Ltd., London, 1960.
86 Recinos, Adrian.
   "The Popul Vuh", (Trs. Delia Goetz &
   Wm. Hodge & Co. Ltd., London. Sylvanua Morley)
87 Taylor Hansen, L.
   "The Ancient Atlantic"
   Amherst Press, Amherst, Wisconsin, U.S.A.
88 Davy, John.
   "New Image of the Earth"
   "The Observer", London, March 22, 1964.
89 Scott-Elliott, W.
   "The Story of the Lost Atlantis and the Lost
   Lemuria".
   Theosophical Publishing Co.
90 "Clypeus", 30.
   Anno VII, No. 5/6,
   P.O. Box 604, Torino.
91 Hills, Lawrence D.
   "Lands of the Morning"
   Regency Press, London, 1970.
92 Taylor Hansen, L.

   "The Ancient Atlantic"
   Amherst Press, Amherst, Wisconsin.
93 Pauwels, L. & Bergier, L.
   "The Dawn of Magic"
   Anthony Gibbs & Phillips, London, 1963.
94 Alder, Vera Stanley.
   "The Initiation of the World"
   Rider & Co., London.
95 Murray, Jacqueline.
   "Daughter of Atlantis"
   Regency Press, London.
96 Ouspensky, J.P.
   "Teritum Organum"
   Routledge & Kegan Paul Ltd., London.
97 Phylos the Thibetan.
   "A Dweller on Two Planets"
   Neville Spearman Ltd., London.
98 Stearn, Jess.
   "Edgar Cayce—The Sleeping Prophet"
   Muller, London, 1967.
99 Michell, John.
   "The View Over Atlantis"
   Sago Press, London, 1969.
100 Servier, Jean.
   "Je ne crois pas au progres"
   Planete, No. 18, S/?, 1964.
101 Zaitzevm Vyacheslav.
   "Visitors from Outer Space"
   Sputnik 1, Jan 1967, Moscow.
102 Blavatsky, Mdm. H.P.
   "The Secret Doctrine"
   Theosophical Publishing Co., Pasadena.
103 "Book of Enoch" (Trans. Canon, H. Charles)
   SPLK, London, 1962.
104 Vermes, G.
   "The Dead Sea Scrolls in English"
   Penguin, London, 1962.
105 David-Neel, Mdm Alexandra.
   "With Mystics & Magicians in Tibet"
   Penguin, London, 1936.
106 De Villars, Montfaucon.
   "Le Comte de Gabalis"
   A.G. Nizat, Paris, 1963.
107 King, Dr. George.
   "The Nine Freedoms"
   The Aetherius Society, Los Angeles, 1963.
108 Kolosimo, Peter.
   "Il Pianeta Sconosciuto"
   Sugar Editore, Milano.
109 St. Mark.
   Chapter XIII v 24-27.
110 Plato.
   "Critias", (Trans. R.G. Bury)
   Heinemann, London, 1921.
111 Blavatsky, Mdm. H.P.
   "The Secret Doctrine"
   Theosophical Publishing Co. Pasadena.
112 Kitto, W.D.C.
   "The Greeks"
   Penguin, London.
113 Mereshkovsky, Dmitri.
   "The Secret of the West"
   Jonathan Cape, London, 1935.

108

114 Donnelly, Ignatius.
"Atlantis, the Antediluvian World"
(Ed. E. Sykes) Sidgwick & Kackson, London, 1930.
115 Churchward, James.
"The Children of Mu"
Neville Spearman Ltd., London. 1959.
116 Mereshkovsky, Dmitri.
"The Secret of the West"
Jonathan Cape, London, 1935.
117 Parisini, Cecile Trilland.
"Atlantide"
Clypeus, 2-3, 1967, Casella Postale, 604, Turin.
118 Homet, Marcel F.
"Sons of the Sun"
Neville Spearman Ltd., London. 1961.
119 Spence, Lewis.
"The Riddle of Atlantis"
Rider & Co. London.
120 Plato.
"Critias".
121 Plato.
"Critias".
122 Trench, Brinsley le Poer.
"Men Among Mankind"
Neville Spearman Ltd., London, 1962.
123 Drake, W. Raymond.
"Gods or Spacemen?"
Amherst Press, Amherst, Wisconsin, U.S.A.
124 Zaitzev, Vyacheslav.
"Visitors from Outer Space"
Sputnik 1, January 1967, Moscow.
125 "Japanese Flying Saucer News"
C.B.A. Yokohama, 9-1, 1966.
126 Bernard, Dr. Raymond.
"The Hollow Earth"
Feldcrest Publishing Co. New York, 10.
127 Blavatsky, Mdm. H.P.
"Isis Unveiled", Vol. 1,
Theosophical Publishing Co. Pasadena.
128 Verrill, A. Hyatt & Verrill, Ruth.
"America's Ancient Civilizations"
G.P. Putnam & Sons, New York.
129 Seneca.
"Medea" (Trs. S. Liebmann & S. Miller)
Bantam Books, New York.
130 Cerve, Wisher S.
"Lemuria"
AMORC, San Jose, California.
131 Eliade, Mercea.
"From Primitives to Zen"
Collins, London.
132 Burland, Cottie.
"North American Indian Mythology"
Paul Hamlyn, London.
133 Spence, Lewis.
"Outlines of Mythology"
Fawcett World Library, New York.
134 Recinos, Adrian.
"Popol Vuh", (Trs. Goetz, Della & Morley Sylvanus)
Hodge & Co. London.
135 Velikovsky, J.
"Worlds in Collision"
Sidgwick & Jackson Ltd., London.
136 Velikovsky, J.
"Earth in Upheaval"
Sidgwick & Jackson Ltd., London.
137 Burland, Cottie.
"North American Indian Mythology"
Paul Hamlyn, London.
138 Nicholson, Irene.
"Mexican and Central American Mythology"
Paul Hamlyn, London.
139 Dayan, Daniel.
"La fin de notre civilization, est-elle per demain?"
Plenete, J/F, 1968.
140 Bellamy, H.S.
"Moon, Myths and Man"
Faber, London.
141 Jessup, M.K.
"The Expanding Case for UFO"
Arco Publications, London, 1957.
142 Churchward, James.
"The Lost Continent of Mu"
Neville Spearman Ltd., London, 1959.
143 Cerve, Wisher S.
"Lemuria"
AMORC, San Jose, California.
144 Ibid.
145 Fort, Charles.
"Works of Charles Fort"
Holt & Co. New York.
146 Cosmic Brotherhood Association.
"Brothers", Vol. 2. 1-4, 1962
C.B.A., Yokohama, Japan.
147 Williamson, G.H.
"Other Tongues, Other Flesh"
Amherst Press, Amherst, Wisconsin, U.S.A.
148 Homet, Marcel F.
"On the Trail of the Sun Gods"
Neville Spearman Ltd., London, 1965.
149 Finneberg, Valentin.
"Don't be downhearted, Polyglot!"
Sputnik, October, 1968.
150 Bergier, J.
"La nouvelle aube des alchimistes"
Planete, 39, M/A 1968.
151 Kolosimo, Peter.
"Non E Terrestre"
Sugar Editore, Milano, 1968.
152 Jocelyn, Daniel W.
"Pebble Tools", INFO Jounral, Vol. 2 No. 1
I.F.A. Arlington, Virginia.
153 Willis, Ronald J.
"The Nampa Image"
INFO Journal, Vol. 1 No. 2.
154 Guilbert, Jean Claude.
"Qui a tire sur Adam?"
Planete, Nr 8, Juin 1969.
155 Churchward, James.
"The Lost Continent of Mu"
Neville Spearman Ltd., London, 1959.
156 Homet, Marcel J.
"On the Trail of the Sun Gods"
Neville Spearman Ltd., London.
157 Verrill, Hyatt A. & Verrill, Ruth.
"America's Ancient Civilizations"
G. Putnam & Sons, New York.
158 Donnelly, Ignatius.

"Atlantis, the Antediluvian World"
Sidgwick & Jackson Ltd., London.

159 Churchward, James.
"The Sacred Symbols of Mu"
Neville Spearman Ltd., London.

160 Wilcox, Elizabeth J.
"Mu, den sjunkna Kontinenten"
Parthenon, Halsingburg, Sweden.

161 Thompson, J. Eric S.
"The Rise and Fall of Maya Civilization"
University of Oklahoma Press, Norman, N.Y.

162 Heyerdahl, Thor.
"Amerindians in the Pacific"
G. Allen & Unwin Ltd., London.

163 Clark, Ella E.
"Indian Legends of the Pacific North West"
University of California, Los Angeles.

164 Williamson, G.H.
"Road in the Sky"
Neville Spearman Ltd., London.

165 Williamson, G.H.
"Other Tongues, Other Flesh"
Amherst Press, Amherst, Wisconsin, U.S.A.

166 Williamson, G.H.
"Secret Places of the Lion"
Neville Spearman Ltd., London.

167 Clark, Ella E.
"Indian Legends of the Pacific North West"
University of California, Los Angeles.

168 Phylos the Thibetan.
"A Dweller on Two Planets"
Neville Spearman Ltd., London.

169 Cerve, Wisher S.
"Lemuria"
AMORC, San Jose, California.

170 Verrill, A. Hyatt & Verrill, Ruth.
"America's Ancient Civilizations"
G.P. Putnam & Sons, New York.

171 Clark, Ella E.
"Indian Legends of the Pacific North West"
University of California, Los Angeles.

172 Burland, Cottie.
"North American Mythology"
Paul Hamlyn, London.

173 Ibid.

174 Page, Curtis Hidden,
"The Chief American Poets"
Houghton Mifflin Co. Boston, Mass. 1933.

175 Taylor Hansen, L.
"He Walked the Americas"
Neville Spearman Ltd., London.

176 Burland, Cottie.
"North American Mythology"
Paul Hamlyn, London.

177 Spence, Lewis.
"Myths and Legends of the North American Indians"
G. Harrap, London, 1927.

178 Ibid.

179 Mapes, Walter de
"De Nugis Curialium", AD 1182,
Camden Society, MDCCCL.

180 Ribera, Antonio.
"El Gran Enigma de los Platillos Volantes", Editorial
Pomaire, Barcelona, 1966. (quoting Cortes, Hernan.

"Cortes de relacion de la Conquista de Mexico",
Esposa Calpe, Argentina)

181 Ibid.

182 Spence, Lewis.
"Myths of Mexico and Peru"
George Harrap, London.

183 Prescott, W.H.
"The History and Conquest of Mexico"
Everyman, Dent, London.

184 Reed, Alma.
"The Ancient Past of Mexico"
Paul Hamlyn, London.

185 Duran, Fray Diego.
"Aztecs The History of the Indies of New Spain!"
Cassell, London, 1961.

186 Spence, Lewis.
"Myths of Mexico and Peru"
George Harrap, London.

187 Reed, Alma.
"The Ancient Past of Mexico"
Paul Hamlyn, London.

188 Williamson, G.H.
"Secret Places of the Lion"
Neville Spearman Ltd., London.

189 Churchward, James.
"The Lost Continent of Mu"
Neville Spearman Ltd., London.

190 Wilkins, Harold T.
"Mysteries of Ancient South America"
Rider & Co., London.

191 Homet, Marcel F.
"Sons of the Sun"
Neville Spearman Ltd., London.

192 Verrill, Hyatt and Verrill, Ruth.
"America's Ancient Civilizations"
G.P. Putnam & Son, New York.

193 Irwin, Constance.
"Fair Gods and Stone Faces"
St. Martin's Press, New York.

194 Taylor Hansen, Lucille.
"He Walked the Americas"
Neville Spearman Ltd., London.

195 Thompson, J. Eric.
"The Rise and Fall of the Maya Civilization"
University of California, Norman, N.Y.

196 Churchward, James.
"The Lost Continent of Mu"
Neville Spearman Ltd., London.

197 Nicholson, Jane.
"The X in Mexico"
Faber & Faber, London.

198 Creighton, Gordon.
"A Russian Wall-Painting and other Spacemen"
Flying Saucer Review, J/A 1965.

199 Nicholson, Irene.
"Mexican and Central American Mythology"
Paul Hamlyn, London.

200 Spence, Lewis.
"Myths of Mexico and Peru"
George Harrap, London.

201 Sejourne, Laurette.
"Burning Water, Thought and Religion in Ancient
Mexico"
Thames and Hudson, London.

110

202 Prescott, W.H.
   "The History and Conquest of Mexico"
   Everyman, Dent, London.
203 Verrill, Hyatt and Verrill, Ruth.
   "America's Ancient Civilization"
   G.P. Putnam & Son, New York.
204 Thompson, J. Eric S.
   "The Rise and Fall of Maya Civilization"
   University of Oklahoma, Norman, N.Y.
205 Irwin, Constance.
   "Fair Gods and Stone Faces"
   W.H. Allen, London.
206 Reed, Alma.
   "The Ancient Past of Mexico"
   Paul Hamlyn, London.
207 Tarade, G. & Millou, A.
   "L'Enigma di Palenque"
   Clypeus, Anno 111 4-5, 1966.
208 Churchward, James.
   "The Lost Continent of Mu"
   Neville Spearman Ltd., London.
209 Wilkins, Harold T.
   "Secret Cities of Old South America"
   Rider & Co. London.
210 Thompson, J. Eric S.
   "The Rise and Fall of Maya Civilization"
   University of Oklahoma, Norman, N.Y.
211 Kunischev, Vladimir.
   "Cracking the Ancient Maya Code"
   "Sputnik", October 1968.
212 Recinos, Adrain.
   "Popol Vuh", (Tr. Goetz, Delia & Morley, Sylvanus.)
   Wm. Hodge & Co., London.
213 Leon-Potilli, Miguel.
   "Mythology of Ancient Mexico", (Mythologies of the Ancient World)
   S.N. Kramer, Anchor.
214 Valin, Claude
   "Des Civilizations Avancees existaient avant le Deluge"
   Planete, M/J, 1968
215 Spence, Lewis.
   "Introduction to Mythology"
   Fawcett Publications, Inc. Greenwich, Conn.
216 Delio, Camillo.
   "La pauvre Colline des Mortes"
   Planete, N/D, 1967
217 Dayan, Daniel.
   "La Fin de notre Civilization"
   Planete, J/F, 1968.
218 Stross, Brian.
   "The Ihkals"
   Flying Saucer Review, M/J 1968.
219 Thompson, J. Eric S.
   "The Rise and Fall of Maya Civilization"
   University of Oklahoma, Norman, New York.
220 Ceram, C.W.
   "Gods, Graves and Scholars"
   Sidgwick & Jackson, London, 1952.
221 Soustelle, Jacques.
   "The Daily Life of the Aztecs"
   Weidenfeldt & Nicolson, London.
222 Collis, Maurice
   "Cortes and Montezuma"
   Faber & Faber, London.
223 Wilkins, Harold T.
   "Secret Cities of Old South America"
   Rider & Co., London.
224 Von Hagen, Victor Wolfgang
   "The Ancient Sun Kingdoms of the Americas"
   Panther, London.
225 Wilkins, Harold T.
   "Mysteries of Ancient South America"
   Rider & Co. London.
226 Jessup, Dr. J.K.
   "The Case for UFO"
   Arco Publications, London.
227 Galindez, Oscar A.
   "Teleportation from Chascamas to Mexico"
   Flying Saucer Review, S/O, 1968.
228 Prescott, W.H.
   "History of the Conquest of Peru"
   G. Allen & Unwin, Ltd., London.
229 Bellamy, H.S.
   "Built before the Flood"
   Faber & Faber, London.
230 Bellamy, H.S. & Allen, P.
   "The Calendar of Tiahuanaco"
   Faber & Faber, London.
231 Churchward, James.
   "The Children of Mu"
   Neville Spearman Ltd., London.
232 Bucknell, G.H.S.
   "Peru"
   Thames & Hudson Ltd., London. 1963.
233 Saurat, Denis.
   "Atlantis and the Giants"
   Faber & Faber, London.
234 Bellamy, H.S.
   "Before the Flood"
   Faber & Faber, London.
235 Bellamy, H.S. & Allen, Percy.
   "The Calendar of Tiahuanaco"
   Faber & Faber, London.
236 Voss, Aage.
   "Et besynderligt Sammentraef"
   UFO Nyt, Oslo, August, 1962.
237 Goddard, J.
   "New Lights on Ancient Tracks"
   Flying Saucer Review, M/A, 1964.
238 Michel, Aime.
   "Flying Saucers and the Straight Line Mystery"
   Criterion Books, New York.
239 Williamson, G.H.
   "Road in the Sky"
   Neville Spearman Ltd., London.
240 Blavatsky, Mdm. H.P.
   "Isis Unveiled"
   Theosophical Publishing Co. Pasadena.
241 Wilkins, Harold T.
   "Secret Cities of Old South America"
   Rider & Co. London.
242 Williamson, G.H.
   "The Rock of the Writings"
   Flying Saucer Review, N/D 1957.
243 Rampa, Lobsang.
   "The Third Eye"
   Secker & Warburg, London

111

244 Verrill, Hyatt & Verrill, Ruth.
   "America's Ancient Civilizations"
   G.P. Putnam & Son, New York.
245 Churchward, James.
   "The Children of Mu".
   Neville Spearman Ltd., London.
246 Perego, Dr. Alberto.
   "Interplanetarischer Verkehr in Erdegeschehen"
   UFO Nachtichten, August 1963, Wiesbaden.
247 Ashe, Geoffrey.
   "Land to the West"
   Collins, London.
248 Homet, Marcel F.
   "Sons of the Sun"
   Neville Spearman Ltd., London.
249 Voltaire.
   "Candide and other Tales"
   Everyman, Dent, London.
250 Arbalaez, Fernando.
   "La deuxieme conquete de l'Eldorado"
   Planete, 24, S/O 1965.
251 Fawcett, Brian.
   "Ruins in the Sky"
   Hutchinsons, London.
252 Ashe, Geoffrey.
   "Land to the West"
   Collins, London.
253 Ribera, Antonio.
   "El Gran Enigma de los Platillos Volantes"
   Pomaire, Barcelona.
254 Verrill, Hyatt and Verrill, Ruth.
   "America's Ancient Civilizations"
   G.P. Putnam & Son, New York.
255 Zarata, Augustin de
   "The Discovery and Conquest of Peru"
   (Tr. J.M. Cohen) Penguin Books, London, 1968.
256 Borland, C.
   "Peru under the Incas"
   Evans, London, 1967.
257 Verrill, Hyatt and Verrill, Ruth.
   "America's Ancient Civilizations"
   G.P. Putnam & Son, New York.
258 Prescott, W.H.
   "History of the Conquest of Peru"
   G. Allen & Unwin Ltd., London.
259 Alder, Vera S.
   "Fifth Dimension"
   Rider & Co. London
260 Wilkins, Harold T.
   "Secret Cities of Old South America"
   Rider & Co., London.
261 Verrill, Hyatt & Verrill, Ruth.
   "America's Ancient Civilizations"
   G.P. Putnam & Son, New York
262 Von Hagen, Victor Wolfgang.
   "The Ancient Sun Kingdoms of the Americas"
   Panther, London.

263 Prescott, W.H.
   'History of the Conquest of Peru'
   G. Allen & Unwin Ltd., London.
264 Lee, Rexy.
   "Cosi gli Inca plasmavano le pietre"
   Clypeus, No. 4-5. Dicembre 1967.
265 Michell, John.
   "The View Over Atlantis"
   Gamstone Press, London, 1969.
266 Verrill, Hyatt & Verrill, Ruth.
   "America's Ancient Civilizations"
   G.P. Putnam & Son, New York.
267 Prescott, W.H.
   "History of the Conquest of Peru"
   G. Allen & Unwin, Ltd., London.
268 Verrill, Hyatt & Verrill, Ruth.
   "America's Ancient Civilizations"
   G.P. Putnam & Son, New York.
269 Jessup, Dr. J.K.
   "The Expanding Case for UFO"
   Arco Publications, London.
270 Zarata, Augustine de
   "The Discovery and Conquest of Peru"
   (Trs. J.M. Cohen) Penguin Books, London.
271 Prescott, W.H.
   "History of the Conquest of Peru"
   G. Allen & Unwin Ltd., London.
272 Centro Unico Nazionale
   "Notizario UFO", 1970, No. 6.
   C.U.N. Casella Postale N. 790, Bologna.
273 Koestler, Arthur.
   "The Ghost in the Machine"
   Hutchinson, London.
274 Herodotus.
   "History", (Trans. E. Powell)
   Oxford University Press.
275 Apollodorus.
   "History"
   Loeb Classics, Heinemann.
276 Graves, Robert and Patai, Raphael.
   "Hebrew Myths, The Book of Genesis"
   Cassell, London.
277 Vesco, Renato.
   "Considerazioni preliminare sulla questione delle
   presunte apparizioni preistoriche degli U.F.O."
   Clypeus, 31, Anno VII 7/8.
278 Japanese UFO News.
   Vol. 4. No. 9, Sept. 1970.
   C.B.A. Yokohama.
279 Pauwels, Louis and Bergier, Jacques.
   "Des doutes sur L'evolution",
   Planete 12, Nov. 1969.
280 Cayce, Hugh Lynn.
   "The Edgar Cayce Reader"
   Paperback Library, New York.
281 Taylor Hansen, L.
   "The Ancient Atlantic"
   Amherst Press, Amherst, Wisconsin, U.S.A.

112

W. Raymond Drake

A British historian (1913-1989), and a disciple of Charles Fort, W.R. Drake is one of the most credible researchers of the "Ancient Astronauts" theory, which maintains that aliens arrived on Earth and interacted with the human race throughout antiquity and in all parts of the globe. Author of a dozen books on the Space Gods phenomenon, Drake's work complements that of "Chariots of the Gods?" author Erich Von Daniken, but Drake's first book appeared in print prior to Von Daniken's international bestseller. In this book about the ancient Mediterranean's strange relationship with the Sky People, Drake utilized over fifty writers of antiquity and scrutinized their main works through a UFO "lens."

Drake spent many years digging through huge archives of material, looking for supposed anomalies that could support his scenarios of space aliens impacting human history. As Drake himself said, "I aspired to collect as many facts as possible from ancient literature to chronicle for the past what Charles Fort has so brilliantly done for the present century."

His published books include: Gods or Spacemen? (1964). Gods and Spacemen in the Ancient East (1968). Mystery of the gods – Are They Coming Back To Earth? (1972). The Ancient Secrets of Mysterious America – Is Our Destiny Upon Us? (1973). Gods and Spacemen in the Ancient West (1974). Gods and Spacemen in the Ancient Past (1975). Gods and Spacemen Throughout History (1975). Gods and Spacemen in Ancient Israel (1976). Cosmic Continents (1986). Several additional manuscripts have been privately circulated and will eventually be published.

ANCIENT SECRETS OF MYSTERIOUS AMERICA

Are You Prepared For The Return of The Ancient Sky Warriors?

By Sean Casteel

✳ Does the misshapen skull of a strange "Star Child" discovered in Mexico serve as proof of interbreeding between Mexican females and people from the sky in ancient times?

✳ Learn about the Incan word "pachacuti" and its frightening meaning for our world today. What awaits us, according to the indigenous prophets of the ancient Americas?

✳ Read about how the so-called "primitive" cultures of the Americas believe a future paradise will be brought into being when their gods of old return. Who will be accounted worthy?

*   *   *   *   *

The ancient astronauts theory of UFOs spans the globe and the outreach of an alien presence has made itself felt everywhere mankind has called home. The Americas are no exception, as this work by W.R. Drake and other contributors testifies.

The Strange Skull

There is at least one unearthly "alien artifact" W.R. Drake would never have heard of during his career that involves a strange skull found in Mexico in the latter part of the 20th Century. Today, the bizarre artifact remains in the care of Lloyd Pye, a crypto-zoologist who specialized in researching hominoids like Bigfoot and the Abominable Snowman. In February of 1999, Pye was contacted by an anonymous couple who said they had something to show him. Pye assumed they wanted to talk about something to do with hominoids, since that was known to be his specialty.

- 115 -

Instead the couple showed him two skulls they had been keeping in a small cardboard box. One skull was obviously human, but the other one completely surprised him. It was extremely small, with strangely-shaped eye sockets and with an even stranger shape to the cranium. The couple had brought the skulls to Pye to ask his advice on what to do with them. He recommended DNA testing of the misshapen skull to see if the bizarre characteristics were the result of a human birth defect or contained a type of alien DNA hitherto unknown.

A Journey Into Mexico

In an interview I conducted with Pye for "UFO Magazine," he explained how the misshapen skull was originally discovered. Many of the details of exactly where and when are now obscured by the passage of time, but at least some of the story has been handed down to Pye, who says he takes it on faith.

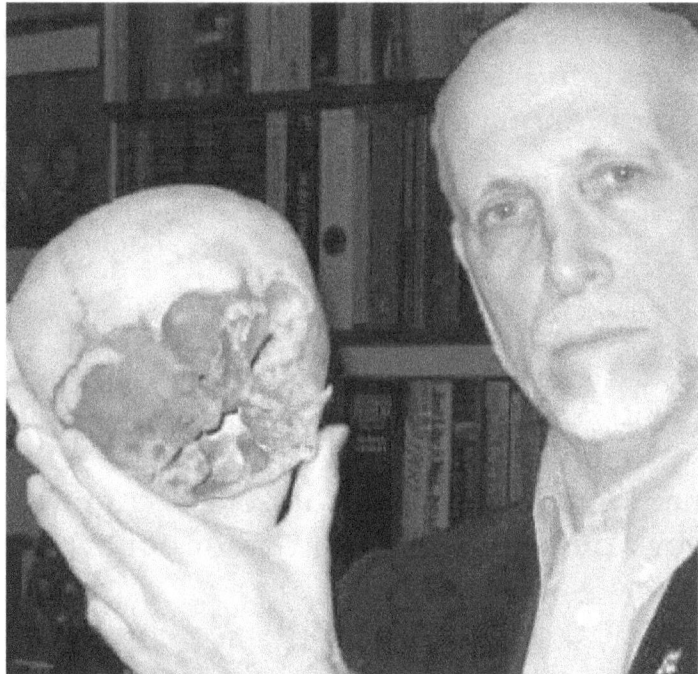

The Mexican parents of a teenage girl had entered the U.S. illegally, but had eventually achieved a legal status after the young woman's birth. They returned to Mexico to visit their family in a small rural village a hundred miles southwest of Chihuahua, Mexico. The exact location is not known, and the woman has since died and cannot be questioned.

Hominoid researcher Lloyd Pye holding the Star Child skull, an artifact that may be the missing link of alien/human hybridization.

"When her family took her down there," Pye began, "the villagers and the people she was staying with told her, 'You don't go in the caves and the mineshafts around here. That's taboo. We don't do that.' So, being a teenager and being told what not to do, that's exactly what she had to do. The first opportunity she had, she sneaked away and explored the caves and the mine tunnels. In one of the mine tunnels, she found a human skeleton lying on its back. At its side was a misshapen hand coming up out of the dirt beside the skeleton."

After digging further down around the misshapen hand, the teenager found more remains in a shallow grave, including a misshapen skeleton and misshapen head to go along with the hand. She put all the bones into a big basket she had brought with her on the pretense that she was going berry picking, then carried the bones back to where she was staying, concealing them behind a tree. Two days later, a heavy rain came and washed most of the bones away. After searching downstream for them, she recovered only the two skulls, then sneaked them into her luggage and back into the U.S.

The woman kept the skulls her entire life, and as she was nearing death, she asked an American friend of hers if he would take them and keep them for her. Some years later, the skulls ended up in Pye's hands.

The Star Child

Pye quickly dubbed the strange skull "The Star Child" because of its anomalous, "alien" appearance. After close examination by Pye, the Star Child skull has yielded up the following facts. First of all, the eye sockets are not human and also do not conform to any known genetic abnormality. The skull was, according to Pye, "completely redesigned from human to Star Child, but it's the same set of bones." The skull is structured so that it may have held three brain lobes rather than the normal two.

Another strange attribute may indicate that the Star Child had no cerebellum at all, "which would not be compatible with life as we know it," Pye said. The neck would likely be only a third the size of a human neck, and the weight of the skull is also much lighter than any human counterpart would be.

"It feels almost like a gourd relative to the real density and heaviness of human bone," Pye said. "Also, the Star Child is completely minus its frontal sinuses. And its brain is a completely different size. An average human brain is 1400 cubic centimeters. The Star Child has 1600 cubic centimeters. It's wall-to-wall brain. It's just completely redesigned to hold an awful lot more brain."

Pye explained that in anthropological terms, a difference of that amount constitutes an entirely different species of human being.

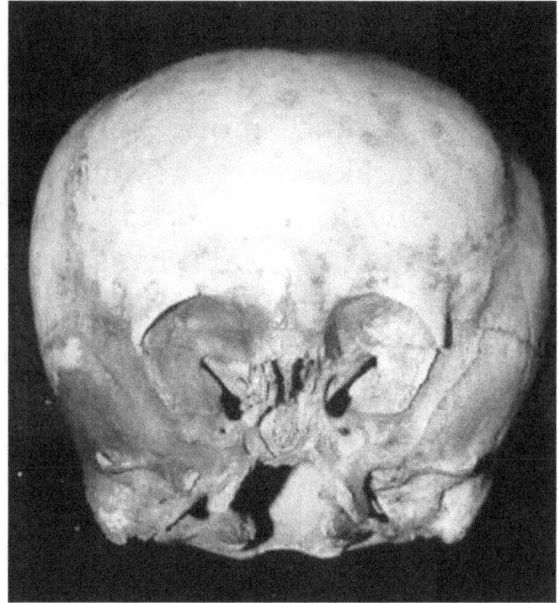

The Star Child skull bears silent witness to what could be the mystery of the ages.

"Homo habilis goes to homo erectus with a leap of 200 centimeters. Homo erectus goes to homo archaic with a leap of 200 centimeters. Homo archaic goes to Neanderthal with 200 cubic centimeters. So if nothing else, we might be looking at a new kind of species here. But at a minimum, we're looking at something that is highly, highly unusual."

The Ways Of The Aliens In Old Mexico

One reason the Star Child's deformities are likely not hereditary has to do with the ways of old Mexico.

"In a primitive society," Pye said, "which is where the Star Child supposedly came from, they wouldn't put up with birth defects. There was no stigma on infanticide. If something came out and it wasn't quite right, they just did away with it and started over, no problem."

According to local legend, those same primitive societies were said to have been in regular contact with aliens conducting genetic experiments similar to those the abduction literature is so full of today, Pye said.

"These are well-known, well-regarded legends with roots spreading throughout Central and South America," Pye wrote on his website. "They are pervasive and longstanding, and in general state that on a regular basis 'Star Beings' come down from the heavens and impregnate females in remote, isolated villages. The women carry their 'Star Children' to term, then raise them to the age of six or so.

"At that point," Pye continued, "the Star Beings return to collect their progeny and remove them to places, and for purposes, not clearly outlined in the legends, though improving a stagnant gene pool is often mentioned as a motivation."

Pye also offers a very interesting scenario on what events may have led up to the death of the Star Child and its mother.

"Many 'intuitives' and 'sensitives' feel the adult skeleton was female," Pye wrote, "and the child was hers, a human-alien hybrid created by a union between her and a Star Being. Some feel that the mother had learned the Star Beings were returning to take her child from her, which she refused to contemplate.

"Panic-stricken and filled with dread, she took her child and fled her village, seeking refuge in the hidden mine tunnel. There she killed it and buried it in a shallow grave, leaving one of its hands out of the ground to hold onto. Then she took a fatal dose of poison and lay down beside her child to die."

The speculative story obviously contains many elements of the modern abduction scenario, including the impregnation of female abductees who then cling stubbornly to their unborn fetuses and who experience a strong emotional bonding with their hybrid children onboard a UFO. Perhaps the presence of a strong maternal-protective drive literally transcends time and place and is a component of the relationship between aliens and humans throughout their mutual history.

"The Star Being legends go back for hundreds of years," Pye said. "In the old days, they could put these kids in these isolated, rural villages and nobody outside of three miles was even going to know about it. They're certainly not going to spread the news all over the world the way it is now with communications being what they are.

"You should understand," he continued, "that the grays apparently don't have an emotional capacity like we do. So they can't nurture a kid. Well, if a kid's got a lot of human in it, it's got to have some nurturing or it isn't going to grow up right. It's going to languish and probably die from failure to thrive."

The aliens at some point figured out that a minimum of six years with a Star Child's mother was necessary for the baby to develop properly. Then they would return to collect what was theirs, which functions as a variation on the overall theme of the aliens coming back and putting the finishing touches on some unfinished business.

The World Turned Upside Down

Attorney Judith Bluestone Polich is the author of "Return of the Children of Light: Incan and Mayan Prophecies for a New World." I spoke to her for a book I wrote called "UFOs, Prophecy and the End of Time" (available from Global Communications) about her mystical experiences south of the border and what she thinks they're all about.

Polich talked about her travels in Mexico and Peru and Central America, and said she definitely feels that some locations have a mystical power all their own.

"I feel they're special places," she said, "and that they may hold special energies. The prophecies of the Incas, for example, are somewhat energy-based, because these people have an ability to perceive reality more energetically than the rest of us. So their prophecies talk about consciousness being divided into seven levels. They believe that most humans are presently in the second and third levels of consciousness. Their prophecies talk about a coming time in which there will be a leap to the fifth level of consciousness, and that this new consciousness is a much more holistic, much more energy-based consciousness – very different than our way of perceiving the world now."

The Inca tradition foretold a series of events that would precede a world age shift.

"They called their world ages 'suns,'" she explained, "a time when they would enter a new sun. It was almost as if they believed that the light coming into our solar system from the broader universe somehow was triggering a change, a shift in perception, a shift in the understanding of space/time."

The Inca called that time preceding a world shift "pachacuti."

"Now 'pacha' means all of the physical manifestations," Polich continued, "and 'cuti' means to turn upside down. So a really tumultuous time, a time of overturning of space/time reality, always preceded a world shift. Sometimes that could take the form of catastrophic physical events in which the threads to the past were broken and so a new understanding of reality emerged. Other times it might be more of a psychic event, something that happened at a deeper structural level, that caused reality to shift. So certainly we're in a time of pacahcuti right now, a time of very rapid change, a change of our understanding of reality."

So when the Children of Light return, as promised in the title of Polich's book, that return may not be Space Brothers in flying saucers openly landing, but rather an evolutionary leap in consciousness that is the natural next phase of humankind.

Similar Prophecies of Chaos and Redemption

A researcher named David Flynn claims to have found newly discovered manmade glyphs in Bolivia that predate commonly accepted theories of just when mankind took his earliest steps and became something truly human. The glyphs were first seen by Flynn when he examined recent satellite photos on the Internet and he believes the carvings are intended to convey a religious meaning.

Just what sort of gods were those ancients trying to placate or communicate with?

"At a site called Ku-e-lap in a remote location in Northern Peru," Flynn told me in an interview, "a site so remote that the only road into it was built a mere 35 years ago, there is an enormous wall speculated to be built of three times more material than Egypt's largest pyramid. This site was built by the Cha-cha-poyan, or Cloud People, who were said to be tall people with very fair hair. There is no evidence suggesting where these people came from.

"The Incas knew of this culture and reported that the Cloud People arrived during a time of 'pachacuti,' or world change," he continued. "This word can also mean extreme changes in space/time, a new era, transformation and plowing, as in the overturning of the earth. In the Inca civilization founding myth, the first Inca was named Manco Capac, and he appeared at the end of a world deluge in which all the races of men and created things perished when the waters rose above the highest mountain peaks in the world.

"No living thing survived, except Manco Capac and a woman who remained in a box. When the waters subsided, the wind carried them to Tiahuanaco, where Viracocha began to create the people and nations of the region. A rainbow, seen in the clouds at the end of the flood, was adopted as the standard for the civilizations of the Andes. The Spanish conquistadors wrote of the rainbow standard of the Incas, who explained its origin from many thousands of years before their culture came into being. It is still in use by Bolivians and Peruvians to this day. The Inca recreation story is consistent with the Genesis 6 flood epic."

The Return Of The Ancient Warriors

When asked whether any of this has a direct link to the UFOs of our time, Flynn responded with an interesting bit of apocalyptic prophecy.

"The greatest UFO flap in modern times," he said, "has been centered over the ancient site of Tenochitlan, where Mexico City is today. The Mayan and Aztec cultures shared many similar legends of creation and world cataclysm with the Incan and pre-Incan civilizations. One Inca myth in particular involves a golden disc that hung in the temple at Cusco, Peru. It was said that during the dividing points of ages, the disc would be activated when the sun rose in the center of the Milky Way and distribute a pure energy of life and thought from the sun to the whole world.

"Also, during this time, the warriors of the god Viracocha would return from heaven to establish the rebirth of civilization. When Pizarro and his soldiers arrived in Peru, the disc was taken to Lake Titicaca, where it was hidden in a temple under the water, awaiting the next global cataclysm. Similarly, the Mayans predicted the return of their god, KuKulcan, or the Quetzacoatl of the Aztecs, from the heavens before the destruction of the earth and the rebirth of civilization.

"These stories combine the ideas of divine intervention from the heavens for humanity during the time of global change," he added. "This is the same message that many researchers in Mexico have derived from the huge increase of UFO activity in the area."

The Hopi Prophets and Their Helpful Gods

The Hopi Indians of the American Southwest also believe in gods from the sky and hold beliefs about the cycles of time similar to their counterparts to the south in Mexico and South America. The Hopi belief is that the world has gone through many different cycles, and they say we are presently at the end of the Fourth World.

"We've gone through three different cycles," author and researcher Gary David told me, "and three different worlds were destroyed. Now we're at the end of the Fourth World, which they say is going to be destroyed."

The Hopis also have beliefs that correspond to the notion of an extraterrestrial presence.

"The Hopis are connected to so many different entities," David said, "that we might think of as extraterrestrial today. They have the idea of the Sky People or Sky Elders coming down to the earth. One particular group of people that the Hopis have talked about in their legends – and I found evidence of this in the rock art there – are the Ant People, a very important group that helped the Hopis out during the destruction of two different worlds."

That Hopis' sense of history goes like this: The First World was destroyed by fire, which may have manifested itself as an asteroid strike or some kind of volcanism. The Second World was destroyed by ice, indicating an Ice Age or an extremely cold period. The Ant people led the Hopis down into caverns where they survived the terrible cataclysm being suffered by the world outside. The Ant People also taught the Hopis to sprout beans in the caverns in order to feed the people, an event commemorated even today by the ritual Bean Dance.

"The Ant People are basically benevolent creatures," David said. "In the pictures I've seen in the rock art, there are antennae on these creatures and they have spindly bodies and large eyes and bulbous heads. Some of these creatures assume what's called a 'prayer stance.' That means that both arms are raised at their sides above their heads and the elbows are at right angles. This is a traditional stance that you see all over the Southwest in rock art."

There is also a linguistic link with the Anunnaki of ancient Sumeria, thought by the late scholar Zechariah Sitchin and others to be the alien race that came down from the sky to teach man the ways of civilization.

"It's funny," David said, "but the Hopi word for ant is 'anu,' and the Hopi word for friends is 'naki.' So you put these two together and you get the Anunnaki, from the Sumerian cylinder seals and so forth, and you see these Sky People came down to earth. So the Ant People might be the same as the Anunnaki of the Sumerians."

Even More Benevolent Gods

The friendly Ant People seem to have left the Hopis to their own devices when the time came for the destruction of the Third World in a terrible flood. In that disaster, the Hopis survived by going across the ocean on bamboo rafts to arrive in our present Fourth World and the Ant People dropped out of the story. But other helpers soon came along.

"The Hopis have other benevolent entities that have helped them," David said. "They have what is known as the sky god Sotuknang. He has a curved headdress – similar to a helmet – and looks very much like an alien being. There's a legend about Sotuknang related to the flood."

According to the story, a great flood was about to engulf a Hopi village and the people were fleeing the coming destruction. There was a little boy and girl, twins, who were somehow left behind. They decided to try to find their parents and escape the flood.

"So they went out across the desert," David recounted, "and during the first night they were camping. They saw what is called a 'flying shield' come down right before them. This being, this sky creature, got out of his flying shield. He was described in the legend as having some kind of clothing or costume that glittered like icicles, and the face shone like a star. That's the way they describe the face.

"So this might be some kind of inter-dimensional being, or it might be that the helmet is lit up in some fashion. But this creature came to the children and said, 'Don't be afraid. I'm going to take you up in my flying shield and we're going to go up above the desert and find your parents.' And this entity Sotuknang gave them something to eat, corn and melon and so forth. And he said that, 'In the future, I'm going to come to you in your dreams and I'll instruct you in the proper way to live and the proper life to pursue.'"

The sky creature located the twins' parents and delivered the children to them, after which the flying shield took off again.

A Hopi Gray?

There is yet another Hopi god with extraterrestrial characteristics named "Masau'u."

"Masau'u was there at the beginning of the Fourth World," David said. "He's the god of the earth and the underworld and fire. This god led the people around and determined where they should build their villages. The people were basically migrating across the desert and building stone pueblos.

"Masau'u is strange-looking creature," he continued. "He has a bulbous head and very large round eyes and a large round mouth. And he's kind of bald. It's said that his skin resembles the texture of a summer squash, kind of bumpy like that. His feet are very long and his body is always described as being gray. In fact, the word 'amaus,' the root word of 'Masau'u, literally means gray in the Hopi language. There are connections with the underworld and death and the kind of subterranean world that Masau'u is supposed to inhabit.

"Artists have made drawings based upon the descriptions that the Hopi elders have made of this particular god, and it really looks like an extraterrestrial gray. Our contemporary idea of what a gray looks like matches this ancient Hopi god perfectly."

The Hopi Prophets Go Public

The Hopis also have a long legacy of prophecy, including dire predictions of the End Times. The prophecies reached the world at large through what is called the Hopi Hearings held in July 1955.

"The Bureau of Indian Affairs," David said, "met with the Hopis to discuss mundane things like grazing rights and stock management and forced schooling, as well as the rise of alcoholism on the reservation. But in the process, some of these spiritual elders began to talk about the End Times, the floods, the famines, all these kind of Biblical-proportion End Time prophecies, great strife among people, the end of all the Hopi ceremonies. They mentioned World War III and images of bombs raining down like hailstones and rivers of blood; very reminiscent of the Book of Revelation with the kind of language they were using."

David remarked that the Hopis are probably the least Christianized of any of the tribes in the American Southwest. Some of the tribes along the Rio Grande were more affected by the Catholicism of the conquering Spaniards and the missionaries. Nevertheless, the Hopis have a tradition of prophecy that resembles a lot of Biblical prophecy.

"The Hopis have been foreseeing the future for perhaps over a thousand years," David said. "They've foreseen what's going to happen. Some of the things that the Hopi people were saying have come to pass. For instance, they made certain prophecies about people in the future speaking through spider webs. You can picture telegraph or telephone lines – and the worldwide web, an actual 'web' of communication.

"Another prophecy is that people will be riding in wagons without horses on black ribbons. These, of course, are automobiles going across the black asphalt. Another prophecy the Hopis came up with before it actually happened was that 'a gourd of ashes will fall on the earth and burn the people. Then the atomic bombs blew up in Hiroshima and Nagasaki, and it was metaphorically the gourd of ashes falling on the earth. The Hopis foretold people living in the sky at the End Times, and we have the International Space Station and the shuttle, so people are living in the sky now."

The Hopis may have foretold the coming of the women's liberation movement when they prophesied that women will start to wear men's clothing.

"The Hopis are a very traditional culture, and the women wear long dresses," David said. "But they said that women will start to dress like men."

The Hopis also prophesied that they would journey to the House of Mica to plead for peace and would be ignored.

"This actually happened," David said, "when Hopi delegations went to the United Nations building, the House of Mica, and they tried to plead for peace and were essentially ignored or patronized. They said that in the End Times, we'll go to this House of Mica and try to get the world to wake up before it's too late."

Promises Of Paradise

In the midst of all the carnage and warfare, the Hopis predict, there will also come a "Purifier" named Pahana.

"And he'll have a certain tool," David said, "that's like a cosmic weapon of destruction. This figure Pahana will destroy all those who were not living the life pattern given to the Hopis at the beginning of the Fourth World. Also, in one account, it says that the wicked will be beheaded. It's kind of a frightening scenario for what is to come. But the Hopis foresee that some of the people will survive, just like they survived the destruction of the three previous worlds. And a few people will go into the Fifth World, and there will be a world of paradise and a new beginning."

Are the Ancient Astronauts, the Sky People, the Space Brothers – whatever name you give them – working us through a coming era of hellish world changes in order to lead us to a heaven on earth? Are the ancient gods of the Americas soon to return to transform a wicked civilization into one that rightfully deserves to know peace and tranquility? Perhaps it is so, that our salvation shall come from the same hands that guided the Incas and the Hopis and the other indigenous peoples of the Americas, whose so-called "primitive" cultures were light years ahead of the oppressors who came so cruelly to rule over them.

Sean Casteel

Sean Casteel has written about UFOs and other paranormal subjects since 1989. He is the author of several books published by Global Communications, to include "UFOs, Prophecy and the End of Time," "Signs and Symbols of the Second Coming," and "The Excluded Books of the Bible." He has a website at www.seancasteel.com and his books are available for purchase there. His work has also been published in the United Kingdom, Italy and Romania, and he continues to work on a freelance basis for numerous magazines in America and the United Kingdom.

Mystery of The Crystal Skulls and Their ET Connection

By R. Joshua Shapiro
a crystal skull explorer

- Does the discovery of the Crystal Skulls throughout the Americas signify a link with the Ancient Sky Gods?

- How could primitive people have created the crystal skulls that duplicate a human skull bone almost perfectly, using primitive tools of the era they were carved in?

- What proof is there of a possible link between the skulls and the Grandfathers of the Pleiades?

*   *   *   *   *

Since 1983, I have had contact with what are called "Crystal Skulls." Perhaps some of the readers of this chapter might not be familiar with what a crystal skull is? Recently however, millions of people learned a bit more about the skulls when the fourth installment of the "Indiana Jones" film franchise was released in May of 2008 by Steven Spielberg and George Lucas. And as it turned out, in the end, they showed thirteen crystal skulls which when brought back together transformed into an alien being that re-activated its spacecraft buried in the ground and left our world. I would say this part of the film did show an aspect of what we believe could be a theory of the origins of the crystal skulls – that there is a definite connection with extraterrestrials but probably not in the way the film portrayed it. Anyway, for those readers not fully knowledgeable about what a crystal skull is, let's see a definition first.

Definition of A Crystal Skull

A crystal skull, as the name implies, is a human-formed skull made from various types of quartz crystals. Although today people are calling crystal skulls any type of skull that is comprised of different type of gemstones (besides quartz) which are being made by modern carvers as well as very old (non-quartz) skulls being found in the ground. We will primarily focus on the quartz skulls as these skulls were the first to be uncovered that were linked to ancient ruins in Mexico and Central America. In the crystal skull community there are three types of crystal skulls defined, according to the Crystal Skull Society International, founded by F. R. 'Nick' Nocerino.

a) <u>Contemporary or New</u> – The crystal skulls being carved using diamond tip tools today by modern carvers, primarily in Brazil and China, which began to be created less then 100 years ago.

b) <u>Old</u> – Representing crystal skulls which were created or carved from 100 years ago to 1000 – 2000 years ago. Different researchers use a different end time frame. Most examples of this kind of skull have been uncovered in Mexico and Central America. (<u>Note</u>: Within the last few years there are many skulls being found in Mexico in particular, so many it is impossible to keep up with them now.)

c) <u>Ancient</u> – Those crystal skulls which I feel are over 2000 years and older. How old? Thousands if not millions of years old, which mostly likely were created through some advanced form technology which we may not be familiar with even using our most modern tools of today. There is a possibility that the ancient crystal skulls either originated from advanced civilizations in the past, like Atlantis or Lemuria/Mu, or were gifts from the Gods that were brought from off-planet.

Links Between The Indigenous Peoples of The Americas With Crystal Skulls

Now it may be impossible to prove where the ancient skulls have come from as well as to prove which of the crystal skulls known today are truly ancient as there is no definitive method to determine this although different crystal skull researchers have their own ideas. As to the locations of where the crystals skulls have been found, they have for the most part primarily come out of Mexico and Central America. This would imply a connection with the various indigenous cultures of Mesoamerica that lived in these areas, including the Toltecs, Aztecs and Mayans. Descendants of these cultures all speak about the crystal skulls but these civilizations did not keep records. This information comes from legends handed down by word of mouth, while it is suspected that the current native population may be guarding various crystal skulls in secret for their own protection.

Additionally, in my personal travels, I have had some contact with Native American Elders or Shamans, who, although their tribe or people may not personally possess a crystal skull, have certainly heard about the skulls. I know of a Native American Shaman from Canada who spoke about 13 crystal skulls he had first learned about from his grandparents. The Shaman also had, let us say, a spiritually-based vision where he had an inner communication with the essence of the skulls. On another occasion, I visited a Navajo tribe outside of Albuquerque. There was a sect of this tribe called Canoncito, but in their language they called themselves To'hajiilee. The boundary of this tribe's land is in the shape of a human skull. An elder of the tribe named Leon Secatero, who I had a chance to meet once, a remarkable man who unfortunately has passed away, stated empirically that his people do have a crystal skull but that to protect its purity they would never show it to others who are outside of their tribe.

However, it is the Mayans who have shared the most information about the crystal skulls, and they acknowledge that they work with the crystal skulls in their ceremonies. Nevertheless, due to the invasion of the Europeans coming to the Americas in the late 1400s and beyond, many of the sacred artifacts of these cultures, especially items of gold, were stolen. For many hundreds of years, the indigenous people have learned to hide and protect these sacred objects in secret – that is until it is time for them to come out or be revealed as is discussed in some of their prophecies.

Now, having shared all of this so far, I can say absolutely that within the last ten years there are many crystal skulls appearing, mostly in Mexico, where they just seem to keep popping up out of the ground. Some of them somehow go to private owners or find their way into stores to be sold. If we use a paranormal procedure to work with and examine the crystal skulls by, let's say, having a sensitive sit with the skulls, then we do get insights about their origins. In the visions of the sensitives, they also see the indigenous people from North through South America having crystal skulls and utilizing them in ceremonies or for spiritual healing and growth. Okay, I would like to move this chapter in a new direction next in order to discuss a few indigenous elders/shamans I have met at various conferences where I have had the honor to attend and be a presenter. I had a chance to speak to these special individuals and here are some other insights I learned from them.

Crystal skull researcher Joshua Shapiro believes that extraterrestrials may be responsible for planting these artifacts in various locales around the earth.

When I attended a crystal skull symposium in Sedona, Arizona, in the spring of 1999, organized by Dr. Chet Snow and his wife (this is where I received my first personal crystal skull as a gift from an ex-wife, "Portal de Luz" {Portal of Light} – a 10 lb smoky quartz skull made by the superior Brazilian carver, Leandro da Silva, a personal friend) – I had a chance to listen to the information presented by two priests who were linked to a group of Mayans in Guatemala led by Don Alejandro. In a message one of the priests was given regarding the skulls, it was said the most ancient skulls were gifts to them from the Grandfather of the Pleiades and that they did not make these skulls themselves. But, since they were sacred objects, they felt they must guard them and protect them. In a book by Morton and Thomas called "Mystery of the Crystal Skulls" (published in 1997) they interviewed Don Alejandro in Guatemala, who stated they did have in their care several crystal skulls which were hidden.

At the crystal skulls conferences in Switzerland and Holland (2006) that a few of us were involved with to setup, I had a chance to meet a Mayan Priest named Apolinario Chile Pixtun. In his talks, translated from Spanish, he called the Crystal Skulls the Crystal Heads. He shared how the symbol of the head (using its Mayan name) is prevalent throughout their spiritual philosophy and sacred books, including links with the Mayan Prophecy. Don Alejandro, again in his interview for Morton and Thomas, stated that there exist 52 sacred crystal skulls, 13 of which this Mayan group in Guatemala were guarding while other indigenous people, perhaps three other groups, might also have sets of 13 skulls. Of course 52 is a sacred number for the Mayans.

There is another Mayan Day Keeper, Hunbatz Men, who lives in the Yucatan in Mexico, that I have had the pleasure to meet a few times, first in Germany and most recently in Mexico City in 2009 for a crystal skull conference. He is also very connected to the crystal skulls. Hunbatz Men has publicly said that in one of their sacred books (he called it the "Chilam Balam") it is specifically stated that it is vital for a specific group of crystal skulls to come together to help take our world into a higher state. He also shared the information that the Crystal Skulls will help to re-activate sacred sites and temples in Mexico, which is why he has organized various gatherings at these sites and invited several crystal skull guardians to join him. Hunbatz Men has also spoken to me (as Don Alejandro also acknowledged) about a link with the crystal skulls and Atlantis. That is, when Atlantis sank and part of the Yucatan was colonized by the Atlanteans, many of their sacred objects were brought to different parts of the world, including crystal skulls which made their way into Mexico and

Central America. Hunbatz Men incidentally was gifted with a crystal skull, made from another form of quartz. The skull was purportedly found in a cave in China, and he now shares the object when he does his public talks.

So, to conclude this section, it is quite clear that many of the indigenous peoples of the Americas do understand and recognize the crystal skulls as sacred tools. They work with the crystal skulls in their special ceremonies. And some of the legends and knowledge held within these cultures seem to indicate that the origins of the crystal skulls either have a connection with so-called ancient astronauts or advanced civilizations in the past or both. It would probably take several books to cover all the knowledge and history that connects the people of the Americas with the crystal skulls – but at least I have given some idea of the key information which has surfaced so far.

Okay, but what about the UFO – Crystal Skull Connection?

Let's explore then the idea that perhaps some of the ancient crystal skulls which are known today either come from an ET source or have an ET connection. I mean, if the indigenous people who have some of the so-called ancient skulls do not have a technology to make the advanced skulls (in form and feature) that have been discovered so far today, then could some of the skulls have been the gifts of the Gods or advanced ET races? There are three crystal skulls I have personally met which I believe have a strong UFO link. Let me tell you their stories and some of my personal experiences with them.

ET – A human-size, smoky quartz skull, guardian Joky van Dieten, the Netherlands

In 1991, I was invited to Los Angeles to participate in a conference and speak about the Crystal Skulls. At this conference I saw my good friend Eric Fintzi, who at this time had a crystal store in Venice, California. He had a booth at this conference and was insisting I come to his store after the conference as he had something important to show me. When I finally arrived at his store, he introduced me to a woman named Joky van Dieten who was familiar with my first book, "Mysteries of the Crystal Skulls Revealed." She told me actually, that this book had mysteriously dropped off of a bookshelf by itself in Banyan Books in Vancouver, and this is why she bought it. She had had some interest in the crystal skulls previously and actually came in contact with Mr. Fintzi through this book, as we had a listing for him in our crystal skull directory in the back. But even after I went to the store and met Joky, I didn't fully understand why Eric was so insistent that I come to the store and join them for dinner at his home. This was cleared up very quickly after he came out in the living room where we were sitting with a box to show both of us after dinner was concluded.

In the box was a human-sized, smoky quartz skull. Miss van Dieten had contacted Mr. Fintzi via the phone number we listed for him in our book and asked if he had any ancient human-sized crystal skulls for sale – which he did not at the time. And since there were only a few skulls of this type known, he didn't know of any in the world that were available. But Miss van Dieten told Mr. Fintzi he would hear about one soon and a few days later, miraculously, he was contacted by a family in Guatemala who had a crystal skull they wanted to sell as they were very poor and needed money. (Author's Note: This is not uncommon for a person who is to become a crystal skull guardian, to have a strong intuition or be guided to a source that has the crystal skull they feel exists.)

Mr. Fintzi told us this family in Guatemala had had possession of this skull since 1906, when members of their family were digging in the ground and a shovel struck the skull. (It still has a chip on the head.) Now, as to why I am discussing this skull for this article: It is because when the skull came out for us to view it, this crystal skull did not have the shape of our modern skull bone at all. It has an overbite in the teeth and the chin and head are slightly pointed. I mentioned to Miss van Dieten that it looked like an extraterrestrial skull – and after seeing her father's face inside the skull (he had passed on some years prior) she decided to call this skull "ET."

Well, you can look at the photo shown here and decide for yourself if it looks a bit like an "ET." But another clue about this skull came when Miss van Dieten decided to go with us (I think it was 1995) to

Australia to participate in offering some crystal skull events around Sydney. I have a good friend, Norm Hacker, who lived in Australia that I had met during one of many trips to Peru. For some reason, he decided to help us get a booth at the Body-Mind-Spirit conference taking place at this time and organized things for us to do a few other small presentations at some local spiritual centers.

So at our booth at this conference, Miss van Dieten had brought "ET" and one of her other ancient crystal skulls to be on display and people were able to have a brief session with these skulls to experience their energy. Well, one person who came was so affected by "ET" that she felt strongly inspired to bring her master reiki teacher back to have a sitting with "ET." So when her teacher came, and kind of went into a trance, I was recording everything she said.

To summarize what the reiki teacher shared: She discussed the idea that "ET," its essence, was a being from another world who, due to some type of misconduct on his home planet, was sent out into the universe to live by "himself" (because we feel a masculine presence) and finally came to the Earth. In order to have contact with the people of the earth (as this "being" existed in another dimension), "he" solidified a part of himself as a crystal skull so that "he" could work with humans. Additionally, in some sessions we had with other people in the presence of "ET," there was a suggestion that this skull came back to Miss van Dieten because she had been its guardian before, possibly the queen of an underwater civilization. Of course these theories of where "ET" came from or has been cannot be proven nor am I sure that Miss van Dieten agrees with them either. But many people have sensed that "ET" has a link with extraterrestrial beings. Besides, Miss van Dieten has been a wonderful guardian of this crystal skull and allowed many people to have a chance to meet "ET" in person. There was an archeologist that Miss van Dieten met once who told her, as far as he knew, there has never been a bone skull of this shape found in the ground.

Windsong – A human-sized clear quartz.

Guardian: Floyd Petri and family, Texas, US

Floyd Petri is a retired secret service agent and police chief. I had my first contact with Mr. Petri in 1996, when we began a series of correspondences via email which eventually led me to visit Mr. Petri in his home in the early part of 1997. Mr. Petri is in the possession of a human-sized clear quartz skull with the "ET" presence within the skull and that has the name of "Windsong." As you can see from the photo of this skull, its facial features are not as distinct as some of the other crystal skulls which are known in the world but the size and shape of a crystal skull is not the most important consideration. But the story of how it found Mr. Petri is pretty amazing. So let me briefly summarize how this happened to him. We see again that when it's time for a crystal skull to find its guardian, all the doors will open to where the guardian is led.

In 1993, while working as a CID special agent in Austin, Texas, Mr. Petri started to have an intuitive compulsion that he must find a certain location in the city but he didn't know why. This compulsion led him to a store that rented videos out front and a rock shop in the back. When Mr. Petri met the owner, he spontaneously asked him if he had any human-sized crystal skulls for sale. He didn't understand why he asked this question but that is what came out of his mouth. The owner said, no, he didn't but he had some small crystal skulls, which of course Mr. Petri declined to purchase. Mr. Petri thought this strange compulsion would then be finished but it was not. He continued to visit the rock shop a number of other times and each time he asked the owner the same question but the owner continued to deny he had such a crystal skull until one time . . .

He brought a friend with him to the rock shop who mentioned to the owner that Mr. Petri was involved with UFO research. And it was like these were the magic words because the owner completely changed and told Mr. Petri that he really did have such a skull and showed it to him inside a box in the back of the store. It became apparent that Mr. Petri, on some inner level, was being called to meet this skull. Mr. Petri asked the owner if the skull was for sale but the owner didn't want to sell it for any price. Again, Mr. Petri thought his compulsion was over but he would still visit the store from time to time to see this crystal skull. Then one day the owner told Mr. Petri that this was his lucky day because this crystal skull had told the owner he must sell the skull to Mr. Petri and even gave the owner a price, which is what Mr. Petri could afford. So this is how "Windsong" and Floyd Petri came together.

Now the owner had worked with two sensitives to determine the history of this crystal skull and where it came from, so here is a summary of what the sensitives received, and which Mr. Petri has confirmed to be accurate as to what he experienced and heard:

"Windsong" is an "Energy of Light Being" who comes from another planet. The name of "Windsong" is the closest we can come to speaking "her" name as it cannot be pronounced in our reality and sounds like the wind blowing through the trees. Windsong's home planet is so far away from Earth that we as humans cannot comprehend the distance. On "her" world they do not know death. Anyway, Windsong traveled with all of her kind from her home planet to experience a region of space which is a physical location known as "The Dark." They felt that they had to travel there to experience "The Dark" so they can know the difference between "The Dark" and "The Light" and then had to make a decision to choose to stay in "The Dark" or return to "The Light." However, halfway they stopped at Earth and deposited Windsong in the largest vein of quartz on Earth after giving her all the knowledge of the universe. She will wait for her fellow beings from her planet to pick her up on their return voyage.

However, for Windsong to exist here, "she" needed a spatial energetic place that resonates with "her" being so "she" could exist for a very long time and this is why she initially chose to stay in a large quartz crystal vein in South America. She was able to move herself anywhere within this vein or leave it for short periods of time. Windsong said to the psychic that in the 1700s, a blind Shaman felt her presence in the vein of quartz and over many years created a crystal skull from the quartz of this vein. Then Windsong decided to vacate the vein and located herself within the skull. She wanted Floyd to be her keeper because Floyd's true soul essence also comes from another planet she sensed and Windsong wanted to be with someone who would better understand her.

To give you an idea of what Windsong is like, here is what I experienced when I first met her in 1997. I had to fly to a local airport in Texas near where Mr. Petri and his family live. He picked me up at the airport and brought Windsong with him so I could view and hold the skull. Many of the old and ancient skulls I have seen have a very strong and intense energy field around them. But Windsong was very calm and gentle. As a matter of fact, when Floyd first received Windsong and brought "her" home, he didn't know how his wife Barbara would respond to having a crystal skull, being that she was a Southern Baptist. So Floyd decided he would leave Windsong in his car until he sorted it out with Barbara, which they eventually did. Being in Texas, which gets quite warm, the inside of the car would be like an oven but this crystal skull was always cool to the touch.

Also when I met Barbara and Floyd's son, they told me that Windsong would speak directly to them; they could "hear" her telepathically. However, Floyd complained he could never hear Windsong, being a nuts and bolts person who is so logical, but I have watched Floyd intuit that Windsong wishes to communicate and what her desires are. Then after we ate dinner one night, I felt like doing a small meditation with Windsong, who was sitting on the dining room table. After we finished the meditation we heard Barbara shout from the kitchen. What had happened is that during the meditation, Barbara, who has bursitis in one arm, which she could never lift straight, all of a sudden while in the kitchen, easily and without any pain at all, lifted her arm up all the way.

In 1999, when I received my first crystal skull ("Portal de Luz") at the crystal symposium in Sedona, I had a chance to do a private session with Windsong and Floyd and a few other people. I believe that Windsong did help in "her" own unique way to assist in awakening the living consciousness linked to "Portal de Luz." In December of 2009, we had another chance to visit Mr. Petri and his wife in their home when my life partner Katrina came with me and saw Windsong for the first time. Well, Windsong was also talking with Katrina and said something like this to her: *"What took you so long? I have been waiting for you."* Now of course we can't prove that Windsong is an extraterrestrial being, but there are so many people who have had contact with an intelligence linked to this crystal skull that it would be hard to believe that Mr. Petri and his family would just be making this up. Especially with Mr. Petri having been in a number of responsible positions linked with government and the police that require integrity and honesty, I have no doubt that this story is true and my own experiences with Windsong support this.

Synergy, Clear quartz larger than human-size skull, Sherry Whitfield, Arizona, U.S.

I first met Sherry Whitfield in Michigan in the fall of 2001, when she was the manager of a craft store for a friend and had her crystal skull "Synergy" (16+ lb) on display. I had a chance to sleep with "Portal de Luz" and "Synergy" during this visit. Sherry had received this skull in the late 1990s from a gentleman named George, who went to South America frequently to obtain various gemstones which he would sell to the public. Sherry met George at a crystal fair in Arizona where George had this crystal skull at his booth. It turned out George felt this large crystal skull should go to Sherry so we have yet another case of how an old or ancient skull is passed from one person to another when it is the right time.

According to George, he came across this crystal skull when he was doing one of his travels through Ecuador and came to a small village. One of the families in the village allowed George to sleep in their small home on a sleeping mat on the floor. When George woke up the next morning, the head of the family presented the skull to him to do with it what he felt he needed to do. He was told this skull was given to this family in the early 1800s by a woman missionary who told them this crystal skull originated with an ancient civilization.

There is a lot more about "Synergy," as well as newer aspects to the subject that Miss Whitfield is continually learning about, so if you wish to know more, you can find Miss Whitfield on Facebook or she has her own websites. Now why I am discussing "Synergy" in this article is because of what I received during a visit with this crystal skull in my hotel room in Tucson, Arizona, in the fall of 2004. Miss Whitfield's ex-husband brought the skull over and allowed photographs to be taken.   Sherry was not present due to a serious health problem she was experiencing at this time but everyone is happy that she fully recovered. As I was meditating with this crystal skull, I had a strong feeling come over me that this skull represented a race of humanoid people not native to the earth but which had a lion head or face. Synergy is definitely not like a human bone skull in any way. The face is out of proportion to a human skull and it does have a bit of an "ET" look which you can see as you view the photo of this skull shown here. What I can tell you is that eventually Miss Whitfield met a man in England who knew of a primitive tribe in Australia. When he showed this tribe the photos of Synergy, they were extremely happy. They claimed they were the Guardians of this crystal skull for many years but they had had to let the skull travel throughout the world. They were happy it was safe and in Miss Whitfield's capable hands and care.

So to summarize this last section, these are three crystal skulls which I have personally met during my travels and which I believe are linked with "ET" or extra-terrestrial beings. I have seen a number of other crystal skulls (quartz and non-quartz) which are older skulls that look extraterrestrial. And finally the modern carvers are also producing ET-looking crystal skulls including duplicating the crystal skull in the Indiana Jones film. Since there are a number of people who are crystal skull guardians who are having some form of inner communications with the crystal skulls (from all three types we defined before) whether it is a form of telepathy, a feeling or intuition – this means for me that quartz is an excellent conduit and medium for contact with spiritual or dimensional beings who are not on our physical level but exist around us.

While it has been speculated that some of the ancient crystal skulls publicly known may be of alien manufacture, due to their advanced design in form, there are definitely a few older crystal skulls which the guardians feel are overshadowed by an ET presence. This can be another indirect type of proof that we are having contact with ETs. Or that the crystal skull being studied which has this type of energy around it truly was a gift left by our so-called Star Brothers and

Sisters to assist humanity in our spiritual evolution and in remembering who we truly are. The UFO – Crystal Skull link is just another mysterious aspect of the crystal skulls that frequently comes up in our research and that we will one day prove to be absolutely true.

A Short History Of How The Crystal Skulls First Appeared In The Americas

The first two crystal skulls to become known to a large chunk of the general public are the Paris Crystal Skull, which currently resides in the Musee du quai Branly in Paris near the Eiffel Tower, where it was first displayed in 1878, and the British Museum Crystal Skull in the British Museum in London, first displayed in 1898. As far as we know, both of these crystal skulls came out of Mexico and were connected to a French antiquity dealer named Boban, who sold them to private owners before they eventually found their way into their current museum homes. They were probably robbed first by local peasants from Mesoamerican ruins and then sold.

Another crystal skull that came out of Mexico in the 19th century (1840s), about which the last I heard is that it is in private hands (although it was for sale in 2009) is known as the Rosary Cross Skull. This crystal skull has been with a family named Redo. The Rosary Cross Skull is a small clear quartz skull with a hole in its top so that a cross made out of quartz and gold (with the year 1571 inscribed upon it) can be placed inside it. I met Norma Redo at a conference in Mexico City in 2009 where she brought another crystal skull which, when I felt it, had a fairly powerful energy connected with it, possibly due to being in the presence of the Rosary Cross Skull.

In the early 1900s, the following crystal skulls emerged, according to their guardians, linked to Mexico and Central America. "ET" (smoky quartz, Guatemala, 1906), the 1920s: Mitchell-Hedges Crystal Skull (clear quartz, Belize, 1924), "Max" (clear quartz, Guatemala), "Ami" (amethyst quartz, Mexico), and "The Mayan Crystal Skull" (clear quartz, Mexico).

As we move forward in time, more and more crystal skulls have been revealed. So many crystal skulls are coming out at the present time that it is impossible to keep track. But there has been a tremendous shift in the awareness of the crystal skulls as now thousands and upon thousands of crystal skulls are being carved by modern carvers each year. And these carvers would not be making this number of crystal skulls unless there were many people who had a desire to have their own. And many people have more than one, like us! This trend did not begin to develop until the middle part of the 1990s, but I don't see it ever stopping now. Just one word of caution – if you decide to become a crystal skull guardian, be ready for your life to change in a big way!

Final Conclusions

Well, I have been involved in the study of researching UFOs and Crystal Skulls for over 25 years. Besides some of the experiences I have shared with the crystal skulls in this article, I have had my share of different types of UFO contact as well. So I would say, modestly, that I believe I understand both of these controversial subjects quite well. I know within my inner being that some of the more advanced crystal skulls have come to us via real life ETs, who I say are the so-called "good ones" who want to truly help humanity and awaken us to our spiritual heritage. While many people now are more open then ever before and believe ETs and UFOs do exist and that we can't be the only intelligent creatures in the whole Universe, still, to have a direct contact with the crafts or the ET's themselves is a big shock. This is probably why the ETs suppress memories of the experiences people have with them so these people (contactees and abductees) can still live a so-called normal life and not go crazy. Of course all the TV shows and movies we have about aliens are helping us to get used to the idea because all the prophecies state a more direct contact is coming in the near future.

Anyway, I offer the idea in this article that the crystal skulls are another type of physical proof of the contact we are having with ET civilizations. That some of the very old or ancient crystal skulls we are aware of publicly have been filled (programmed) with incredible knowledge and information which was placed in these ancient computers, if we can call them that, by our extraterrestrial friends. And in which, when it is the proper time, will be revealed to our world to assist us in creating a world of peace and to better understand our true spiritual nature. For I believe that we are galactic citizens with a spiritual heritage and destined to be infinite beings that exist simultaneously on many levels and are divine children of the Creator.

Now I do have a vision or a movie that plays in my head. Perhaps this vision or movie is inspired by the contact with the hundreds and hundreds of crystal skulls I have been fortunate to see and be in the presence of, or perhaps it comes from one of my spirit guides, some of which I believe are Interdimensional. Let me share this vision with you. If you don't think I am too crazy from what I have written so far, then maybe this vision will make sense to you.

What I see is that one day there will be a crystal skull that we will understand how to activate or "turn on," and we will obtain the information encoded within the skull. The form this information will take will be like a movie or video that plays inside of the skull in 3D. This will be just another version of a viewing screen like we have on our TVs, screens in the theaters, on the computers, tablets or cell phones. Oh, and when this video plays, it will be interactive, meaning that when you talk to the person who appears, they will answer you. The closest I can come to an example of what this might look like is from the first "Superman" movie. Remember where Superman's (Kal-El, his name on Krypton) parents put into the spacecraft with their son, before their planet Krypton exploded, special crystals? These crystals build Superman's Fortress of Solitude in the North Pole and also allow him to interact with his Father to learn the knowledge of Krypton even though his father is long gone.

And when this special day comes and we have the technology to activate this living movie inside one of the crystal skulls, then we will know the history of humanity, where we come from and how the ETs have guided us and helped us to develop as galactic citizens. Will you ready on this day?

Thank you, all the best, peace and light always

Joshua Shapiro
A Crystal Skull Explorer.

====================

Joshua Shapiro has been involved with the crystal skulls since 1983, when he saw an amethyst skull called "Ami" which he believes is an ancient crystal skull. "Ami" triggered an inner awareness within Joshua that the crystal skulls are vital for the future of humanity and world peace so he has dedicated his life to the exploration of the crystal skulls and sharing the best information he has collected with the public. He and his partner Katrina Head are known as the crystal skull explorers and travel the world to do presentations and private sessions with their personal crystal skulls. Joshua is the co-author of three books on the crystal skulls and has had the honor to visit in person (and sometimes do research) with most of the well known crystal skulls in the world. To learn more about the crystal skulls or contact Joshua you can:

Visit his website at: www.whatarecrystalskulls.com
Or email at: crystalskullexplorers@gmail.com

Visitors From Hidden Realms: The Origin and Destiny of Humanity, As Told By Star Elders, Shamen and UFO Visitors

By Brent Raynes

My Sweat Lodge Related Vision

The following happened back in February 1993. It was only a few hours after the first sweat lodge that my wife and I had ever participated in, conducted by people of Native American ancestry near the northern edges of Alabama's Bankhead National Forest. I awoke after a few brief hours of sleep (after returning home from our late night sweat) to a "vision." In my "vision" I perceived a round white disc-shaped object in the sky. Below it I could see some trees. Inside the round disc was what looked like an image of the legendary Phoenix. The disc itself was enclosed by a U-shaped structure.

Soon after perceiving this, I took pen and paper in hand and drew out what I "saw" as best I could. (See reproduction of my drawing) In a recent follow-up telephone conversation with Richard Barnhouse (the Ohio petroglyph researcher) I briefly described my "vision" to him and how its similarity to Portsmouth's horseshoe mound (which I had not known about at the time of my "vision") had intrigued me somewhat since I first learned about it a few years ago through Greg Little. My wife Joan and I had actually visited it with Greg and Lora Little back in 2001.

When I first told Richard about my "vision," I wasn't sure what sort of reaction that I might get. "That is a really good vision," he exclaimed. Since he didn't dismiss it out-of-hand or laugh it off, I proceeded to question him further as to what, in his view, it might have meant. He began to explain, then seemed to hesitate slightly, and then said: "That's just one of the constellations I have problems with. It's Ophiuchus. It's called the 13th constellation. That's one of the alignments I think that's coming up on this December 21st, 2012 date where everything lines up in the universe. The U is an alignment and then that disc, that circle, most of the time is a reference to a soul." He felt that my phoenix was likely actually a thunderbird, and he pointed out that there was even a bird effigy mound on the outskirts of Portsmouth.

"Ophiuchus is the portal," Richard stated at one point, "the doorway." He believes that he has figured out some things about a ceremony that was done with what he calls "stone eggs." "When you died they collected your soul into one of these eggs," Richard explained. "It was kept in what they called the ghost lodge. They could only keep it for a year and then in a

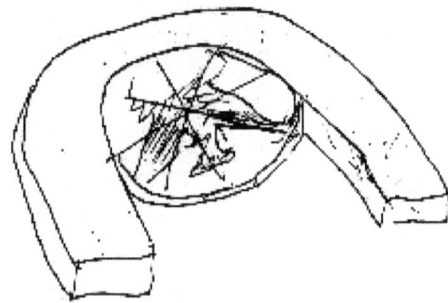

Brent's drawing of the Phoenix vision.

ceremony it was sent on its way to heaven and released out of the stone egg. It was then just another empty, useless rock until it was time to put another soul into it."

Richard described how he believes that tobacco and prayers were used to "carry their spirit" up to "the gate of heaven." He added, "They don't go directly to the Creator. It goes to the gates of heaven, to the thunderbird, and the spirit, like I told you, that was in that egg and is the spirit of the wind."

Does all of this sound strange? Well, if you've studied shamanic belief systems much at all you have to acknowledge that Richard may be on to something here. For example, following this conversation, I was reminded of an interview with one Brant Secunda who had lived among the people of Huichol, Mexico, and for 12 years apprenticed under an elderly healer named don Jose Matsuwa. In an interview in

"Magical Blend" magazine (No. 64, 1999), when asked about the Huichol view of death and an afterlife, Secunda replied: "When someone dies, we do a ceremony within five days to escort the spirit to the realm of light or what we call the Sky Realm. After five years, a shaman can bring your spirit back in the form of a little quartz crystal. It's a totally magical ceremony. The spirit actually comes down from the sky in a crystal: a physical crystal manifests in the sky and lands there on the altar. It's very wild. It defies our model of reality."

Richard Barnhouse

Richard thinks that the ancient shamans/priests were doing "ceremonies" in which they were "raising power." "So they were using these sacred items or objects of power, placed in certain locations, to control what was going on.

"Of course, Native Americans believe that there is a living something inside of everything that there is and they were using that," Richard stated. "On all of these rocks there's this constant thing about collecting the soul of something, or creating something and then capturing it, and capturing its soul and putting it in to one of these eggs, so that it can be used. That's at the very heart of the religion. But see, that's unknown to most people."

Petroglyph Manipulation

Finally I had to ask Richard if in his half a century of visiting ancient mounds, earthworks and petroglyph sites whether he had ever had something unusual or unexplained occur to him. Richard told me that he had coined a new term: petroglyph manipulation. "That's my name for it," he said. "They would arrange certain symbols in certain patterns to make something happen, whether it's for magic, to raise power, open doorways, capture spirits, who knows?

"I was kneeling on the floor, playing with this and moving the symbols around, and I had an out of body experience. I've always heard about these experiences but I had never had one myself. I think that's what triggered it.

"I was trying to find patterns that would go together, so I would draw the patterns and then cut them out and place them in what I thought was the correct flow to make what I call like a sentence, or to put them together in a group that belonged together, and that's when I had that happen."

Then, about a week later, he had taken a friend somewhere at night and was waiting alone outside in his car when he decided again to give this process another try.

"It was dark and I was arranging this stuff in patterns again and playing with it. Here comes what I thought were two animals running side by side down the street, out of the darkness. When they get close to the car they're running but it's almost like watching them running in slow motion. Their leg movements were very slow, yet they were covering distance in a hurry. When

Joan Raynes with feather in Portsmouth horseshoe earthwork

they got even closer I realized that they weren't even touching the ground. They were a foot above the ground. Then I thought that they looked more like wolves. I couldn't make up my mind whether they were a dog or a wolf, or something in between, and I'm actually wondering what in the devil am I looking at. Then I looked in the side mirror as they went by and it was a boy and a girl, I'd say somewhere between 18 and 20. Naked, no clothes, no fur, and they're still running. Kneeling down but they're still running, just like I had seen coming up the street. Healthy, muscular, but definitely a boy and girl. When they got past the car, well, I actually looked out the window once I'd seen that in the mirror. All of this was happening in a heartbeat and I stick my head out the window, I'm looking back at these wolves or dogs, whatever they are, with the fur all over them. So they're past the car and then I look up in the rearview mirror and I can see the boy and the girl again and then in the darkness behind me they were gone.

"I was out of my league," Richard said. "I didn't know what I was doing or what happened, but I just simply wasn't going to do it again."

I asked Richard if he had used the same symbols during this incident as he did the time he had the out of body experience. "They were the same type," he explained. "They weren't the same ones.

"All of these symbols are also objects. I call them objects of power, sacred items, and what all of them were designed to do I don't know. But I think that they were arranging them in patterns around on the rocks when they were doing the ceremonies and when they were using them in the earthen encirclements and squares."

These two episodes happened about 12 years ago. I asked Richard if he had had anymore out of body episodes. "That was the only one that I have ever had in my lifetime," he said.

A few years ago, Joan and I met Terra Manasco, a talented craftsperson of Cherokee ancestry, and talked with her about Kinlock Shelter, considered by many an ancient Native American "power spot" in the dense Bankhead Forest of Alabama. It seems that Terra held views similar to what Richard had described to me. In a statement that had been published in the local "Wild Alabama" magazine in 1996, she stated: "It was the Uchee, who called themselves the Children of the Sun, who first used this site to Walk the Rainbow. Inducing themselves into a trance of blue-blackness formed by a series of sacred number patterns, a cord of white light would shoot out from their navels and arc out into the universe. It was upon this cord that they 'Walked the Rainbow' and visited many worlds. The symbols carved on Kinlock's rocks are the magic symbols used in the trance as well as recreations of spirits encountered beyond the Rainbow."

Many people even today it seems have been drawn to Kinlock and have had rather profound spiritual, mystical experiences. One man who had performed a "vision quest" there described how at one point he had found himself in an out-of-body state, rising up to the treetops. The experience soon became a cosmic consciousness type of event. "It seemed as if the molecules of my body dispersed and split apart, and integrated, and became part of all that I saw," this man recalled later. "I have never again been the same person that I was before that experience. I am better."

I was once drawn to visit Kinlock too. Soon after a sweat lodge ceremony (which had become fairly routine by that time) I had the impression that I needed to go there, that there was a certain petroglyph in the rocks that was very significant. I honestly had no idea why or what it was and I had never visited this site before. In fact, when I went there our Native guide and friend, Wanda "Dove" Reed, told me to sit and meditate, get out of my head, but I was intrigued by all of the awesome rock carvings, busily taking photographs and drawing what I was seeing on a pad of paper. I just couldn't get into my right mind! (Pun intended, of course) When I left there, I had no idea what symbol was significant. They had all been neat and interesting, but nothing stood out as one that deserved special attention. Not long afterwards, I was in another sweat lodge again and I had a vision of a cactus, like you see in the American Southwest, and it was in the shape of a bird's foot, of which I had seen several bird-foot rock carvings at Kinlock. Instantly I knew that was the symbol that required my special attention!

The same day that we visited Kinlock we visited another site with beautiful ancient rock carvings a few miles away. It was there that Joan had a "vision" of three star like patterns, in a triangular type formation, associated with some sort of wavy energy field. She has, since then, been able to "see," on occasion, similar wavy energy patterns around people, trees, rocks, etc. On the other hand, I got the impression of a circle divided into four quarters and the words "Southern Cross." A few years later, I would meet and interview Andrew Collins while he was visiting with Greg and Lora Little at their home in Memphis. He had a book soon to be published, entitled "The Cygnus Mystery." I learned that the star constellation of Cygnus, also called the "Northern Cross," was a cross-shaped arrangement of stars that ancient people worldwide associated with a portal or gateway to the afterlife through which their souls would go upon death. It was often symbolized as a bird's foot. Another portal along the Milky Way was a near twin cross-shaped formation of stars known to us today as the "Southern Cross." There were other things that I saw that day too that upon talking with Andrew and later reading his book seemed to pull more pieces of the puzzle together.

Jungian synchronicity? Spirit contact? Whatever the explanation, these experiences do occur and can have a fairly profound impact on people.

====================

Brent Raynes

Brent Raynes is the author of "Visitors From Hidden Realms" (2004) and "On The Edge of Reality" (2009), and the editor of the popular online magazine "Alternate Perceptions" (www.mysterious-america.net). Brent has been investigating and researching UFOs since 1967. His interests have included the full spectrum of paranormal phenomena. He's been involved in a good many haunted house investigations, has been doing EVP (Electronic Voice Phenomena) work, as well as crypto-zoological studies, plus met many Native American practitioners and been involved in visiting sacred sites and taking part in their ceremonies. In November 2010, Brent was a keynote speaker at the ARE (Association for Research and Enlightenment) in Virginia Beach, Virginia, where a special UFO conference was held. It was called "Visitors From Hidden Realms," in honor of Brent's book.

References
Alternative Perceptions Magazine – Free Online Subscription At:
http://www.mysterious-america.net/

The Native American Kachina and the Extraterrestrial Relationship

By Angela Sangster

The nations indigenous to the land that is now the United States gave great respect and credence to the laws of nature, as is evident from the remains of ancient pottery, crafts and drawings. What of the laws of the universe, though? What evidence is there that the nations of this land believed in celestial life forms?

Petroglyphs found in ancient rocks of the Hopi regions of the Southwest have shown figures that appear to be ant-like. There are many legends of the Ant People, who were a benevolent race that aided humans during the destruction of the First World. Gary David, an author and researcher, has examined the connection between these ant-like drawings and the masks worn for the Kachina dance. Were these masks actually representations of a belief in extra-terrestrials?

When David was living among the Hopi, he came to some interesting conclusions. He noted that the villages, or ruins of villages, lined up specifically to stars in the Orion belt constellation. This got him studying further, and in looking at the ancient rock art and carvings, he saw many that corresponded with star charts and drawings of creatures that appeared to be extraterrestrial in nature. He then began to look at the connection between the popular Kachina dance and the spirits they represented, along with a possible link to another planet.

History of the Kachina

As far back as 1300 A.D., the Kachina cult has been in existence. Ancient drawings of the masked figures have been found in the ruins of Hopi villages and are always associated with the rain so desperately needed in the arid environment. Allegedly it was believed that the visits would come from the Kachinas themselves during the first of the four worlds they believe to have existed, and now come in the form of carefully chosen masked dancers.

In Hopi and Navajo beliefs, Kachinas are quite simply messengers between this world and the next. The masks have many designs on them that appear otherworldly. No two Kachina masks look alike as each are specific to different entities and elemental factors that have been part of their history. Separate from the Kachina masks that are thought to represent the deities themselves, the popular Kachina doll is more of a teaching tool. It is not to be confused as representative of the ancient deities. It does however give young children an insight into these beliefs and instructs them on how to interact with nature deities.

The Hopis revered the Kachina and believe they descended from the sky.

Sotuknang, The God of the Sky

Most notable among the masks is the representation of Sotuknang, or the God of the Sky. Like many other ancient societies, the stories are told through the petroglyphs and the cave drawings. These drawings, like those of the Egyptians and ancient Chinese, depict objects that appear to be aircraft of some kind. In the legends of Sotuknang, it is said that he comes to the people on a "flying shield." It is reminiscent of other legends and religious histories where it was evident that at the very least, people were thinking about existences outside this particular realm.

One of the more controversial aspects of the Kachinas is the presence of a deity known as the Blue Kachina or the Blue Star. There are those, such as Dan Katchongva, the leader of the Hopi Sun Clan in the early 1900's, that claim this Blue Star or the Eye of God is an ancient legend foretelling the End of Times. It is thought by some that the Blue Star Kachina is simply an extension of the Ghost Dance movement that swept across the nation during the latter part of the nineteenth century. It is true that the prophecy was foretold by Katchongva during this time; however, there are other mentions of this prophecy, especially in Frank Waters "Book of the Hopi." There have been spheres of blue discovered in the solar system that are speculated to signal the coming fulfillment of this prophecy. It is also quite possible that the blue hues of an exploding comet or meteor could create this effect.

Masks of the Kachina

Regardless, the Kachina masks that are still used today very much resemble the stories of the Four Worlds that are told on the ancient walls of ruined cities. The legends also resemble others that have come to light, such as the Annunaki, or the extraterrestrial race that is thought to come from the planet of Nibiru. This belief, while science has yet to fully substantiate it, was evidenced in the drawings of Ancient Sumeria. Just as the Annunaki were believed to possess great knowledge that was taught to humanity before the worlds began to be destroyed, the Ant People, and later the Kachinas also were teachers and mediators. It is also important to note that it was the "Anasazi" that the Hopi descended from, which when pronounced, is not a far stretch from "Annunaki".

Looking at these masks, it is easy to speculate that the inspiration for them must have been something not seen in this world. Many of the masks for the warrior Kachinas (directly below the chiefs) resemble what has come to be known as the "grays" or the extraterrestrials that are believed by some to have come to this planet. The dances and the languages spoken are of an ancient form that is only understood by the ones doing the dance. It is thought in this state that the dancer is overtaken by the spirit of the Kachinas and becomes one with whatever element it represents.

One thing is evident, and that is that the ancient Hopi thought far beyond the world around them and believed that life existed everywhere. It is also evident that there are many stories that, while they may differ in ways that are specific to their beliefs, they share many common points. These points seem to indicate that life in other parts of the universe has been something speculated on for many, many centuries.

Strange and spooky to outsiders, members of various Native Tribes treated the Kachina with great reverence.

The Kachina dances still take place today in the Southwest Hopi, Navajo, and Pueblo areas, especially in the Hopi Mesas. Kachina dolls are intricately designed and sold to the many tourists that flock there every year to take part in witnessing these dances and ceremonies of a people rich in wisdom and culture. Many of them do not know the ancient ways that these ceremonies represent, because so much of the culture itself was ignored by those who sought control of this land. As we sift through the artifacts and legends that have survived time and the elements, we can only piece together the story of these remarkable people that believed in living in harmony with the earth's gifts – and quite possibly in harmony with the rest of the universe as well.

Ant People of The Hopi and The Annunaki

The works of Zechariah Sitchin present his theory of a twelfth planet in our solar system that was instrumental in creating the Earth. The race of extraterrestrials that he believed to be the ultimate originator of the human race he referred to as the Annunaki.

Zechariah Sitchin's work is a subject of great debate, either with those who call it pseudoscience or those who have determined his translations of ancient texts are incorrect. It is however interesting to note that other civilizations besides the ancient Sumerians had similar creation stories recorded through petroglyphs and wall drawings. One of these civilizations originated in the land now known as the United States and eventually became the Hopi nation. The ones that the Hopi descended from were known as the Anasazi.

Author and researcher Gary David lived among the Hopi in South Dakota as an English teacher. In meeting and talking with these people, he found the philosophy of "as above, so below." In essence, this means that the constellations in the sky reflect the geography of the Earth. This is something that has been theorized about regarding the three Giza Pyramids and their relation to the stars in the Orion belt. While that theory in and of itself has come under scientific scrutiny (mainly in the studies that show the pyramids were added on to for those points to match up), it is interesting to note that David noticed a similar correlation between the Hopi Mesas in the Southwest and the same constellation.

Members of the tribe would dress up in costume to look exactly like the gods from upon high who visited them in the past.

Orion's Belt

The three stars that make up the Orion belt are brightly seen in the early part of the year, and line up exactly with each other. Many different cultures have given meanings to this particular group of stars and it is evident that the skies have fascinated people for centuries. Gary David thought so as well, and began to study the sky charts and the locations of Hopi villages and ruins. He noted that these villages lined up with all the major stars in the Orion constellation. He also studied the rock art that was on the caves and ruins. In this, he came to some very interesting conclusions, which led him to think about just how seriously the Hopi had taken extraterrestrial life and the significance of the other planets in the solar system. In the rocks and caves of the Mesa villages, he found many petroglyphs that matched up with modern star charts and constellation patterns.

Sotuknang, the Sky God in Hopi legend, taught that the world has gone through several phases or cycles already, and we are in this time living in the Fourth World. In the original world, which was according to legend destroyed by fire, the benevolent Ant People sequestered everyone underground with them and shared what they had. The people were safe from the fire and destruction above. It is said that the Ant People even sacrificed their own food to aid the people. As the Sky God Sotuknang systematically destroyed the world above, the people waited patiently for the fires to burn and the earth to cool before they came up from above.

When the earth was completed, the Sky God gave the blessings and told them to love and nurture the earth so that destruction was not warranted again. The Ant People took their place as ants, and new life began in the Second World. Humanity being what it is, there have been two worlds destroyed since then, and this, the Fourth World is set for the appearance of the Fifth and final world. This can be compared to the Christians awaiting the rapture, where the Creator comes back and the ultimate world begins. This was prophesied to happen when the Blue Kachina or the Blue Star appeared. This was to signify the end of the Fourth World, and would be foretold by the Kachinas removing their masks and becoming one with the powerful beings they are said to represent.

In another part of the world, other drawings and carvings would give Zechariah Sitchin the spark for his theory on the race of beings that were here to teach humanity about the land in Ancient Sumeria. This race was believed to be superior and was thought to originate from the skies. It was through their teachings that the Sumerians were able to learn how to live in the world and take care of it until the gods of creation returned. Just like the Ant People of the Hopi, they were there to teach mankind about their planet and how to use its resources.

An interesting note is that the Hopi word for ant is "anu." The word for friends is "naki." There is also the similar pronunciation of the Hopi ancestors, the Anasazi. Again we see this phrase in another belief in another part of the world. This is not to say that it proves anything, but is just simply an interesting note. Is it possible that these stories are interrelated somehow? Or is it simply coincidence that there are so many points of connection?

Whether or not there is an actual connection between the Hopi of the Southwest and the ancient Sumerians and Egyptians, it certainly gives one pause that their creation stories were very similar. It also makes it apparent that celestial communication has been a curiosity of mankind for much longer than UFO sightings in the 20th century. As we continue searching in the skies for answers, it is humbling to think how many centuries the questions have possibly been asked.

=====================

References
Copyright 2010 www.TrueGhostTales.com
www.tntparanormal.com

Angela Sangster

Angela Sangster was born and raised in Decatur, Illinois, and grew up in a house that she believes was haunted. She has four beautiful children and has happily been a single mother for several years. Her ten-year-old daughter has Autism Spectrum Disorder, which has been both a challenge and a learning experience for Angela. Angela enjoys hiking, camping, fishing, NASCAR and researching all kinds of information, but especially that related to the paranormal and new treatments for Autism. She classifies herself as a skeptical believer and feels that you really don't need proof to believe in the paranormal. However, she would like to gain a better understanding of the paranormal and learn more about what is not paranormal. That way we can study more of what "is" paranormal.

Bonus Section - Crystal Skulls The Extraterrestrial Connection

Tim Beckley – A Special Report

There appears to be a remarkable connection between the sudden appearance of the mysterious crystal skulls, UFOs and the return of the ancient visitors we call "aliens," for lack of a more appropriate identification.

On 10-10-10, a group of Mayan elders visited the United Nations on Manhattan's east side to tell representatives of countries willing to listen that, while 2012 would not bring about a catastrophic end of the world, it could open humankind to a totally new spiritual awareness, including the return of the sky visitors who were more visible in the cultures of Central and South America in ages past. They reminded us that we do indeed stand at the crossroads of evolution today, that while we may be on the cusp of international disaster, still nothing is inevitable, and that as individuals and members of a global society, we can pull ourselves together and ultimately enter a golden age like that which has never existed before.

Timothy Green Beckley

As part of their visit to the

seat of America's financial and business institutions, the Mayans and the skulls they carried with them were hosted by the Association of Research and Enlightenment at a seminar in the Chelsea section of the City. The affair attracted over 500 visitors, most of who had come to see and touch the skulls for the first time. On several occasions during the weekend, jubilant attendees told others in attendance that they had seen unidentified craft – UFOs – hovering over the apartment buildings in the neighborhood; it was as if the UFOs were drawing upon the power and energy emitted by the many skulls on the premises.

For the next 48 hours, the New York City press reported, hundreds gathered on the streets in Chelsea, looking and pointing up into the sky at what seemed to be a fleet of mysterious objects which drifted about as if they owned the airspace over Manhattan. While no one in the press knew of the association between the crystal skulls and their Mayan handlers, there was obviously a connection that could not be disputed.

(See ABC newscast
http://www.youtube.com/watch?v=1TA_pKVKgKg).

The skulls on display at the symposium were of various sizes and appearances, but all were said to exude tremendous psychic energies that could be felt by most participants at the conclave. There were those who said the unidentified objects seen over Chelsea were balloons sent aloft from a nearby party in New Jersey, and while this may have accounted for some of the sightings, there were other orbs that appeared under intelligent control.

* * * * *

Joshua Shapiro has long been collecting extensive data on Crystal Skulls from around the world. He has traveled to meet and spoken with various owners and caretakers of the skulls all of whom have a unique narrative to tell about their adopted property. The photos that are displayed are from his personal property.

© Joshua Shapiro, gift from Al Ramirez
"Ami" - an ancient amethyst crystal skull found in Mexico in the 1920s and the first ancient crystal skull Joshua Shapiro met in person in 1983.

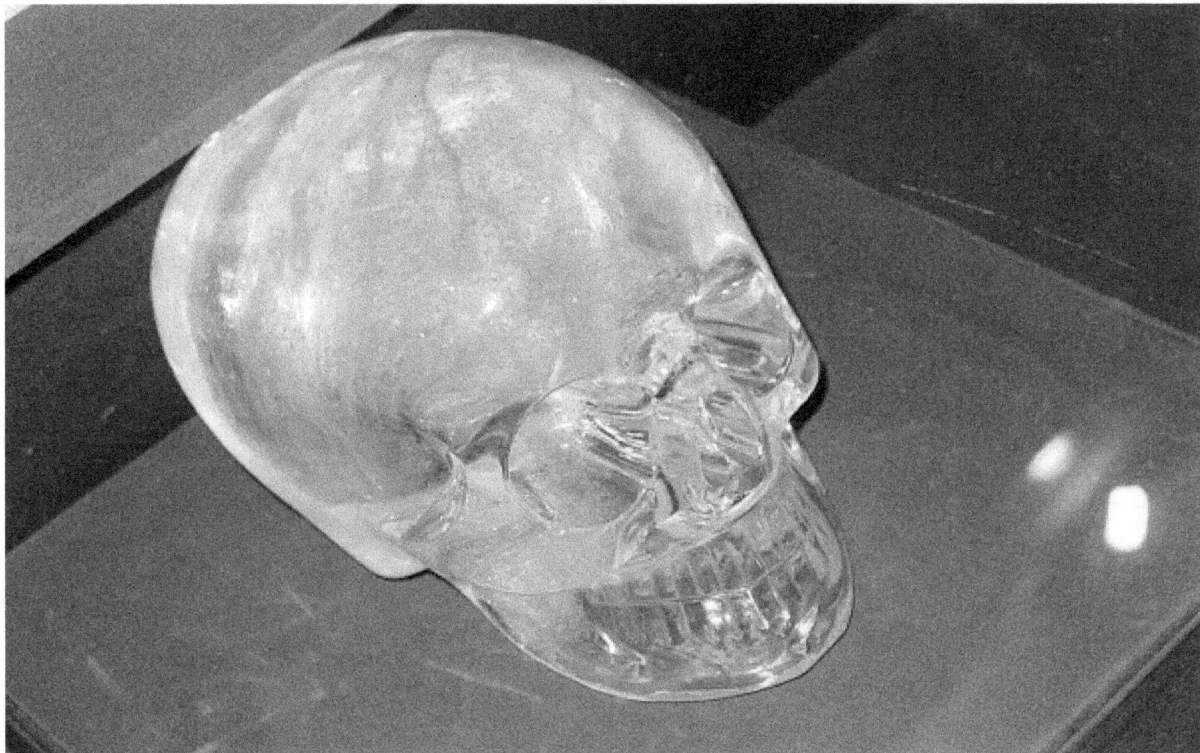

© Joshua Shapiro
"The British Museum Crystal Skull" - a clear quartz skull on display in the British Museum in London since 1898. The skull is human-sized and was found by a soldier of fortune in Mexico.

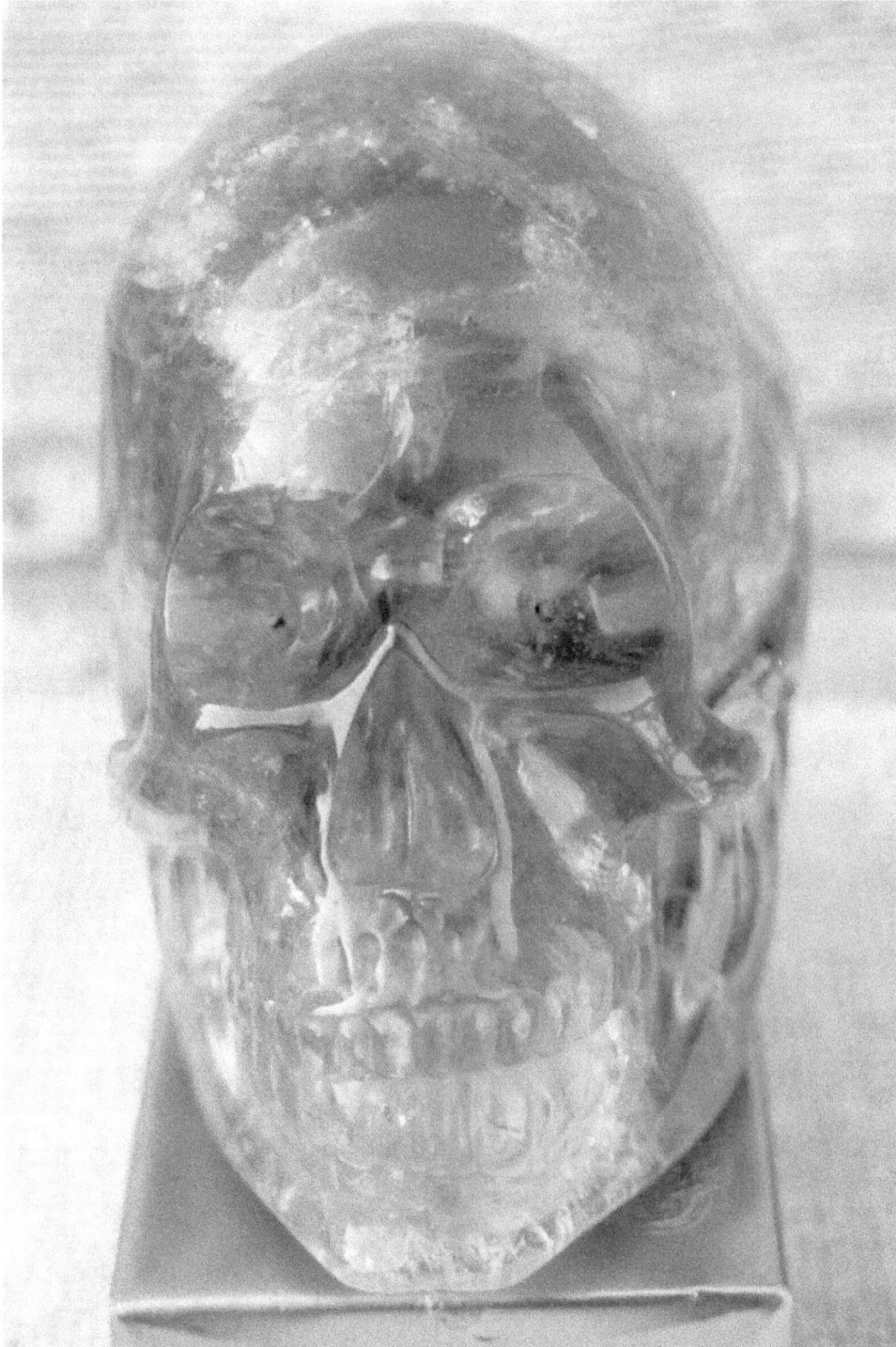

© Joshua Shapiro, permission Joky van Dieten
"ET" - an ancient smoky quartz crystal skull found in 1906 on the property of a
Mayan family in Guatemala. The skull's current guardian is
Joky van Dieten, of the Netherlands.

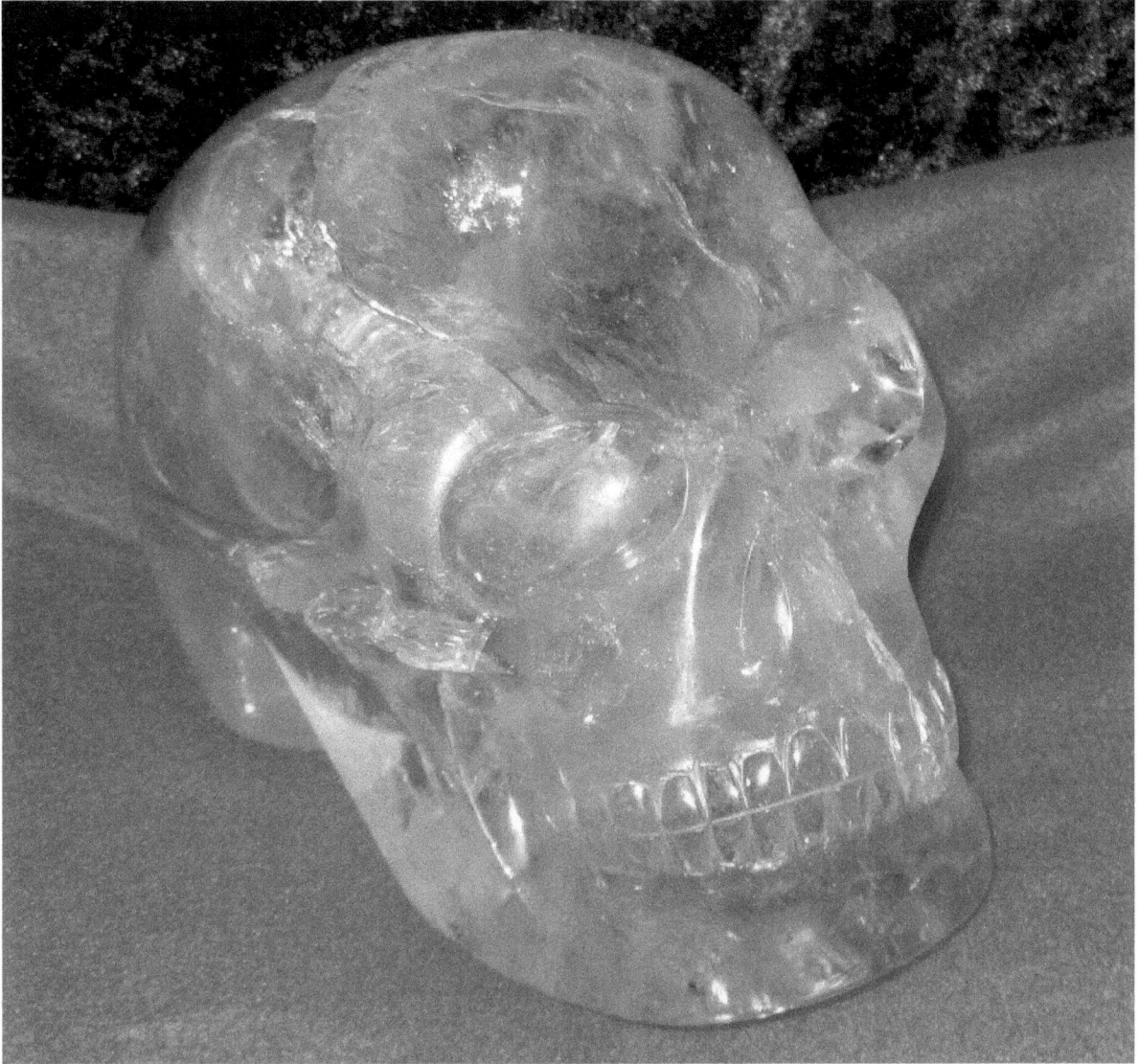

© Joshua Shapiro & Katrina Head
"Portal de Luz" (Portal of Light) - an example of a modern carved smoky quartz skull
by a Brazilian carver, Leandro da Silva in 1998. Part of the collection of crystal
skulls held by Joshua Shapiro.

© Joshua Shapiro & Katrina Head
An example of both modern and old crystal skulls that are shown on this table on display at a Crystal Skull Conference in Mexico City in the fall of 2009 at which Joshua Shapiro was a speaker.

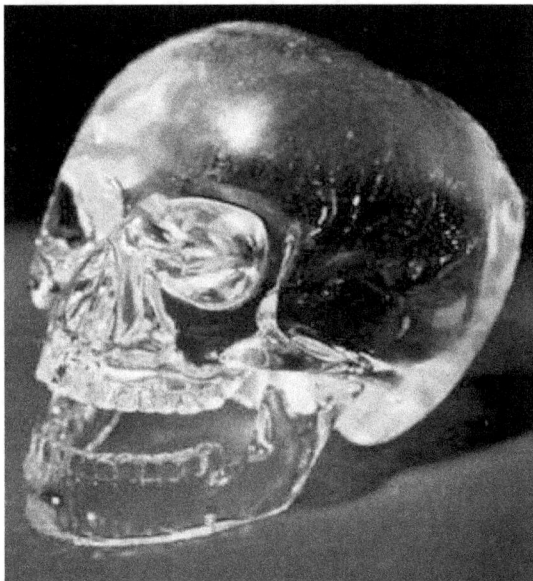

The Mitchell-Hedges Crystal Skull

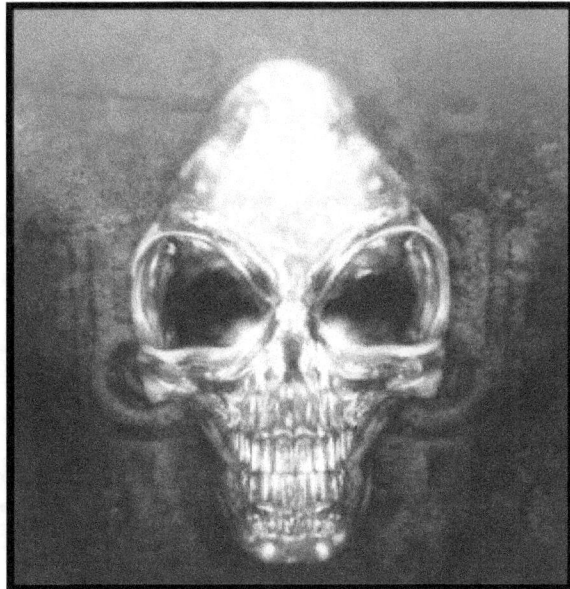

South American Mayan Skull

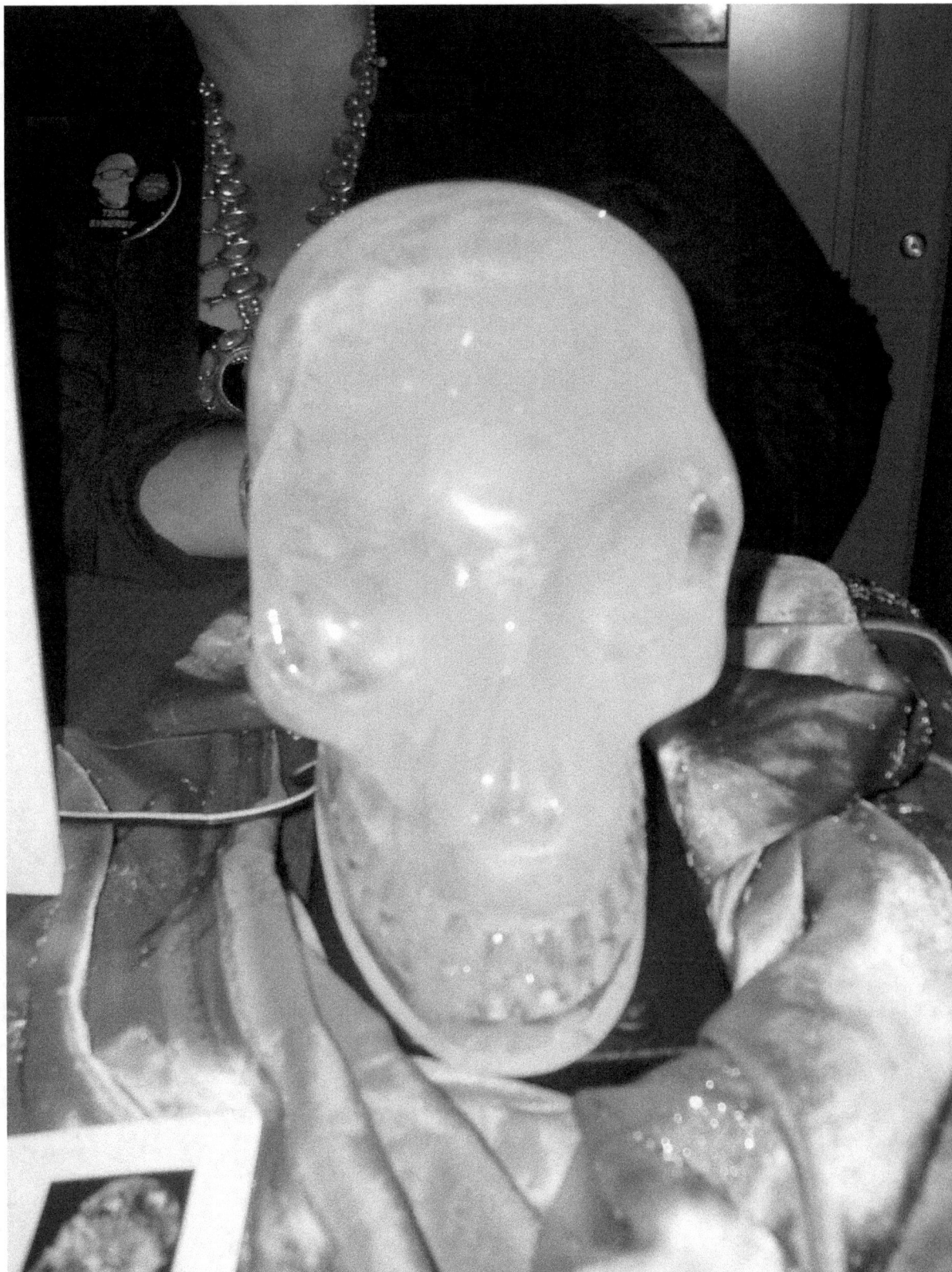

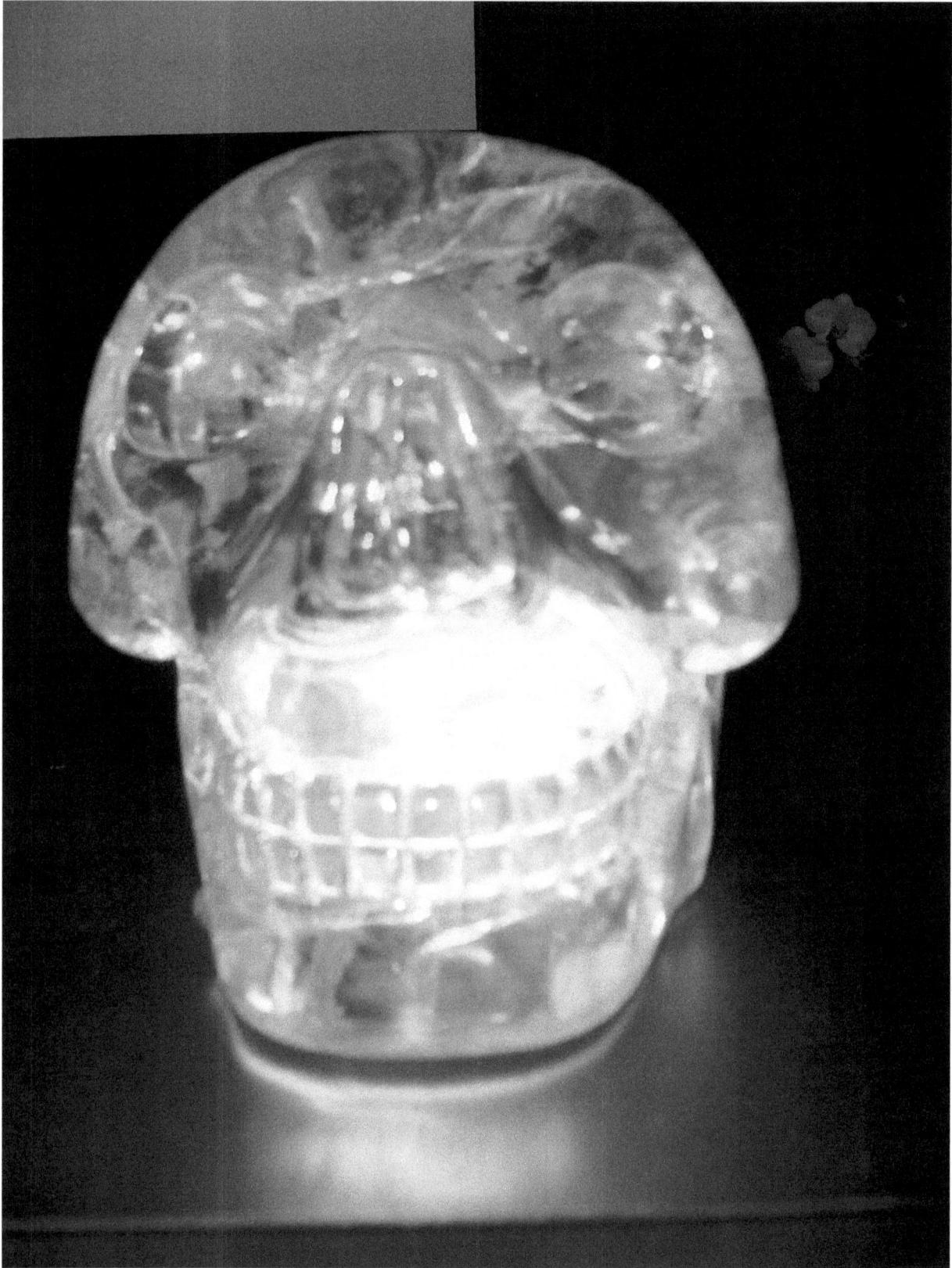